"WOMEN'S WORKING LIVES"

Edited

by

John Kremer

&

Pamela Montgomery

BELFAST: HMSO

FOREWORD

Women's experience of employment is different from men's. In general, women remain marginal and often invisible in terms of the labour market. Official statistics and research too often ignore the influence of women's domestic roles and the unpaid work they carry out in the home. Even sympathetic research can perpetuate stereotypes by describing an undifferentiated 'working woman' without reference to the individual's unique experience.

The Equal Opportunities Commission for Northern Ireland commissioned the survey on which this book is based in order to uncover the realities of women's employment. Much of the discrimination which women experience in the workplace stems from unacknowledged, and often unrecognised, prejudice; and prejudice feeds on ignorance – the Commission meets the myths and misunderstandings every day in its enforcement and its promotional roles.

We felt it vital that an accurate picture be painted of women's experience of work, and also their attitudes to it. What is revealed is a scene of women of courage, skill and determination challenging the stereotypes and managing their lives with extraordinary agility. The picture also however contains images of women facing an endless series of barriers and hurdles on their path to equality. There are no 'new men'; employers are not fulfilling even the letter let alone the spirit of the law; the changing patterns of work outside the home have not led to significant changes in terms and conditions of employment. The state, through the social security system, mirrors the inequalities of employment.

The book draws attention to a range of measures of which two are highlighted here. The first is a complete overhaul of the sex discrimination and equal pay legislation to produce a unified code which will comply with both the spirit and intent of European Community law; the second is to develop policies which take account of women's lives as they are lived in the 1990's. These are significant changes, and they would help us all to move towards an economy and a society in which women can play their chosen part, neither penalised for their domestic role nor barred by discrimination from an equal place in the workforce.

Joan Smyth
Chair and Chief Executive

iii

CONTENTS

THE CONTRIBUTORS

Carol Curry   Research Officer, School of Psychology, The Queen's University of Belfast, Belfast BT7 1NN.

John Kremer   Senior Lecturer, School of Psychology, The Queen's University of Belfast, Belfast BT7 1NN.

Donal McDade   Senior Research Officer, Department of Public Health Medicine, Eastern Health and Social Services Board, Belfast.

Eithne McLaughlin   Lecturer, School of Social Sciences, The Queen's University of Belfast, Belfast BT7 1NN.

Robert Miller   Senior Lecturer, School of Social Sciences, The Queen's University of Belfast, Belfast BT7 1NN.

Pamela Montgomery   Chief Investigation Officer, Equal Opportunities Commission for Northern Ireland, 22 Great Victoria Street, Belfast BT2 2BA.

Sheila Rogers   Senior Equality Officer, Equal Opportunities Commission for Northern Ireland, 22 Great Victoria Street, Belfast BT2 2BA.

Ann Toman   Investigation Officer, Equal Opportunities Commission for Northern Ireland, 22 Great Victoria Street, Belfast BT2 2BA.

Janet Trewsdale   Lecturer, School of Social Sciences, The Queen's University of Belfast, Belfast BT7 1NN.

Irené Turner   Senior Lecturer, School of Psychology, The Queen's University of Belfast, Belfast BT7 1NN.

Peter Ward   Managing Director, Research and Evaluation Services, 391 Lisburn Road, Belfast.

List of Tables

CHAPTER 5:   EMPLOYMENT

CHAPTER 6:   TRADE UNION INVOLVEMENT

CHAPTER 7:   UNEMPLOYMENT

CHAPTER 8:   CHILDCARE

CHAPTER 9:   INFORMAL CARE

CHAPTER 10:   ATTITUDES AND MOTIVATIONS

CHAPTER 11: EQUAL OPPORTUNITIES

APPENDIX 1: TECHNICAL REPORT

Chapter 1

INTRODUCTION

John Kremer and Pamela Montgomery

This book is based primarily on a survey, the Women's Working Lives Survey (WWLS), which was commissioned by the Equal Opportunities Commission for Northern Ireland in 1990. The WWLS was designed to identify the various factors which determine whether or not women participate in paid work and how the unpaid work which women carry out in the home influences their lifetime involvement in the labour market. It was also intended that the WWLS would document the type of paid work women have done and currently do, and women's attitudes and experiences of employment.

The WWLS can be seen as part of a tradition of research on women's employment, a tradition which stretches back to at least 1945 (see Dex, 1988, pp. 20-45). Early reports, including those by Thomas (1948) and Hunt (1968) were important in providing data on employment patterns and attitudes to work but it was not until 1984 that a truly comprehensive account of women and employment in Great Britain became available. This was based on the 1980 Women and Employment Survey (WES), carried out for the Department of Employment and the Office of Population and Censuses and Surveys by Jean Martin and Ceridwen Roberts (1984).

The development of the 1980 WES was informed by a growing recognition of the limitations of official statistics and government surveys in relation to women's employment. Increasingly the view had been expounded that women's position in, and experience of, employment could not be understood without reference to their domestic roles and the unpaid work which they carry out in the home. This was a relationship which official statistics and government surveys offered little scope for exploring. Fundamental questions had also begun to be asked about the way in which government statistical information was collected and compiled, in particular with regard to women (Oakley and Oakley, 1979; Hunt, 1980; Nissel, 1980; Allin and Hunt, 1982). As a result of this process, official statistics and surveys came under severe criticism for using definitions and classifications which were often inappropriate to women, and which had limited value in addressing questions regarding women's employment. Pursuing this argument, Beechey (1986) has maintained that an underlying assumption in routine statistics is a view of work which is predicated upon men's typical experience of the labour market, namely continuous full-time employment outside the home from education to retirement. For a variety of reasons, but most especially because of childcare and domestic responsibilities, women's work histories do not correspond to this male pattern. It has been far more common for women to have interrupted careers and to engage in forms of work which can accommodate childcare or care for other dependants.

Veronica Beechey continues this theme by demonstrating how this male-oriented model of work results in either a failure to take account of or an underestimation of, women's economic activity. As the yardstick against which employment is measured is full-time, year-round employment outside the home, alternative forms of employment are likely to be unrecorded, under-represented or distorted. These forms of work include homework, casual work, seasonal work, irregular work and part-time work, and are patterns of employment which are predominantly and traditionally seen as women's work. In practical terms, these forms of work are likely to be under-represented in official statistics for three reasons. Firstly, by its very nature the work may fall entirely outside the net of statistics (for example, homework). Secondly, as the categories which are used to record employment implicitly reflect upon types of men's work and recognition of men's skills, they are generally not suited to categorising women's work. Thirdly, under-representation may occur because atypical work may not be declared. Such work is invisible in official statistics and at the same time is often carried out in inadequate working conditions. It is also the case that those engaged in part-time work may fall outside statutory protection relating to certain employment rights (see Chapter 5). An additional distortion to employment statistics arises from the official definition of unemployment as a count of those registered as unemployed. Married women in particular are less likely than men to register as unemployed because fewer women are eligible for unemployment benefit. Furthermore, in periods of high unemployment women may be discouraged from seeking work and may not consider themselves to be unemployed in the same sense as male breadwinners (Beechey, 1986). By thus reflecting men's position and work experiences and by ignoring women's experiences of the labour market, women are often invisible in official statistics or at best marginal. One ramification of this practice may be that women's employment is kept off the policy agenda entirely, or is relegated to a minor concern (Davies, 1991).

It was against this debate that Martin and Roberts's 1980 WES was undertaken. By focussing specifically on women's work, both paid and unpaid, and by framing categories and questions which took account of women's experiences, their survey played a significant role in increasing our understanding of women's position in employment and the complex range of factors influencing women's participation in paid work. An interview-based study of 5588 women and 799 of their partners, the WES yielded a wealth of information on issues ranging from basic economic activity rates through to lifetime patterns of employment, and documented the experience and attitudes of women to home and work. The WES was also highly influential in challenging many unhelpful and inaccurate stereotypes about the woman worker and her attitudes to employment.

What has happened in terms of primary research in the intervening years since 1980? Certainly the decade has witnessed no shortage of interesting analyses and commentaries on women's employment, both in Great Britain (for example, Brown, Curran and Cousins, 1983; Dex, 1985; 1987; 1988; Beechey and Whitelegg, 1986; Beechey and Perkins, 1987; Webb, 1989) and in Northern Ireland (for example, Trewsdale and Trainor, 1979; 1981; 1983; Trewsdale, 1987; 1990; McWilliams, 1991). However, almost invariably the most significant sources for these analyses have been official statistics and government surveys. In the Republic of Ireland, a similar picture emerges. Blackwell's (1989) report for the Irish Employment Equality Agency provided a thorough statistical digest of material on women's work but this in turn was gleaned from several government sources and most notably the Irish Census of Population (1983) and the Irish Labour Force Survey (1983; 1984).

As regards other types of research on women's attitudes to, and experience of, work, in terms of the European scene, since 1979 the Commission of the European Communities has published a number of reports on women's and men's attitudes to work and politics across Europe, based on questions included in the Eurobarometer survey (Commission of the European Communities, 1979; 1980; 1983; 1987). Interesting as this material is, it has not reached a wide audience and publication of reports based on subsequent surveys has been somewhat sporadic. The International Social Survey Programme (ISSP), launched in 1983, gathers comparative data from research teams in 11 countries and between 1988 and 1989 specifically addressed the issue of women and the family. However, the range of questions included in this survey appears to be limited and reports based on this material are scarce (Scott and Duncombe, 1991). To begin to fill the gap in Great Britain, the introduction of the British Social Attitudes annual surveys in 1983 was welcome. The surveys have been based upon approximately 2000 annual face-to-face interviews, and cover a wide range of topics relating to various social and political issues including work, education, housing, health, the family, welfare and the environment. The results of these surveys are normally selectively reported each year as edited books, and various chapters have on occasion dealt with women's paid and unpaid work (for example, Witherspoon, 1985; 1988). Whilst originally the survey was confined to Great Britain, a separate Northern Ireland Social Attitudes Survey was initiated in 1989. Annual editions have started to appear based on these results (Stringer and Robinson, 1991; 1992), within which one chapter has addressed women's and men's attitudes to paid work (Montgomery and Davies, 1991).

Interesting as these findings may be, given the broad remit of the surveys the goal of encompassing women's employment comprehensively was never realisable. Primary research which is dedicated exclusively to women's work is far less easy to locate, and when found it is usually more modest in terms of sample size, objectives and budget. Often such projects have been directed towards single issues (for example childcare services, sexual harassment, training or employment in a particular industrial sector). Less often, they have aimed for a broader sweep. One example in Northern Ireland is the work of Kremer and Curry (1986) which considered attitudes towards women amongst the general population as well as selected professional groups. The postal survey was based on a random sample taken from the Electoral Register for Northern Ireland, eventually yielding replies from 1000 men and women. Items covered a wide range of issues relating to work, including experiences and attitudes to training, promotion, working conditions, sexual harassment and equal opportunities. A number of interesting findings emerged from this survey, one of the most significant being that attitudes were not found to be more traditional in comparison with Great Britain.

Reviewing the available literature as a whole, it is fair to say that a reliable and comprehensive picture of women and work has not been developed since 1980. To fill this gap requires a consideration of the broad canvas of women's lives as a whole and where paid work features within this picture, hence the development of the WWLS.

The Women's Working Lives Survey

In view of the dearth of recent research, together with the scope of their work, it is not surprising that Martin and Roberts's WES has continued to enjoy such prominence. However, it is now over ten years since that survey was undertaken and during this time, spanning the Thatcher years, the United Kingdom has witnessed a remarkable number of political and socio-economic changes. For example, the European dimension has become increasingly significant, trade union influence has declined, and at the same time Western economies in general have experienced at least two major recessions. The backcloth against which the WES was written seems somewhat distant today. For example, in their Introduction the authors noted:

> *By the end of the 1970s not only had the rate of increase in the number of women in the labour force slowed down .... but the rate of unemployment amongst women was rising and had begun to cause concern (Martin and Roberts, 1984, p.2).*

During the 1980s, regardless of the ongoing debate as to how to define and quantify female employment, it is accepted that women moved into paid employment in increasing numbers, albeit often part-time work (see Chapter 5). The decade also saw a further decline in the traditional manufacturing industries, the growth of service sector employment and an increase in what have been called "flexible" patterns of work, namely part-time, fixed-term contract, temporary, seasonal, casual and home-based work. The economic forces which determined movement towards these patterns of employment opened the way for more women to enter the labour market. It is somewhat paradoxical that on the one hand, the economic climate was precipitating women's movement to work but at the same time politically, the Conservative government was pursuing policies which conspired to make women's working lives that much more difficult. At best the Thatcher government could be described as having been ambivalent towards working women, on the one hand espousing a value system predicated upon the fictional Victorian family, on the other hand having to deal with the economic necessity of encouraging women to work. Far from advancing the cause of women's rights, many would argue that the political rhetoric which lauded traditional values and which described the family as the primary social institution during the Thatcher years was instrumental in further marginalising women workers and in halting progress along many equal opportunities fronts (Wicks, 1990). The changes in legislation regarding the "availability for work" of women with children (see Chapter 7) exemplify the shift in government thinking, as does the lack of regard for state childcare facilities for the under fives (see Chapter 8).

It was against this socio-political context and against continuing limitations of existing government surveys and statistics that the Equal Opportunities Commission for Northern Ireland commissioned a survey to examine the issue of women and employment, focussing on both attitudes and experiences. Based on a representative sample of 1,000 women of working age in Northern Ireland, the broad aims of the project were to explore the characteristics of women's employment, the extent of and reasons for women's unemployment and economic inactivity, the influence of the life cycle on women's movement in and out of employment, and the influence of domestic life on women's participation in paid work. To address these concerns, the WWLS was planned to generally chart similar territory to the WES. At the same time, the overall structure of the interview schedule, the sequencing and format of questions, the areas of interest and the type of questions themselves were altered in response to the WES itself and later survey work, as well as social trends and shifting priorities during the 1980s.

The Geographical Context

This then places the WWLS within its historical context, but what of its geographical context, Northern Ireland? Many readers will have first-hand experience of life in Northern Ireland, and for these readers this section may be largely redundant. For those whose acquaintance is less intimate and whose knowledge is based on more indirect sources, it may be important to set the scene in a very general sense, and simultaneously to lay a few ghosts to rest.

To begin, in what respects is Northern Ireland either similar to or different from the rest of the United Kingdom? In very general terms, it should not be forgotten that Northern Ireland is subjected to roughly the same economic forces as Great Britain. However, as one of the most remote parts of the celebrated Celtic fringe, the region has been especially vulnerable to the slings and arrows of economic fortune and misfortune. For example, Northern Ireland has consistently endured a higher rate of long term male unemployment and it has the lowest per capita income in the United Kingdom. These are coupled with the highest birth rate (Compton and Coward, 1989), the poorest childcare services (Hinds, 1989), the lowest divorce rate, the highest church attendance and religious observance (Cairns, 1991), and the most traditional moral codes and social norms governing sexual behaviour and birth control (Sneddon and Kremer, 1991).

At the risk of pre-empting discussion or detracting from existing commentaries on women's lives in Northern Ireland (for example, Montgomery and Davies, 1990; Davies and McLaughlin, 1991), all these factors in their different ways will impact upon women's experience of work and opportunities for work. Therefore it could be argued that Northern Ireland genuinely presents a fascinating location for research on women's working lives, a location where factors which universally play their part in determining women's employment opportunities may be revealed most starkly and vividly.

In many other respects, Northern Ireland offers itself as an ideal venue for social research. For example, it has a discrete, self-contained and stable population. Those who currently live in Northern Ireland are more than likely to have been born there and hence to have been subjected to its influences throughout their lives. In research terms, it is a manageable population of approximately 1,500,000, and cost effective to the extent that survey research is relatively cheap given the size of the population. At the same time, Northern Ireland is a separate jurisdiction with its own government agencies, albeit that these are similar in many respects to those operating in Great Britain.

As regards factors which mark Northern Ireland out as particularly special, most obviously, religion cuts a deep and well documented swathe through the society, manifesting itself in many social and political institutions and processes, including differential employment opportunities for Catholics and Protestants (see Chapter 7) and a school system which is largely segregated into the Catholic and non-Catholic sectors (see Chapter 4).

Northern Ireland's education system is also remarkable in other respects. For example, unlike Great Britain's predominantly comprehensive secondary school system which is not based on selection, at the age of eleven children in Northern Ireland are tested, graded and then awarded places in grammar or non-grammar schools, a selection process which itself has been shown to be terminally infected by gender bias (see Chapter 4). A high proportion of secondary schools in Northern Ireland are also single sex, and the effects of single-sex and mixed-sex schooling have long been shown to have an impact on women's lives, attitudes and opportunities.

In terms of the world of work, long term unemployment has been a serious and persistent problem (see Chapter 8). This problem is also endemic to many Western economies at the present time but in Northern Ireland it is not likely to be ameliorated by the effects of a declining birth rate as is true in many other parts of Europe. This is because of relatively high fertility rates in the region (Compton and Coward, 1989). On a more positive note, however, a high percentage of the Northern Irish labour force is employed in the public sector, a sector which has been less prone to job losses in times of recession (see Chapter 5 for further discussion).

When all these issues are considered in concert, Northern Ireland presents itself as a fascinating arena for discussion of women's issues and for consideration of the interaction between factors in the determination of experiences and opportunities and it was against this background that the WWLS was undertaken.

About This Book

The WWLS yielded a great deal of information on a wide range of issues relevant to understanding women's employment, past and present. This edited book is not offered as a summary of all the findings nor as a compendium of all the possible stories which are embedded in the data. Instead, through a collaborative venture involving both the Queen's University of Belfast and the Equal Opportunities Commission for Northern Ireland, a number of authors with an active involvement in gender research or policy in Northern Ireland, were invited to use the survey data to construct pictures of women's working lives in the early 1990s. On certain occasions, the focus of interest has been narrow, dealing with a relatively small section of the survey. On other occasions, contributors have felt it was appropriate to range more widely across the data. Likewise, on certain occasions the findings tell us something about Northern Ireland alone but in the majority of cases the issues which emerge have universal applicability. It may be useful to picture the book in terms of a three dimensional matrix. Horizontally, the book is divided into chapters, each of which deals with a major topic such as trade union involvement, childcare, education and training or employment. At the same time, an extra dimension is offered by the vertical themes which run down through the book and which appear and reappear at regular intervals, some of which are outlined below. Finally, the academic backgrounds of the different authors give the material its third dimension, namely the bringing together of multiple perspectives from across the social sciences. The contributors come from diverse backgrounds, and the alternative slants, priorities and perspectives which each brings to this material aim to be refreshing rather than bewildering.

The Themes

It is relatively easy, and tempting, to simply use new data to confirm and reinforce our existing ideas. At the same time, as analysis proceeds it becomes plain just how dangerous and misleading preconceptions can be when trying to interpret social research. To move forward it is essential to tackle analysis with an open mind, to put aside suppositions and to genuinely "play it as you see it". Bearing this in mind, what themes emerge from the data? Four are highlighted here, although this is very much a personal selection from amongst numerous stories which could be told.

Marginality and Invisibility

Despite the progress which has been made in terms of equal opportunity's legislation and despite a belated public recognition by governments across Europe of the important role which women must play in the workforce in the 1990s, women as a whole remain marginal and often invisible in terms of the labour market. This is revealed in many ways. Some forms are obvious, some are more covert, some are structural, some are attitudinal, some are predictable, and yet others are unexpected. Looking first at the more blatant evidence, the disregard which government and employers alike show towards the needs of working women with children leaps from the page, including most noticably the continuing inadequacies of childcare provision (Chapter 8). In addition, the lack of investment and serious, practical action to improve girls' education and training as a preparation for work in general, and for non-traditional employment in particular, remains apparent (Chapter 4). In a more covert way, women are still regarded as marginal when they continue to be perceived in terms of traditional yet inappropriate stereotypes. There remains a lack of understanding of women's work orientation and a disregard of women's commitment to work, and yet, when asked, women demonstrate extremely positive attitudes to so many aspects of the world of work.

Women are also likely to remain on the margins so long as the criteria for advancement and promotion at work are premised upon men's employment. A woman may decide to take time off to raise children, or she may find it difficult to attend residential training courses or to work late should the need suddenly arise, but these actions should not be interpreted as a lack of motivation, ambition or commitment. Instead the need to balance a number of responsibilities and commitments inevitably shapes day-to-day plans and schedules. At the extreme of this continuum are those women who have been obliged to give up work or curtail careers in order to care for others (Chapter 9). In terms of marginality, here are a group of women who fulfil a vital function within our redefined welfare state but who remain, without question, close to the edge.

Women's peripherality in the labour market is also revealed less directly through the ongoing debate as to how to define female economic activity (see Chapters 3, 5 and 7). It would be easy, and in many respects reassuring, to look upon the debate and wrangles over what constitutes female economic activity as an academic game, as a problem for statisticians and social scientists but with little significance to the real world. In actual fact, this debate strikes to the heart of a central concern; it is difficult to classify and pigeonhole women's employment and unemployment primarily because the system of categorisation was built upon the world of men's work. The ensuing problems, for example, in knowing when to define a woman who is not in paid employment as unemployed, demonstrates all too clearly that the square peg of women's work fits uneasily in the round hole of male employment statistics. Significantly this problem has become worse rather than better over recent years, as the criteria for determining eligibility for unemployment benefit have become more stringent (see Chapter 7) and the perceived value for many women of registering as unemployed becomes less obvious, despite the long term consequences for them in terms of pension entitlements.

As a further demonstration of peripherality it is certainly true that women are more likely to be found in those jobs characterised by poorer working conditions and contracts, shorter hours and fewer career prospects. This is not in dispute but the inferences which can be drawn from this finding in terms of individual orientation and priorities are more invidious. For example, it is all too easy to continue to fuel the fire of androcentrism, to see male employment as the norm against which comparisons are drawn. Women's work is accordingly regarded as less important, and following on immediately, women's unemployment is likewise regarded as less significant. Unfortunately, academics themselves may well have contributed to this model of marginality, for after all, the popular and oft cited dual labour market model has been used to traditionally draw a line of demarcation between characteristically men's work and typically women's work (Barron and Norris, 1991). This model may be useful as a very general descriptive guide to the labour market but it is no more than this and should not be used to attempt to understand individual experience or attitudes, nor as a pitprop for traditional stereotypes of men and women. Research on work commitment and job satisfaction has consistently failed to reveal sex differences, and whilst our understanding of these concepts and their significance remains poor (see Chapter 10), the lack of significant differences should not be ignored (Hakim, 1991).

Inequality in the Workplace

Following from this issue, it remains true that the world of work continues to be predominantly a man's world (see Chapter 11). As Chapter 6 demonstrates, the trade union movement has historically been run by men for men, and campaigning has been most active for issues which were the direct concern of men. This has almost inevitably meant that progress along other fronts, for example, campaigning for better childcare services, has lagged seriously behind. Although relatively few women identified overt manifestations of discrimination at work (see Chapters 10 and 11), the structural barriers to progress within work and to entering and re-entering the world of work remain firmly in place. For example, education and training remain the preserve of the young, with older women in particular possessing very few qualifications to equip them for employment (Chapter 4). In addition, given average women's wages and the cost of formal childcare, the financial constraints which this imposes on many women's opportunities to take up work cannot be ignored (Chapter 8).

The picture which finally emerges is certainly not one festooned with attitudinal or motivational barriers but instead it is the practical and structural impediments which are far more prominent. For example, the number of women with access to employment facilities such as flexitime, job sharing, career break schemes and childcare was consistently low (see Chapter 5). For those women in work, 87% work sufficient hours to qualify for full statutory rights as employees (Chapter 5) but a considerable number of these women are not aware of their entitlement. Until government genuinely recognises the difficulties which traditional, inflexible work routines present to women, and until employers act in concert to address these concerns, then it will still be the case that women work despite their conditions of employment and not because of them.

Understanding the Woman Worker

In the light of this analysis, is it possible to put together a profile of "the typical woman worker" and to outline her motivations and priorities? The answer to these questions must be quite bluntly, no. Instead the research demonstrates that it is futile to try to engage in such enterprises given widely differing life experiences. Beyond this, the results show how inhibiting stereotypes can be, for behind stereotypes live individuals with unique experiences, attitudes and priorities. To use one example, as a generality it would be possible to say that women have taken or expect to take time away from paid employment to raise children, but who, how, when, why and for how long is almost impossible to predict. In addition, the likelihood of a career break in the first instance is increasingly less easy to determine. At the same time, and as already mentioned, a career break should not of itself imply less commitment to work. Any heuristic model which assumes that an individual's "commitment" is a finite substance which can only be distributed so far and no further is naïve. Women may have a strong commitment to their families but this should not be seen as necessarily detracting from their commitment to their paid employment.

Since the industrial revolution, it is true that women have predominated in the secondary employment sector, but research over the years has not shown women's attitudes and commitment to their work as reflecting upon this disadvantage. This is regarded by many as paradoxical and particularly when set alongside women's strong commitment to the family. Whilst our understanding of work motivation and orientation remains poor, the seeds of confusion may have been cultivated by a popular model of human motivation which implicitly underpins our interpretation of these results. Needs and motivations were traditionally thought of as being organised into a rigid hierarchy but more recently attention has turned to the processes by which we are able to accommodate and balance various needs simultateneously. The determination and definition of work commitment and orientation as an expression which is inversely related to commitment to other concerns may have dogged interpretation in the past but should not in the future. Within the discipline of psychology there is a growing acknowledgment of our skills, complexities and capacities as information processors. Possibly the time has come for this recognition to gain wider acceptance across the social sciences.

To explore these complexities and to move forward will necessarily require a careful reappraisal of accepted research methods. The standard survey is well able to describe social trends and generalities but at the same time the danger lies in ignoring the individual experience and differences which go to make up the summary statistics. Social researchers may thus not only reflect upon but indeed reinforce stereotypes. With this in mind, the shift towards combining both quantitative and qualitative techniques in research projects is to be encouraged.

Women's Working Lives in the 1990s

Comparing earlier research with the WWLS findings, what changes have occured and what do these changes mean for women in the 1990s? Most immediately and obviously, the survey has once again confirmed the increasing participation of women in the labour market, and although the numbers in part-time work are substantial, there is greater evidence of career continuity.

Chapter 2 demonstrates that in Northern Ireland, as in Great Britain, the so-called "M" profile of female economic activity across the life cycle is not an accurate representation of reality. By the mid 1980s, it was becoming evident in Great Britain that the dip in female activity rate, associated with women taking time away from work for childcare, was becoming less pronounced (Webb, 1989). In addition, the second peak of female empoyment, beyond the age of 40 was becoming higher before falling away steeply after 55. Such a pattern has also emerged from the WWLS. Fewer women now routinely take time out to have children, with over 60% of those in their twenties remaining in employment, falling only to 57% between the ages of 30 and 34. With this in mind it is noteworthy that recent government statistics (Office of Population, Censuses and Surveys, 1992) have recorded the lowest birth rates for women in their twenties since 1945, with births rates for women aged 20 - 24 and 25 - 29 falling by 19% and 8% respectively during the 1980s. Simultaneously birth rates for those aged 30 - 34 have risen by 27% and for those aged 35 - 39, by 44%. Given these trends, it is likely that the profile of female economic activity by age will show even less variation during the 1990s.

Irrespective of reality, the stereotypical image of the married woman's work career has normally included a lengthy career break to look after children. Chapter 3 shows that this stereotype is increasingly redundant. At the same time, many women are still having to cope with the demands of domestic and childcare responsibilities alongside full-time work (Chapter 2) or more normally part-time work, with very little help from their employers or partners. To expect women to deal effectively with these competing demands on their time and energy without fundamental structural changes to their contracts and conditions of employment is unrealistic. It is likely that the pressure for change will continue to grow, and in particular as the pace of liberalisation in terms of attitudes towards women and work during the 1980s has been so dramatic. How women in the 1990s fare in the light of these changes remains to be seen but the forces for change are potentially powerful.

References

Agassi, J.B. (1982). *Comparing the Work Attitudes of Women and Men*. Lexington, Mass.: Lexington Books, D.C. Heath.

Allin, P. and Hunt, A. (1982). 'Women in official statistics'. In E. Whitelegg, M. Arnot, E. Bartels, V. Beechey, L.Birke, S. Himmelweit, D. Leonard, S. Ruehl and M.A. Speakman (eds.), *The Changing Experience of Women*. Milton Keynes: Open University Press.

Barron, R.D. and Norris, G.M. (1991). 'Sexual divisions in the dual labour market.' In D. Leonard and S. Allen (eds.), *Sexual Divisions Revisited*. Basingstoke: Macmillan Press.

Beechey, V. (1986) 'Women's employment in contemporary Britain.' In V. Beechey and E. Whitelegg (eds.). Op. cit.

Beechey, V. and Whitelegg, E. (eds.) (1986). *Women in Britain Today*. Milton Keynes:

Open University Press.

Beechey, V. and Perkins, T. (1987). *A Matter of Hours: Women, Part-time Work and the Labour Market*.   Cambridge: Polity Press.

Blackwell, J. (1989). *Women in the Labour Force*.   Dublin: Employment Equality Agency.

Brown, R., Curran, M. and Cousins, J.   (1983).   *Changing Attitudes to Employment? Research Paper No. 40*.   London: Department of Employment.

Cairns, E.   (1991).   'Is Northern Ireland a conservative society?'   In P. Stringer and G. Robinson (eds.), *Social Attitudes in Northern Ireland: 1990/91 Edition*.   Belfast: Blackstaff Press.

Commission of the European Communities   (1979).   *European Men and Women in 1978*.   Brussels: CEC.

Commission of the European Communities   (1980).   *Women of Europe: Supplement No. 5*.   Brussels: CEC.

Commission of the European Communities   (1983).   *European Women and Men in 1983*.   Brussels: CEC.

Commission of the European Communities   (1987).   *Men and Women of Europe in 1987. Supplement No. 26. Women of Europe*.   Brussels: CEC (Women's Information Service).

Compton, P. and Coward, J. (1989). *Fertility in Northern Ireland*.   Aldershot: Gower.

Davies, C. and McLaughlin, E.   (eds.) (1991).   *Women, Employment and Social Policy in Northern Ireland: A problem postponed*.   Belfast: Policy Research Institute.

Dex, S.   (1985). *The Sexual Division of Work*.   Brighton: Wheatsheaf Books.

Dex, S.   (1987). *Women's Occupational Mobility: A Lifetime Perspective*.   Basingstoke: Macmillan Press.

Dex, S.   (1988). *Women's Attitudes Towards Work*.   Basingstoke: Macmillan Press.

Feldberg, R. and Glenn, E. (1979). 'Male and female: Job versus gender models in the sociology of work.'   *Social Problems*, 26, 5,   524 - 538.

Fine-Davis, M.   (1983). *Women and Work in Ireland: A Social Psychological Perspective*.   Dublin: Council for the Status of Women.

Hakim, C. (1991). 'Grateful slaves and self-made women: Fact and fantasy in women's work orientations.'   *European Sociological Review*, 7, 2, 101 - 121.

Hinds, B. (1989). *Women and Social Policy in Northern Ireland: Childcare Provision and Employment*.   Belfast: Gingerbread (NI).

Hunt, A. (1968). *A Survey of Women's Employment (Vols I and II)* London: HMSO.

Hunt, A. (1981). 'Some gaps and problems arising from government statistics on women at work.'   *Equal Opportunities Commission Report Bulleting No. 4*.   Manchester: Equal Opportunities Commission.

Jowell, R. and Witherspoon, S. (1985). *British Social Attitudes: The 1985 Report*.   Aldershot: Gower.

Kremer, J. and Curry, C. (1986). *Attitudes towards Women in Northern Ireland*.   Belfast: Equal Opportunities Commission for Northern Ireland.

Kremer, J. and Curry, C. (1986). 'Attitudes towards women in Northern Ireland.' *Journal of Social Psychology*, 127, 5, 531 - 534.

McWilliams, M. (1991). 'Women's paid work and the sexual division of labour.' In C. Davies and E. McLaughlin (eds.), *Women, Employment and Social Policy in Northern Ireland: A Problem Postponed*.   Belfast: Policy Research Institute.

Martin, J. and Roberts, C. (1984). *Women and Employment: A Lifetime Perspective*.   London: HMSO.

Montgomery, P. and Davies, C. (1990). *Women's Lives in Northern Ireland Today: A Guide to Reading*.   Centre for Research on Women, University of Ulster at Coleraine.

Montgomery, P. and Davies, C. (1991). 'A woman's place in Northern Ireland.' In P.

Stringer and G. Robinson (eds.), *Social Attitudes in Northern Ireland: 1990/91 Edition.* Belfast: Blackstaff Press.

Morrissey, H. (1989). *Women in Ireland: The Impact of 1992.* Belfast: ATGWU.

Nissel, M. (1980). 'Women in government statistics: Basic concepts and assumptions.' *Equal Opportunities Commission Report Bulletin No. 4.* Manchester: Equal Opportunities Commission.

Oakley, A. and Oakley, R. (1979). 'Sexism in official statistics.' In J. Irvine, I. Miles and J. Evans (eds.), *Demystifying Social Statistics.* London: Pluto Press.

Office of Population, Censuses and Surveys   (1992). *Population Trends.*   London: HMSO.

Scott, J. and Duncombe, J. (1991). 'A cross-national comparison of gender-role attitudes: Is the working mother selfish?' *Working Papers of the ESRC Research Centre on Micro-social Change.* Paper 9. Colchetser: University of Essex.

Sneddon, I. and Kremer, J. (1991). 'AIDS and the moral climate.' In P. Stringer and G. Robinson (eds.), *Social Attitudes in Northern Ireland: 1990/91 Edition.* Belfast: Blackstaff Press.

Stringer, P. and Robinson, G. (1991). *Social Attitudes in Northern Ireland: 1990/91 Edition.* Belfast: Blackstaff Press.

Stringer, P. and Robinson, G. (1992). *Social Attitudes in Northern Ireland: 1991/92 Edition.* Belfast: Blackstaff Press.

Thomas, G. (1948). *Women and Industry.* London: The Social Survey.

Trewsdale, J.M. (1987). *Womanpower No. 4: The Aftermath of Recession; Changing Patterns in Female Employment and Unemployment.* Belfast: Equal Opportunities Commission For Northern Ireland.

Trewsdale, J.M. (1990). 'Labour force characteristics.' In R. Harris, C. Jefferson and J. Spencer (eds.), *The Northern Ireland Economy: a Comparative Study in the Economic Development of a Peripheral Region.* London: Longman.

Trewsdale, J.M. and Trainor, M. (1979). *Womanpower No. 1: A Statistical Survey of Women and Work in Northern Ireland.* Belfast: Equal Opportunities Commission For Northern Ireland.

Trewsdale, J.M. and Trainor, M. (1981). *Womanpower No. 2: Recent Changes in the Female Labour Market in Northern Ireland.* Belfast: Equal Opportunities Commission For Northern Ireland.

Trewsdale, J.M. and Trainor, M. (1983). *Womanpower No. 3: The Impact of Recession on Female Employment and Earnings in Northern Ireland.* Belfast: Equal Opportunities Commission For Northern Ireland.

Webb, M. (1989). 'Sex and gender in the labour market.' In I. Reid and E. Stratta (eds.), *Sex Differences in Britain; 2nd Edition.* London: Gower.

Wicks, M. (1990). 'The battle for the family.' *Marxism Today*, August, 28-33.

Witherspoon, S. (1985). 'Sex roles and gender issues.' In R. Jowell and S. Witherspoon (eds.), *British Social Attitudes: The 1985 Report.* Aldershot: Gower.

Witherspoon, S. (1988). 'Interim report: A woman's work.' In R. Jowell, S. Witherspoon and L. Brook (eds.), *British Social Attitudes: The 5th Report.* Aldershot: Gower.

Chapter 2

PAID AND UNPAID WORK

Pamela Montgomery

Introduction

One of the most dramatic changes in the Northern Ireland labour market over the last three decades has been the increase in the numbers of married women in employment. In 1961, just under 30% of married women had a paid job. By 1971, this had risen to 47%, with the majority of married women (just over 59%) in paid work by the 1980s (Equal Opportunities Commission for Northern Ireland, 1990). This trend is a reflection of a restructuring of the Northern Ireland economy which has resulted in an increase in female employment, particularly part-time work, together with an increase in male unemployment (see Chapter 5). These changes mirror similar movements in the United Kingdom as a whole from manufacturing to services, from full-time to part-time work and from secure to casual employment (Dex, 1985; Morris, 1990). Clearly the so-called traditional pattern of "male breadwinner, female homemaker" has been under challenge in Northern Ireland as elsewhere for some time and the indications are that the movement towards increased participation in employment amongst married women is set to continue (See Chapter 3).

Taken together, these trends would seem to raise fundamental questions about the sexual division of labour and the continued validity of the traditional model of the family. Recent research by McWilliams (1991) suggests that, as in Britain, the "male breadwinner, female homemaker" model has indeed been overtaken by what she has termed the dual earner couple, couples in which both partners have a paid job. Dual earner couples are now the most prevalent form of family organization in Northern Ireland, comprising 43% of all economically active couples in 1985. Nevertheless, the male breadwinner model still represents 40% of economically active couples but the majority of families in Northern Ireland are now characterised by other forms of organization. To this extent then, the traditional male earner, female carer pattern is being eroded in Northern Ireland as elsewhere.

The implications of such trends have been the theme of much research in Britain and the U.S.A. Early studies interpreted the increasing employment of married women as evidence of a gradual breaking down of the sexual division of labour which it was felt would lead to more sharing of domestic work and ultimately a more egalitarian family (Blood and Wolfe, 1960; Rapoport and Rapoport, 1971; Young and Wilmott, 1973). Subsequent studies suggest a much more complex relationship between paid and unpaid work and how changing roles relate to gender relations in the family and marital power. Research on the position of women in the labour market has shown that overall, women have made few inroads into traditional male occupations and that married women have been drawn into a labour market which is highly segregated into "women's jobs" and "men's jobs" (see for example Martin and Roberts, 1984).

To a large extent the jobs performed by women mirror those tasks and roles traditionally carried out by women in the home. Further evidence points to the constraints on women's access to and experience of paid work, including, for example, whether or not her partner works, the age of her children and in particular the nature of women's role as unpaid workers in the home. Indeed, a central theme in accounts of married women's employment has been the impact of women's continued responsibility for the home and family. This is supported by a wide range of studies which have focussed on the domestic division of labour in the home and which have provided the opportunity to explore in detail the relationship between home and work, and its effect on women's employment patterns over the life cycle (for a review of this work, see Morris, 1990). Such studies, together with work on the organization of household finances (see Pahl, 1989) have also provided the opportunity to explore the relationship between work and home; that is, the impact of changing patterns of employment on the gender division of labour and more broadly on gender roles and relations in the home.

Exploration of these themes within Northern Ireland itself has been limited by a lack of specific research on the domestic division of labour. Thus while it is possible to draw on a growing literature on the general pattern of women's employment, often in comparison to that in Britain (Trewsdale and Trainor, 1979; 1981; 1983; Trewsdale, 1987; Maguire, 1987, 1989; Morrissey, 1989; McWilliams, 1991) or on the experience and position of women in particular occupations or sectors (Larmour, McKenna and Hastings, 1985; Kilmurray and Edgerton, 1985; Watson, 1985, McEwen, Agnew, Fulton and Malcolm, 1987; McLaughlin; 1991), there is little information which can be brought to bear on the precise relationship between paid and unpaid work in Northern Ireland. Given the interest such themes have generated elsewhere, this gap in knowledge is surprising. This lack of information is not, however, confined to the domestic division of labour. Rather, there is a general paucity of research on the family and of the role and experience of family members in Northern Ireland (Montgomery and Davies, 1990). When set alongside the tremendous growth of publications and journals devoted to understanding family life and the current role and experience of women as wives, mothers, daughters and carers in Britain, it is tempting to speculate why these issues in general appear to have generated relatively little research effort in the context of Northern Ireland.

Part of the explanation may lie in what McLaughlin (1991), in her introduction to a recent volume on women and social policy, has referred to as the:

> *accepted wisdom that women in Northern Ireland are particularly oppressed by the influence of conservative religious ideologies and by the parochial or inward-looking nature of life in a divided and troubled society (McLaughlin, 1990, p.6).*

Certainly, the conclusion that Northern Ireland is a more traditional society within which women's primary role is defined as homemaker and mother is a theme which permeates accounts of the position of women in the 1960s, 1970s and early 1980s (see for example, Ward and McGivern, 1982; Fairweather, McDonough and McFadyean, 1984; Edgerton, 1986; McWilliams, 1987; Mitchison, 1988; Roulston, 1989; McWilliams, 1990) and, it could be argued, is one which has inhibited research of the type carried out elsewhere. To this extent then, a lack of empirical work on the variety of roles actually adopted by women and how these may be changing reflects but also reinforces what has been coined the "traditionalism thesis" which, with few exceptions, has dominated debate (Montgomery and Davies, 1990). More recently, writers have begun to question this accepted wisdom and have drawn attention to the need for research to critically examine the reality of women's lives. For example, reviewing recent demographic, social and economic trends, Gray (1991) concludes that, as in the United Kingdom as a whole, Northern Ireland families are also undergoing a transformation so that:

> *The myths surrounding the concept of the so-called "normal" family that exist in some quarters are being replaced by the realisation that the meaning of the family in the 1990s is changing (Gray, 1991).*

McLaughlin (1991) argues that across a range of relevant areas of social and economic life (for example, participation in women's organizations, employment, fertility rates, family size, births outside marriage, numbers of lone parents), the direction and rates of change in the last three decades have been the same in Northern Ireland and Great Britain. While studies have consistently revealed that women in Northern Ireland, particularly married women, are both less likely to be in employment (Trewsdale and Trainor, 1979; 1981; 1983; Trewsdale, 1987) and to return to work when their children are of school age than are their counterparts in Britain (Cohen, 1988; Hinds, 1991), McWilliams (1991) questions whether these trends can really be interpreted as evidence of a greater "traditionalism" in Northern Ireland. She suggests that lower economic rates may be less an indication of traditional attitudes and more a reflection of greater family responsibilities in the context of particularly low levels of childcare provision and/or poorer job opportunities. Focusing on attitudes, Montgomery and Davies (1991) have documented a considerable diversity in attitudes to such issues as divorce, sexual relationships, abortion and pornography between men and women, between the young and old, and between religious persuasions, and have drawn attention to the need to explore how attitudes may be changing in response to actual changes in how life is experienced in the home and the labour market.

Drawing on these themes of diversity and change, this chapter sets out to explore the reality of family life in Northern Ireland in 1990 and the validity of the traditionalism thesis. Using information which was collected on women's career histories, the chapter begins by exploring changes in the primacy of the homemaker role for women in Northern Ireland, and the impact of home on paid work over time. Focusing on married and cohabiting couples below the age of retirement, the remaining sections explore the relationship between the work which husbands and wives carry out in the labour market and in the home. The emphasis will be on how changes in the labour market have impacted on how life is organized and experienced in the home. The first of these sections concentrates on paid work and the extent to which the traditional male breadwinner, female homemaker model of the family reflects on the real life experience of most women and men. The second section focuses on unpaid work and examines whether changes have taken place in terms of the traditional roles of husbands and wives in the home and a final section explores the implications of these trends.

Mothers and Paid Work

A key explanatory factor in accounts of women's employment is the impact of children over the life cycle. For example, evidence from the 1980 Women and Employment Survey (WES) in Great Britain (Martin and Roberts, 1984) indicated that while the majority of women returned to work at some point following the birth of children, almost all took a break from employment. Only 4% of mothers who participated in the survey had remained in continuous employment throughout their working lives. It has been argued that the relationship between women's economic activity and the incidence of dependent children is a reflection of women's responsibility for the home, and for childcare in particular. Low levels of childcare provision effectively inhibit women's ability to participate in the labour market. The WES did, however, also point to changes in the impact of children on women's labour market activity over time. By focusing on the employment histories of different cohorts of women in the survey, they found that successive cohorts were returning to work sooner after having a child and that increasingly women were returning to work between births. In the light of these findings, they argued that the bimodal pattern of participation, which was previously assumed to characterise patterns of participation over women's working lives, specifically work after school followed by a period of economic inactivity until the last child is of school age was, "increasingly a less accurate description of how a large group of women behave in the labour market" (p.187).

Information collected on women's employment histories in the WWLS gives an insight into the changing impact of dependent children on women's labour market activity over time in Northern Ireland. Table 1 shows the impact of children on participation in paid work for successive cohorts of women at specific points in time from 1959 to 1989.

Table 1: Percentage of women in employment by year, by age of youngest child

	Age of youngest child		
	0 - 4	5 - 10	11 - 15
Year	%	%	%
1959	12	56	-
N	*88*	*18*	-
1969	23	53	27
N	*199*	*60*	*15*
1979	30	49	56
N	*200*	*139*	*85*
1989	43	54	57
N	*218*	*128*	*94*

Change is most striking for mothers with a child under school age. Starting with the cohort of women in the WWLS who had a youngest child under five years of age in 1959, it is clear that combining work and motherhood was relatively rare, with working mothers representing only 12% of all mothers with pre-school age children. By 1969, the employment rate for this group had risen to just under a quarter with only a slight increase to 30% by 1979. A comparison of the employment rate for mothers with very young children for 1989 indicates that the next ten years saw a dramatic increase in the proportion of working mothers with pre-school age children, with 43% of mothers with children in this age group in employment.

This trend towards an increase in the proportion of mothers, and in particular mothers with young children, participating in paid work across the United Kingdom has been noted by Cohen (1990). Comparing employment rates throughout the United Kingdom in 1985 and 1988, she found that the percentage of mothers of pre-school children in employment increased from 29% in 1985 to 37% in 1988, and for mothers with children aged 5 to 9, from 45% in 1985 to 53% in 1988 (see also Equal Opportunities Commission, 1991). Full-time employment for mothers with children in both age groups was considerably less common than part-time employment, with just over 11% of women with children under five and nearly 14% of women with children aged five to nine in full-time work. The higher participation rates of mothers with children aged five to nine was due almost entirely to their higher participation in part-time work. Disaggregating employment rates by region, Cohen reports an employment rate of just under 43% for mothers with children under nine in Northern Ireland. While these figures represent one of the lowest rates in the United Kingdom, the difference is accounted for by the much lower participation of mothers in part-time employment in Northern Ireland. When participation in full-time employment is considered, mothers with children aged nine or under have in fact the highest participation rate of any region in the United Kingdom. Although not directly comparable with all of Cohen's (1990) breakdowns, evidence from the WWLS confirms these general trends and provides evidence of the continued trend towards employment, both full-time and part-time, for mothers with very young children (Table 2).

Table 2: Proportions of women with dependent children in employment by age of youngest child

	Full-time work	Part-time work	All work
Age of youngest child	%	%	%
0 - 4 years	24	20	44
5 - 10 years	20	37	57
11 - 15 years	29	32	61
All	24	28	52
N	*111*	*130*	*241*

The WWLS indicates that nearly half (44%) of women with pre-school age children are in employment and of these the majority are in full-time employment. The relatively higher rates of participation in full-time work for mothers with pre-school children in the context of a lower overall participation rate for mothers in Northern Ireland compared with Great Britain is interesting. It may, as McWilliams (1991) proposes, reflect less opportunity for part-time work and/or the negative impact of male unemployment on take up of part-time work by wives (see next section for further discusion).

Overall, while the data suggest that having a young child in the home continues to exert an impact on women's economic activity, this effect has been less significant over time so that many women with children under five not only work but do so full-time. This is not to say that combining the burden of paid work and childcare has become any easier. Indeed, when asked about the impact of bringing up a family on availability for work, the majority of women (62%) agreed that having children had a detrimental effect, and younger women in particular appeared more likely to report that raising a family had been a major obstacle (Table 3). This may reflect changes in women's labour market behaviour, since a higher proportion of younger women with dependent children are now in paid work. Alternatively it may reflect on the immediacy of day-to-day problems faced by those currently with young children, as opposed to remembered difficulties.

Table 3:   Impact of children on availability for work

	Age of respondent					
	21 - 30	31 - 40	41 - 50	51 - 60	60+	All
Impact on work	%	%	%	%	%	%
Hindered a lot	31	32	30	25	20	29
Hindered a little	31	33	33	33	35	33
No effect	38	33	34	41	42	36
Helped a little	-	1	2	-	3	1
Helped a lot	-	1	1	1	-	1
Total %	100	100	100	100	100	100
N	*108*	*164*	*183*	*100*	*40*	*595*

In addition to the dramatic behavioural changes of mothers, attitudinal changes have also taken place. For example, in reviewing British evidence Witherspoon (1988) notes changes in attitudes to working mothers in general, and to the employment of mothers with young children in particular, since the early 1980s. While not directly comparable, evidence from the WWLS would indicate a similar pattern of response in Northern Ireland, with no evidence of greater traditionalism on the part of Northern Irish women (see Chapter 11).

Therefore, while women's responsibility for childcare continues to impact on their participation in paid work, the impact of home circumstances on work opportunities appears to have changed dramatically over recent years with the proportions of working mothers, particularly working mothers with very young children, increasing substantially. Attitudes to working mothers have also become more positive. With these trends in mind, it is clear that the notion of the traditional homemaker role is one which is no longer applicable to, nor to be expected of, a significant proportion of mothers. This is not to say that family responsibilities no longer impact on women's participation in paid work; the findings clearly indicate that for the majority of women with children, domestic responsibilities do influence availability and type of work. This issue will be explored later in the chapter, as will the relationship between changes in women's take-up of paid work and changes in the relative participation of men and women in unpaid work in the home. However, beforehand the chapter next addresses women's increasing participation in paid work and how these changes may be impacting on family life.

Husbands, Wives and Paid Work

Evidence from the WWLS confirms that, as in Great Britain, participation in paid work is the experience of the majority of married or co-habiting women in Northern Ireland, with 62% of married and co-habiting women under 60 economically active and 56% in paid work. Table 4 confirms the prevalence of dual earner households reported by McWilliams (1991), based on her analysis of the Continuous Household Survey (CHS), the Northern Ireland Housing Executive's Survey (HES) and the Labour Force Survey (LFS), and shows that while the male breadwinner model is still important, the majority of families in Northern Ireland are now characterised by other forms of organization.

Table 4:   **Households with an economically active couple, comparative data**

	CHS 1985	HES 1985	LFS 1985	WWLS 1990
	%	%	%	%
Dual earners	43	39	55	51
Male breadwinner	40	38	33	29
Both unemployed	14	18	9	14
Female breadwinner	3	5	3	6

Source: McWilliams, 1991, Tables 2.1 and 2.2.

While dual earner couples are the most common form of family organization across the four surveys, evidence from the WWLS suggests a further decline in the proportion of male breadwinner couples and an increase in the prevalence of female breadwinner couples. However, female breadwinner couples continue to be relatively rare, comprising only 6% of households in the WWLS.

Morris (1990) notes that early reactions to the restructuring of the labour market were underpinned by the assumption that women would take over from men as principal earners. McWilliams (1991) draws attention to a similar reaction in Northern Ireland during the 1980s, when, in response to both increasing unemployment for men and increasing employment for women, women were often described as "taking men's jobs". In fact, research on the position of women in the Northern Ireland labour market (Trewsdale and Trainor, 1979; 1981; 1983; De Frinze, 1986; Trewsdale, 1987; Morrissey, 1989) has consistently shown that, as in the United Kingdom as a whole, women have not replaced men in the labour force. Rather, women have benefited from an expansion of the service sector and the growth of part-time work. As such women are concentrated in a narrow range of "women's jobs", jobs characterised by low pay and poor prospects (see Chapter 5). It would seem that women have neither replaced men in the labour market nor replaced them as principal earners. Female breadwinner couples continue to represent a small minority, as they do in the United Kingdom as a whole (McWilliams, 1991) and rather than replacing their unemployed partners as principal earners, Table 4 indicates that the wives of unemployed men are likely to be unemployed themselves (see also McLaughlin, 1987; 1989; McLaughlin, Millar and Cooke, 1989). Studies of the impact of male unemployment in Britain point to the conclusion that when husbands lose their jobs, wives are also likely to leave employment (Bell and McKee, 1985; Morris, 1985; 1987). The finding that wives are extremely unlikely to replace their partners as principal earners, even when their partners are unemployed, should not be surprising in the context of a highly segregated labour market in which the earning potential of wives is limited relative to that of their husbands. For example, evidence from the WWLS on the net weekly earnings of husbands and wives in dual earner couples shows that only 4% of women earned the same as their partner and only 6% earned more.

This limited earning potential interacts with a state benefit system which acts as a disincentive to women taking up paid work when their partners are unemployed (see Chapter 8). Not only are wives unlikely to earn enough to support the family, the amount of benefit which husbands can claim falls in direct proportion to his wife's earnings. Despite these constraints, a small number of women (6% of the total) were breadwinners. This raises the question as to what differentiates this group from women in unemployed couples. It could be hypothesized, for example, that female breadwinners have higher incomes and earnings large enough to offset loss of benefits. A comparison of the net weekly incomes of women in dual earner and female breadwinner couples does not, however, substantiate this view (Table 5). Female breadwinners were as likely to work part-time (47%) as women in dual earner couples (50%) and, contrary to expectations, they were not high earners. Indeed a higher proportion of female breadwinners were concentrated in the lowest income groups. These lower earnings are a reflection of the occupations of female breadwinners with over a third (39%) of these women concentrated in catering, cleaning and hairdressing, traditionally low paid jobs. This compares with only 22% of women in dual earner couples. An alternative explanation for the interaction between women's participation in paid work and husbands' employment status is suggested by research which has shown that unemployed couples tend to have larger families than other couples, including female breadwinner couples (see for example, McWilliams, 1991). While the sample

Table 5: **Net weekly earnings of women in dual earner couples and female breadwinner couples**

	Couples	
	Dual earner	Female breadwinner
Net weekly earnings	%	%
<£50	19	31
<£100	37	33
<£15	23	19
<£200	12	8
<£250	6	3
<£300	2	3
<£500	1	3
Total %	100	100
N	*291*	*36*

size of both unemployed and female breadwinner couples was small in the WWLS, there appears to be a tendency for unemployed couples to have had larger families. As such it may be that benefit regulations, coupled with women's limited earning potential, results in a situation where there are fewer material benefits associated with wives' employment when their husbands are unemployed, as family size increases.

For the majority of couples in which husbands are unemployed, the WWLS therefore confirms that wives are also likely to be without paid employment. Conversely, for the majority of couples in which husbands are employed, the WWLS indicates that wives are also likely to be in paid work.

The contribution made by women's earnings to the family income and its effect on alleviating family poverty has been well documented (see Chapter 8 for further discussion). In addition, the impact of wives' participation in paid work on how couples organize their money has been the subject of much empirical research in Britain and the U.S.A. Pahl (1989) has argued that knowing about the financial arrangements couple make within marriage provides insights into the nature of relationships and gender relations in the home. The extent to which each partner has control over household finances is indicative of where power over decision making actually lies. Studies of couple's financial arrangements have identified four main types. The whole wage system is one in which one partner, usually the woman, is responsible both for managing family income and for all expenditure. The allowance system involves the main earner, usually the man, handing over a set amount for housekeeping with the remainder kept by him to cover his own expenditure. These types contrast with the joint management system in which both partners have access to all household income and are jointly responsible for management of, and expenditure from, a common pool. The final system, independent management, is relatively rare, and in this case each partner retains a separate income and designated areas of responsibility for expenditure.

The power implications of each of these models are clearly very different. In both the whole wage and the allowance system it is the male earner who decides how much, when and if money will be handed over. Pahl (1989) notes that it is important to distinguish between control of resources and management of resources as while women may have access to all or most of the income in the whole wage system, this form of organization is most likely when money is short and so financial management is a burden rather than a source of power or pleasure. These systems contrast with the joint management system in which both partners have equal access to the household income. Reviewing studies which have focused on the patterns of money management prevalent from the 1950s to the present day, she has drawn attention to an increase in the proportions of couples jointly managing or pooling household income. This raises the question of whether, and to what extent, greater sharing of paid work has impacted on the organization of household resources and what conclusions can be drawn as regards the extent of equality in marriage (Table 6).

Table 6:   Organization of household finances by economic activity of couple

	Dual earners	Male breadwinner	Both unemployed	Female breadwinner	All
	%	%	%	%	%
Shared	77	65	81	94	75
Wife allowance	17	27	5	6	18
Husband allowance	3	7	12	-	5
Other	2	1	2	-	2
Total %	100	100	100	100	100
N	*308*	*176*	*82*	*36*	*602*

Looking at the organization of income, overall 75% of women reported that income is shared. While not directly comparable, similar findings were reported by Witherspoon (1989) who noted some form of pooling of income in 69% of couples. While joint management does then appear to be the most dominant form of organization, some differences do emerge when husband's and wive's participation in paid work are considered. Considering first of all dual earner and male breadwinner couples, joint management is more likely when the woman has a paid job, with a higher percentage of wives receiving an allowance in male breadwinner couples. This said, the difference is not as large as may have been expected so that even in male breadwinner couples, 65% of women reported joint management of money. In contrast to research which has found financial management by the wife to be more common in low income couples, only 12% of women with an unemployed partner reported this type of organization. In fact a higher percentage of these women (81%) reported that money was shared. An interesting finding is the high level of sharing reported in female breadwinner couples, 94%. Part of the explanation here may lie in Stamp's (1985) finding that female breadwinners tend to involve their husbands in financial responsibility as a way of compensating for their husbands loss of breadwinner status.

These differences aside, it is clear that sharing of income is reported by the majority of women regardless of the economic activity of themselves and their partners. Given these findings what can then be inferred about gender relations in marriage in Northern Ireland today? Any inferences are necessarily speculative at this point, however, drawing on Pahl's (1989) in-depth study of 102 couples' organization of finances, it could be argued that responses to this item are indicative of women's and indeed men's aspirations rather than the reality of their experience. On the basis of her study, she concludes that the financial arrangements which couples make reflect not only such issues as choice, convenience, and their economic circumstances but also their ideas about the nature of marriage and relationships between men and women. On the basis of women's reports of how money is organized in the family, it would appear that at the very least, there are aspirations for equality in roles and relationships within the home. These aspirations for equality can also be explored in relation to domestic work and it is to a discussion of this topic that the chapter now turns.

Husbands, Wives and Unpaid Work

Underlying early accounts of the sexual division of labour was an assumption that changes occurring in the labour market would be mirrored by changes in domestic life and role relationships in the home. Studies focusing on the division of household tasks, decision making and the organization of household finance were interpreted as providing evidence of a gradual breaking down of the traditional model of family organization. Husbands and wives were portrayed as increasingly likely to share paid and unpaid work in a more egalitarian family (Blood and Wolfe, 1960; Fletcher, 1973; Young and Wilmott, 1973). The previous section illustrates clearly the limitations of this approach in relation to the sharing of paid work. Subsequent work considering the impact of labour market changes on the division of labour and gender relations in the home has revealed similar problems and has challenged the view that changes in the labour market will bring about a revolution in the organization of work in the home. In fact, overwhelmingly the evidence in Britain points to the continued persistence of the traditional homemaker role for women regardless of whether or not women have a paid job, with women continuing to have responsibility for domestic work and for childcare (Witherspoon, 1985; 1988). While it is the case that, overall, women continue to carry out their traditional responsibilities in the home, research points to variation both within couples over the life cycle and between dual earner and other forms of household organization (Morris, 1990).

The WWLS provides the first opportunity to explore the domestic division of labour in detail in Northern Ireland. It provides the chance to consider not only who does what in the home but also women's perceptions of how work should be carried out in an ideal world, whether women's participation in paid work has had any significant impact on the way families organize their lives and whether different patterns of domestic work have emerged in households in which husbands are unemployed or in which there is role reversal in terms of the breadwinner role.

Housework

Turning to aspirations first of all, the WWLS included one question on how housework should be shared when a woman goes out to work. The WWLS indicates clearly that in an ideal world, overwhelmingly women perceive housework as work which should be shared equally with their partners (Table 7).

Table 7:   % agreeing that housework should be shared

	%
Strongly agree	62
Agree	32
Neutral	3
Disagree	2
Strongly disagree	1
Total %	100
N	*600*

94% of women who were interviewed stated that they agreed that husbands should share housework and of these women, the majority stated that they "strongly agreed" that this should be the case. This consensus of opinion was in evidence regardless of whether or not a woman was herself in paid work or whether or not her partner was currently in paid work. Interestingly, there were no major differences by age in terms of the percentage of women agreeing or disagreeing. There was, however, a slight tendency for more younger women to agree strongly, particularly those women under 40. It would appear then that one response to women's increased participation in paid work is the fostering of an aspiration for the sharing of domestic work. The question then must be asked as to what extent these aspirations of equality or complementarity in marriage are matched with the reality of women's experience as wives within the family. These issues can be explored through responses to a number of questions on how housework is shared between husbands and wives. The first of these was a general question which asked women to think about jobs which need to be done around the home such as shopping, cooking and cleaning and asked respondents how this work was shared between them and their partner (Table 8).

Table 8:   Sharing of housework by economic activity of couple

	Dual earners full-time	part-time	Male breadwinner	Both unemployed	Female breadwinner	All
Housework	%	%	%	%	%	%
Woman does all work	11	16	33	22	17	21
Woman does most work	47	70	49	37	28	50
Work shared equally	40	14	16	36	39	26
Man does most Work	1	-	2	5	17	3
Total	100	100	100	100	100	100
N	*153*	*154*	*176*	*83*	*36*	*602*

The table indicates that such aspirations were not met by the reality of women's experience as wives and mothers in the home. Overwhelmingly, it was women who continued to carry out household chores. Overall, 71% of women indicated that they either carried out all housework themselves or carried out most of this work themselves with only around a quarter stating that housework was shared with their partners. While there were some differences by age, these were less significant than may have been expected and related largely to the proportions of women who stated that they carried out all the housework versus those who stated that they carried out most of the household chores, with sole responsibility less likely to be reported by younger respondents. In order to explore whether men participate more at different stages of the life cycle, when, for example, there are young children in the household and the burden of domestic work is likely to be heaviest, the relative contribution of men and women was compared for women with dependent children by the age of the youngest child in the household. Overall, no clear pattern emerged and although women with a young child were most likely to report sharing (31%), the majority of this group (66%) were responsible either solely or partly for household chores.

Turning to the impact of paid work on the division of unpaid work in the home, male participation in housework was more likely to be reported by couples in which there was a female breadwinner than any other form of family organization, with 39% of respondents stating that housework was shared between themselves and their partners and 17% stating that their partners carried out most of the domestic work. However, from Table 8 it is clear that while role reversal may have occurred in relation to participation in the labour market, even for this relatively small group, role reversal in the performance of unpaid work in the home was not in evidence, with none of the women stating that their partners carried out all such work.

Amongst dual earner couples, there was a clear distinction between those couples in which women worked full-time and those couples in which women worked part-time. Dual earner couples in which the wife worked full-time had a domestic division of labour most similar to that found in female breadwinner couples. A similar percentage of these women reported that domestic work was shared equally with their partners. However, for the majority of this group housework remained either totally or mostly the responsibility of the woman. For women working part-time, a different picture emerges, with sharing of domestic work considerably less likely. In terms of sharing, this group had more in common with male breadwinner couples, with women in both groups unlikely to report sharing. While women working part-time were less likely to report having sole responsibility for housework than women in male breadwinner couples, the low rates of sharing for this group, coupled with their additional responsibilities as paid workers in the labour market, make this form of family organization the most over-burdening for women. Finally, while couples in which both partners were unemployed appear to show a more equitable division of labour than either dual earner couples in which the woman works part-time or male breadwinner couples, this is offset by the fact that because neither partner was in employment, each should be equally available to carry out domestic work in the home. In fact, only 36% of women reported their partners sharing domestic work, with the majority stating that they either had sole responsibility for housework or carried out most of this work themselves.

Looking at the results as a whole, it would appear that it is still the case that the majority of women continue to carry out the bulk of housework regardless of whether or not they have a paid job. This said, participation in housework varied somewhat according to the economic status of both husbands and wives. While role reversal may not have occurred in the way predicted by early commentators, it appears that in households where women work full-time or as sole earners, there is likely to be a more equitable division of labour in the home. Taken together, these findings confirm the general patterns of change found in Britain. There is a greater likelihood of male participation in household chores when wives have a full-time paid job (Pahl, 1984; Gershuny, Miles, Jones, Mullins, Thomas, Wyatt, 1986; Laite and Halfpenny, 1987), and women working part-time receive little help from their partners despite the fact that the domestic burden is likely to be high for these women, many of whom will be combining paid work with caring for young children (Pahl, 1984; Witherspoon, 1985; 1988). While evidence from small scale studies of unemployed couples suggest that despite their greater availability unemployed men do not take on more domestic work, (Pahl, 1984; Morris, 1985a) the WWLS findings indicate that over 40% of men in unemployed couples and over half of men in female breadwinner couples were reported as sharing housework.

So far, this discussion on the division of housework has focussed on whether this work is, in general, shared between women and their partners. Sharing may, however, be interpreted in different ways by different women. For one woman it may mean her husband "helping out" occasionally, for example, when he is asked, when he chooses to do so or when she is ill. For another woman, it may mean shared responsibility. In this regard, it is interesting to compare the proportions of women who reported sharing of housework in the WWLS with those who reported sharing in the 1989 Northern Ireland Social Attitudes Survey (Montgomery and Davies, 1991). Women and men who participated in that survey were asked a general question as to who was mainly responsible for general domestic duties. Using this measure only 8% of women and 10% of men stated that responsibility for household duties was shared. Taken together, evidence from both surveys suggests that while some husbands may participate in housework, in the majority of relationships responsibility for the work being carried out continues to rest with wives.

Information from the WWLS on how often partners actually perform a range of household tasks (washing, ironing, cooking, cleaning, shopping) goes further to confirm that some household tasks remain the sole reserve of women, even in the least traditional of couples (Table 9).

Overall, men would appear to have made few inroads into the traditional female tasks of washing and ironing. 73% of women interviewed stated that their partners never did the washing and 82% stated that their partners never did the ironing. Over a third of husbands never carry out the basic household chores of shopping and cleaning and a quarter never cook a meal. While men appear to be more likely to carry out the latter tasks, particularly cooking, only around a fifth were rated by their partners as carrying out these tasks on a

Table 9: How often husbands carry out housework by age of respondent

	Age				
	21-30	31-40	41-50	51-59	All
	%	%	%	%	%
Ironing:					
Never	76	81	86	81	82
Sometimes	18	18	12	15	15
Often	7	1	2	4	3
Washing:					
Never	63	72	75	82	73
Sometimes	27	24	18	12	21
Often	11	3	7	6	6
Shopping:					
Never	39	34	36	48	38
Sometimes	34	45	40	33	39
Often	27	21	24	19	23
Cleaning:					
Never	27	29	36	50	34
Sometimes	49	52	49	36	48
Often	24	19	15	14	18
Cooking:					
Never	22	17	24	39	24
Sometimes	52	57	60	43	55
Often	26	26	16	18	21
Total %	100	100	100	100	100
N	*131*	*176*	*192*	*100*	*599*

regular basis with the majority replying "sometimes". Taken together, these findings suggest that in the majority of households while men do participate in household chores to some extent, this participation is not only confined to specific tasks, it is discretionary in that overall responsibility for housework remains with women.

However, there was considerable variation by age. Overall, younger respondents were more likely to report that their partners did the ironing, washing, shopping, cleaning, or cooking although the impact of age varied across tasks. For example, there was less variation in reports of how often husbands did the ironing, with 76% of those under 30 stating that their partners never did the ironing and only 7% reporting that they did the ironing "often". For the remaining tasks, age exerted a greater impact with older husbands less likely to carry out domestic chores "sometimes" or "often" and with participation in housework least likely for the over 50s. Again the presence of a young child in the household appeared to exert little impact on the relative contributions of husbands and wives to housework. The exception was cleaning, with more participation by fathers in households with a child under five.

Turning to the extent of male involvement in specific tasks by the economic activity of the couple, the WWLS indicated that regardless of the relative employment status of partners, washing and in particular ironing continued to be "women's work" (Table 10). Only a small percentage of women reported that their partners did the ironing often and while more women in female breadwinner couples reported their partners as doing the washing than in other forms of family organization, even in this group, this was less than a fifth.

Table 10: How often husbands carry out housework by economic activity of couple

Housework	Dual earners full-time	part-time	Male breadwinner	Both unemployed	Female breadwinner	All
	%	%	%	%	%	%
Ironing:						
Never	79	80	82	84	89	82
Sometimes	18	17	17	10	3	15
Often	3	3	1	6	8	3
Washing:						
Never	64	75	76	78	70	73
Sometimes	29	20	20	13	14	21
Often	8	5	4	8	17	6
Shopping:						
Never	35	40	38	45	28	38
Sometimes	39	40	44	29	33	39
Often	26	20	18	26	39	23
Cleaning:						
Never	22	36	44	37	28	34
Sometimes	50	54	45	39	40	48
Often	29	10	11	23	33	18
Cooking:						
Never	18	20	33	24	22	24
Sometimes	52	64	53	52	39	54
Often	30	16	14	24	39	21
Total %	100	100	100	100	100	100
N	153	154	176	83	36	602

For the remaining tasks of shopping, cleaning and cooking, female breadwinners were more likely than any of the other groups to report that their partners often carried out these chores. However, even in these couples, around a quarter of women reported that their partners never performed these tasks.

Again, dual earner couples in which the wife works full-time are most similar to female breadwinner couples as regards male participation in domestic work. In contrast, in dual earner couples in which the woman is working part-time, husbands are less likely to do the shopping, cleaning and cooking and where they do, they are less likely to do so "often". Turning to couples in which both partners are unemployed, it is clear that while both are equally available to carry out domestic work, overwhelmingly men's contribution remains more sporadic with less than a quarter carrying out these tasks often. In her study of unemployed couples, Morris (1985) found that while some men will respond to unemployment by participating in domestic work, this is usually shortlived and often a response to boredom. While it is not possible to explore changes in the extent of participation by individual men over time using the WWLS, some indication of the impact of length of unemployment on participation in domestic work can be obtained by a comparison of the participation of men who have been unemployed for varying lengths of time (Table 11).

The majority of women's partners in the WWLS had been unemployed for more than a year. While few men had been unemployed for less than a year, the WWLS indicates that there may be a relationship between extent of participation in domestic work and length of unemployment, with participation and frequency of participation highest for all tasks amongst those who had been unemployed for less than a year. With the exception of cleaning, participation in all tasks showed a gradual decline over time with the percentage of women reporting that their partners never carried out domestic work increasing with the duration of unemployment.

Childcare

As with domestic work, the WWLS included a number of questions dealing with childcare. Women were first asked a general question on childcare and how much of this was or had been shared with their partners. Table 12 sets out the how childcare is or has been organized by all married or cohabiting women below the age of retirement.

Overall, women were more likely to report sharing of childcare than housework, with 40% stating that childcare was or had been shared equally and only 9% stating that it was, or had been, carried out by the woman without any contribution from her partner. As with housework, in most cases it was women who carried out childcare but unlike housework the extent of sharing varied considerably with age. Initially, looking at the percentages of those women who reported sharing of childcare (Table 12) it is clear that sharing

Table 11: How often unemployed husbands carry out housework by length
of time unemployed

	< 1 year*	1-5 years	> 5 years	All
	N	%	%	%
Ironing:				
Never	[13]	87	87	86
Sometimes	[1]	9	6	8
Often	[3]	4	6	7
Washing:				
Never	[9]	78	81	76
Sometimes	[5]	13	8	13
Often	[3]	9	11	11
Shopping:				
Never	[5]	36	47	39
Sometimes	[6]	31	28	30
Often	[6]	33	25	30
Cleaning:				
Never	[8]	20	47	34
Sometimes	[4]	54	28	39
Often	[5]	25	25	26
Cooking:				
Never	[2]	16	36	24
Sometimes	[7]	53	45	48
Often	[8]	31	19	29
Total %		100	100	100
N	[17]	55	47	119

* Presented as raw data given N < 20

Table 12:   Sharing of childcare by age of respondent

	Age				
	21-30	31-40	41-50	51-59	All
Childcare	%	%	%	%	%
Woman solely	7	7	6	23	9
Woman mostly	41	50	58	49	51
Shared equally	53	43	36	28	40
Man mostly	-	-	-	-	-
Man solely	-	-	1	-	0
Total %	100	100	100	100	100
N	106	163	179	89	537

decreases markedly with age. Over half of women aged under 30 stated that childcare was shared, versus only 28% of the over 50s. In addition, the majority of women who reported that their partner had not contributed at all to the rearing of children were aged over 50 with only a small percentage of the younger age groups stating that they had reared or were rearing the children themselves.

In order to explore life cycle effects and the impact of participation in paid work on childcare, the relative contributions of husbands and wives with dependent children living in the household were explored. While the presence of a young child in the household exerted little impact on the reported sharing of household chores, in terms of men's contribution to childcare, evidence from the WWLS suggests that husbands may be more likely to help with childcare when the children are young. Sharing of childcare was most likely to be reported by mothers of children under 5 with nearly half (48%) reporting that childcare was shared. Sharing decreased for those with older children, with sharing reported by 42% of mothers of children aged 5-10 but only 35% of those aged 11-16. The impact of economic activity of couples on the sharing of childcare is evident, though to a lesser extent than for domestic work with sharing of childcare more evident across all forms of family organization (Table 13).

Table 13: Sharing of childcare by economic activity of couple

	Dual earners full-time	part-time	Male breadwinner	Both unemployed	Female breadwinner	All
	%	%	%	%	%	%
Women does all work	2	4	12	6	5	7
Woman does most work	38	54	59	41	43	50
Work shared equally	60	42	29	53	52	43
Man does most work	-	-	-	-	-	-
Man does all work	1	-	-	-	-	-
Total %	100	100	100	100	100	100
N	89	113	129	49	21	401

As with domestic work, sharing is most likely to be reported in dual earner couples when the woman works full-time (60%) and least likely in male breadwinner couples (29%). Over half of the female breadwinners and women in couples in which both parties were unemployed stated that childcare was shared. Interestingly, while women working part-time were again less likely to report sharing than women working full-time, it would appear that, unlike housework, men's participation in childcare may increase in such circumstances.

Women working part-time were more likely to report sharing (42%) than women in male breadwinner couples (29%).

The discussion of how "sharing" may have been interpreted by women who responded to the survey is relevant with regard to childcare as to housework. In this regard, the Northern Ireland Social Attitudes Survey (Montgomery and Davies, 1991) indicates that when asked who was mainly responsible for the general care of children, while men were more likely, and women were slightly more likely, to report the sharing of childcare duties than household chores, overwhemingly the majority of men (84%) and women (89%) reported that the responsibility for the general care of children rested with wives. As such, while it is the case that some husbands do participate in childcare and that they seem to be more likely to participate in childcare than in housework, in the majority of relationships responsibility for the work carried out continues to rest with wives.

In addition to a general question on childcare, women in the WWLS were also asked about the extent of their partners participation in specific tasks (Table 14). With the exception of taking children to the doctor, the majority of husbands were perceived as having participated in each of the tasks to some extent. However, men's participation varied widely between tasks. Thus, for example, 51% of fathers had never taken their children to the doctor whilst 3% of fathers had never played with their children. It is noteworthy that between a quarter and a fifth of fathers had never carried out the basic childcare tasks of washing or bathing their children, changing a child's nappy, getting up at night to attend to a child or reading to their children.

In addition to variation in reported participation rates between tasks there was also variation in the extent of involvement between tasks. Overall, there was a tendency for men to have a higher rate of participation and a greater involvement in what could be regarded as "fun" activities associated with rearing children, namely playing with children, putting the children to bed and reading to the children. For the remaining activities, there was a tendency for a higher proportion of women to report that their partners had never carried out tasks, or had carried out these tasks "sometimes" rather than "often". While husbands did show both a higher rate of participation and greater extent of involvement in childcare than in housework, the findings indicate that on most of the tasks investigated, responsibility remained with mothers in the majority of relationships.

As to whether men's participation on specific tasks may change over the life cycle this was not investigated. Many of these tasks are only relevant to raising younger children, and as the survey asked women to relate their experience over the life cycle and not with regard to specific points, it is likely that women with older children would refer to their experience when their

Table 14: How often husbands have carried out childcare by age of respondent

	Age				
Childcare	21-30	31-40	41-50	51-60	All
	%	%	%	%	%
Taken to doctor:					
Never	60	48	42	66	51
Sometimes	29	38	47	26	37
Often	11	14	11	8	12
Taken children to school:					
Never	47	29	29	44	35
Sometimes	30	43	39	35	38
Often	23	28	32	20	27
Washed/bathed children:					
Never	26	18	29	42	27
Sometimes	37	42	38	39	39
Often	37	39	32	19	33
Changed a nappy:					
Never	17	20	25	41	24
Sometimes	35	43	46	32	41
Often	48	37	29	27	35
Got up at night:					
Never	19	22	25	37	25
Sometimes	36	46	45	35	42
Often	45	32	31	27	33
Read to children:					
Never	22	17	18	18	18
Sometimes	36	34	40	44	38
Often	42	49	42	37	44
Fed children alone:					
Never	7	6	9	18	9
Sometimes	38	44	54	54	48
Often	55	50	36	27	43
Taken children to bed:					
Never	7	6	5	14	7
Sometimes	39	42	50	52	46
Often	54	52	45	34	47
Played with children:					
Never	3	4	2	6	3
Sometimes	21	25	31	40	29
Often	77	71	66	54	68
Total %	100	100	100	100	100
N	*107*	*162*	*179*	*88*	*536*

children were young. Similarly, it was not possible to explore the impact of economic activity of couples on childrearing since the current economic activity of husbands and wives tells us little about the economic status of partners when these tasks were relevant. Comparing women's reports of their partner's participation by age, for some tasks, namely washing or bathing their children, reading to children, taking children to school or to the doctor, no clear pattern emerged. For the remaining tasks there was an inverse relationship between age and the extent of participation, in that younger women were more likely to report that their partners carried out childcare "often" rather than "sometimes". Further, in relation to two of these tasks, changing nappies and getting up at night to attend to children, the percentage of women reporting that their partners never carried out these tasks decreased with age.

Conclusion

This chapter set out, amongst other things, to critically examine the concept of the traditional family and what this means in Northern Ireland today. It has been shown that the stereotypical perception of the Northern Ireland family as "male breadwinner, female homemaker" has been eroded in Northern Ireland as elsewhere. It has been shown that in relation to paid work at least, this image of the prototypical family is no longer accurate. The evidence suggests that the last decade in particular has seen a further erosion of rigid role stereotypes so that mothers of even very young children are now remaining in paid work. However, while sharing of paid work is presently the experience of the majority of married and co-habiting women in Northern Ireland, and while working and non working women would appear to have aspirations for equality in the home, there is little evidence to support the view expounded by early researchers that changes in the labour market would inexorably lead to a revolution in the organization of unpaid work in the home. Overall, the majority of women in Northern Ireland continue to have responsibility for the home and family regardless of whether or not they have a paid job. The WWLS has, however, provided evidence of a degree of diversity in men's participation and extent of involvement in housework and childcare between couples. On the basis of the reports of working and non-working women, it seems that changes in the labour market may have impacted on the roles of husbands and wives in the home. Thus, for example, men are more likely both to participate and be more involved in housework and childcare when full-time work is shared by husbands and wives, when role reversal in the breadwinning role has occurred or when the couple are sharing unemployment, albeit that in the latter case this participation may be shortlived. Based on the experience of different age groups of women, it seems that men's participation in the home is also more evident now than previously.

An interesting finding is that overall men are more likely to take part in childcare than in domestic chores. This high rate of participation and greater involvement in childcare has to be viewed, however, in the context of the tasks actually carried out by men. On the basis of the women's reports in this study, these are most often what could be regarded as the "fun activities" associated with the rearing of children.

Taken together, the evidence from the WWLS points to the conclusion that, as elsewhere, family life has been undergoing change for some time and seems set to continue to do so. Change is most apparent in relation to the breadwinning role, one which is being increasingly shared by husbands and wives. Despite these changes, the evidence points to the conclusion that for the majority of couples in Northern Ireland, childcare and in particular household chores remain women's work.

References

Bell, C. and McKee, L. (1985). 'Marital and family relations in times of male unemployment.' In B. Roberts, R. Finnegan and D. Gallie (eds.), *New Approaches to Economic Life*. Manchester : Manchester University Press.

Blood, R. O. and Wolfe, D. M. (1960). *Husbands and Wives*. Glencoe: Free Press.

Cohen, B. (1988). *Caring for Children: Services and Policies for Childcare and Equal Opportunities in the United Kingdom*. London: Commission of the European Communities.

Cohen, B. (1990). *Caring for Children: The 1990 Report. Report for the European Commission's Childcare Network on Childcare Services and Policies in the United Kingdom*. Edinburgh: Family Policy Studies Centre.

De Frinze, M. (1985). *Sex Differentials in the Northern Ireland Economy 1963-1978*. Unpublished MA thesis, University of Ulster at Jordanstown.

Dex, S. (1985). *The Sexual Division of Work: Conceptual Revolutions in the Social Sciences*. Sussex: Wheatsheaf.

Edgerton, L. (1986). 'Public protest, domestic acquiescence : Women in Northern Ireland.' In R. Ridel and H. Calloway (eds.), *Caught up in Conflict: Women's Responses to Political Strife*. London: Macmillan.

Edgerton, L. (1987). 'Women in medicine.' In R. D. Osborne, R. J. Cormack and R. L. Miller (eds.), *Education and Policy in Northern Ireland*. Belfast: Policy Research Institute.

Equal Opportunities Commission (1991). *Men and Women in Great Britain*. Manchester: Equal Opportunities Commission.

Equal Opportunities Commission for Northern Ireland (1990). *Where do Women Figure?* Belfast: Equal Opportunities Commission for Northern Ireland.

Fairweather, E., McDonough, R. and McFadyean, M. (1984). *Only the Rivers Run Free*. London: Pluto Press.

Fletcher, R. (1973). *The Family and Marriage in Britain (3rd Edition)*. London: Penguin.

Gershuny, J. I., Miles, I., Jones, S., Mullins, C., Thomas, G. and Wyatt, S. M. E. (1986). 'Preliminary analysis of the 1983/8ESRC time budget data.' *Quarterly Journal of Social Affairs, 2*, 13-39

Gray, P. (1991). 'The changing family in Northern Ireland.' *Childcare (Northern Ireland) Newsletter, 18*.

Hinds, B. (1991). 'Childcare provision and policy.' In C. Davies and E. McLaughlin (eds.), *Women, Employment and Social Policy: A Problem Postponed?* Belfast: Policy

Research Institute.

Kilmurray, A. and Edgerton, L. (1985). *Cut and Dried: Apprentice Hairdressers in Northern Ireland.* Belfast: Equal Opportunities Commission for Northern Ireland.

Laite, J. and Halfpenny, P. (1987). 'Employment, unemployment and the domestic division of labour.' In D. Fryer and P. Ullah (eds.), *Unemployed People.* Milton Keynes: Open University Press.

Larmour, R., McKenna, M. and Hastings, J. (1985). *Women in Hotel and Catering Management.* Jordanstown : University of Ulster at Jordanstown.

Maguire, M. (1987). 'Making your minutes: Women's piecework in a Northern Ireland telecommunications assembly plant.' In C. Curtin, P. Jackson and B. O'Connor (eds.), *Gender in Irish Society.* Galway: Galway University Press.

Maguire, M. (1989). *What Price Women? A Study of Women's Employment in the Retail Trade in Northern Ireland.* Belfast: Equal Opportunities Commission for Northern Ireland.

Martin, J. and Roberts, C. (1984). *Women and Employment: A Lifetime Perspective.* London: HMSO.

McEwen, A., Agnew, U., Fulton, J. and Malcolm, S. (1987). *Women in the Professions.* Belfast: Equal Opportunities Commission for Northern Ireland.

McLaughlin, E. (1987). *Maiden City Blues.* Unpublished PHD thesis, Queens University of Belfast.

McLaughlin, E. (1989). 'In search of the female breadwinner: Gender and unemployment in Derry City.' In H. Donnan and G. McFarlane (eds.), *Social Anthropology and Public Policy in Northern Ireland.* Aldershot: Ayesbury.

McLaughlin, E., Millar, J. and Cooke, K. (1989). *Work and Welfare Benefits.* Aldershot: Gower.

McLaughlin, E. (1991). 'A problem postponed.' In C. Davies and E. McLaughlin (eds.), *Women, Employment and Social Policy in Northern Ireland: A Problem Postponed?* Belfast: PRI.

McLaughlin, E. and Ingram K. (1991). *All Stitched Up: Sex Segregation in the Northern Ireland Clothing Industry.* Belfast : Equal Opportunities Commission for Northern Ireland.

McWilliams, M. (1987). 'The world of work.' *Studies, Summer.*

McWilliams, M. (1990). Women in Northern Ireland : An Overview. In E. Hughes (ed.), *Culture and Politics in Northern Ireland.* Milton Keynes: Open University Press.

McWilliams, M. (1991). 'Women's paid work and the sexual division of labour.' In C. Davies and E. McLaughlin (eds.), *Women, Employment and Social Policy in Northern Ireland: A Problem Postponed?* Belfast: Policy Research Institute.

Mitchison, A. (1988). 'Ulster family feminists.' *New Society, 19,* 17-19.

Montgomery, P. and Davies, C. (1990). *Women's Lives in Northern Ireland Today: A Guide to Reading.* Centre for Research on Women, University of Ulster at Coleraine.

Montgomery, P. and Davies C. (1991). 'A women's place in Northern Ireland.' In P. Stringer and G. Robinson (eds.), *Social Attitudes in Northern Ireland: 1990/91 Edition.* Belfast: Blackstaff Press.

Morris, L. (1985). 'Renegotiation of the domestic division of labour.' In B. Roberts, R. Finnegan and D. Gallie (eds.), *New Approaches to Economic Life.* Manchester: Manchester University Press.

Morris, L. (1987). 'Local social polarisation.' *International Journal of Urban and Regional Research, 11,* 333-352.

Morris, L. (1990). *The Workings of the Household: A US-UK Comparison.* Cambridge: Polity Press.

Morrisey, H. (1989). *Women in Ireland: The Impact of 1992.* Belfast: ATGWU Research Department.

Pahl, R. E. (1984). *Divisions of Labour.*   Oxford: Basil Blackwell.

Pahl, J. (1989). *Money and Marriage.* London: MacMillan.

Rapoport, R and Rapoport, R. N. (1991). *Dual Career Families.* London: Robertson.

Roulston, C. (1989). 'Women on the margin: The women's movement in Northern Ireland 1973 - 1988.' *Science and Society, 53,* 219-236.

Stamp, P. (1985). 'Balance of financial power in marriage.' *Sociological Review, 33,* 546-557.

Trewsdale, J. and Trainor, M. (1979). *Womanpower No 1: A Statistical Survey of Women and Work in Northern Ireland.* Belfast: Equal Opportunities Commission for Northern Ireland.

Trewsdale, J. and Trainor, M. (1981). *Womanpower No 2: Recent Changes in the Female Labour Market in Northern Ireland.* Belfast: Equal Opportunities Commission for Northern Ireland.

Trewsdale, J. and Trainor, M. (1983). *Womanpower No 3: The Impact of the Recession on Female Employment and Earnings in Northern Ireland.* Belfast: Equal Opportunities Commission for Northern Ireland.

Trewsdale, J. (1987). *Womanpower No 4: The Aftermath of Recession; Changing Patterns in Female Employment and Unemployment.* Belfast: Equal Opportunities Commission for Northern Ireland.

Ward, M. and McGivern, T. (1982). 'Images of women in Northern Ireland.' In M. P. Hederman and R. Kearney (eds.), *The Book of Irish Studies.* Dublin: Blackwater Press.

Watson, T. (1985). *Cleaning Up: Women and the Contract Cleaning Industry in Northern Ireland.* Belfast: Northern Ireland Women's Rights Movement.

Witherspoon, S. (1985). 'Sex roles and gender issues.' In R. Jowell and S. Witherspoon (eds.), *British Social Attitudes: The 1985 Report.* Aldershot: Gower.

Witherspoon, S. (1989). 'Interim report: A woman's work.' In R. Jowell, S. Witherspoon and L. Brook (eds.), *British Social Attitudes: The 5th Report.* Aldershot: Gower.

Young, M. and Willmott, P. (1973). *The Symmetrical Family.* London: Routledge and Kegan Paul.

Chapter 3

WORK HISTORIES

Janet Trewsdale and Ann Toman

Introduction

The position occupied by the female labour force within the Northern Ireland economy has been shaped by many factors. These include fluctuations in the social, economic and political climate, as well as shifts in attitudes to women and work over time. This chapter endeavours to trace the changes which have taken place in the female labour market over the last fifty years, alongside the reasons which women gave for having changed jobs, left work or returned to work. This analysis of mobility within the labour market is based principally on one section of the WWLS, a section which was designed to provide information on women's employment histories from the day they left school to the time of the survey, and including movement between full-time and part-time employment. Although reservations may be expressd as to the reliability of recall data which potentially spans such a long period of time, a recent review of retrospective research of this type (Dex, 1991) indicates that the accuracy of recall data is generally good and particularly when dealing with broad outlines and summaries of employment histories.

As well as charting change over time, the analysis may also be able to address other concerns. For example, it is persistently argued that women are less reliable as long term employees than men (see Chapter 10), and that there is a higher probability that they will leave jobs for domestic and health reasons (Joseph, 1983). As a consequence they are often seen by employers as poor investments in terms of training and promotion. On the other side of the coin, it is maintained that women returning to work after having raised a family often find themselves under-employed (McEwan, 1987), insofar as they take part-time jobs in which they do not fully utilise their skills or build on their experience. In order to deal with these issues comprehensively, the most accurate way to gather information would be to carry out longitudinal research, interviewing a cohort of women repeatedly as they move from adolescence to old age. Given the paucity of early databases, such an enterprise is not possible but the WWLS endeavoured to do the next best thing by asking women to describe their careers to date. Most studies of the female labour market have tended to concentrate on aggregate flows into and out of paid employment but have not looked at how individuals have responded to changing circumstances. It is hoped that this chapter will begin to go some way towards filling this gap by considering the history of women's employment, as well as their internal movement within an employing organization.

The chapter begins by scene setting, offering a brief synopsis of the Northern Ireland economy from 1940 to 1977, followed by a more detailed analysis from 1977 to 1990. This summary presents the economic background against which the one thousand women questioned in the WWLS have lived out their economic lives.

The Northern Ireland Economy (1940-1990)

The economic backdrop against which to consider changes in the female labour market is of vital importance. For example, in times of economic recession and uncertainty, it is more difficult to eliminate sex discrimination and to promote equality of opportunity between women and men in the labour market. A downturn in economic growth and an increase in male unemployment often gives rise to demands that women, and in particular married women, should leave the labour force to make way for men to fulfil their "inalienable right to work". This simplistic view of women's role in the economic process is both naïve and wrong. For the first half of the present century the proportion of women working in the manufacturing industry in Northern Ireland was substantially higher than in the rest of the United Kingdom (Isles and Cuthbert, 1957). This, in the main, reflected the industrial structure that had developed in the Province since the middle of the nineteenth century. Although shipbuilding and engineering have long been important activities, the peripheral location of the region favoured the development of light manufacturing sectors producing goods that could be transported easily to major markets in Britain and abroad. Even as late as 1952, for example, the textile and clothing sectors accounted for 43% of all employees in manufacturing, and of this group, more than 70% were women (Isles and Cuthbert, 1957).

At the same time, the proportion of employment in service industries which is accounted for by women has tended to be somewhat lower in Northern Ireland than in the rest of the United Kingdom. In part, this may have reflected upon the particular structure of the service sector in the Province as the public sector only expanded after a shift in government policy in the 1970s (McWilliams, 1991). It seems probable, however, that it also reflected upon the intense competition for service sector jobs amongst women and also men who were in substantial and persistent over-supply in the labour market.

Because of the heavy male unemployment rates endemic to Northern Ireland, industrial development policy during the 1960s and early 1970s gave a high priority to the provision of jobs for men. A substantial proportion of newly created jobs were in synthetic textiles, light engineering and associated activities. With the decline in the traditional textile and clothing sectors the balance of employment opportunities in the manufacturing sector shifted against women.

This trend was offset to some extent by an increase in female jobs in the service sector, particularly in public sector services, but as we shall see below, the main expansion in female employment did not arrive until the late 1970s and early 1980s.

In the years since the establishment of the Equal Opportunities Commission for Northern Ireland under the Sex Discrimination (Northern Ireland) Order 1976, the economy of the Province has experienced first a "mini boom" in 1979, then the recession of 1981, followed by a partial recovery, and finally, in 1986, a further prolonged recession, the severity of which has been likened to the depression of the 1930s (Trewsdale, 1987). From the middle of 1987 there was a slow and prolonged upturn, which lasted until Autumn 1990, since when the economy of the United Kingdom has declined and unemployment has risen sharply. The recession of the 1990s is different from those immediately preceeding it, in that the spectacular increase in interest rates led to a downturn in consumer expenditure which in turn resulted in a sharp reduction in employment in the service sector. This new phenomenon of unemployment in services has had a profound effect on female employment as it is that sector which had been the steady growth area for female employment since the 1960s.

The economy of Northern Ireland maintains a very close relationship with that of the United Kingdom as a whole. Not only does it operate within the same monetary and fiscal framework but the majority of its wage rates are negotiated by United Kingdom based unions. On the marketing side, over three-quarters of Northern Ireland's manufacturing output is sold on, or through, British mainland markets. Despite these close links, the structure of the Province's economy has an important influence on the extent to which changes in the United Kingdom are transmitted through the system. During 1978 the United Kingdom economy showed signs of a moderate recovery. Northern Ireland's participation in the recovery was, however, delayed and fitful, unemployment rose and total manufacturing production remained static at the 1977 level. The total number of employees in employment rose by approximately 10,000 during 1978 and by a further 19,000 during 1979 (Table 1), a period which has subsequently become known as the year of the "mini boom". Closer inspection of the data reveals that approximately 9,000 of the increase in 1978 and 13,000 of the increase in 1979 can be attributed to a rise in the number of women employed. From June 1979 until June 1987 the male component of the total fell steadily to a low of 267,400, representing a loss of some 36,400 jobs. The number of women employed fell by 8,500 between 1980 and 1981 to a low of 222,700; however, by 1990 the numbers had increased by just under 33,000 from the 1981 trough, to 255,600.

The explanation for this increase in women's jobs at the apparent expense of men's jobs lies in the changing structure of the Northern Ireland economy.

Table 1: Northern Ireland employees in employment*

	1977	1979	1981	1984	1987	1990
Sex	000s	000s	000s	000s	000s	000s
Males	296.1	303.8	283.2	269.0	267.4	274.1
Females	209.4	230.8	222.7	227.6	236.7	255.6
Total	505.5	534.6	505.9	496.6	504.1	529.7

* June each year, in thousands

Source: NIAAS No. 9, 1990; and Statistics Notices, DED.

In common with most Western economies, Northern Ireland has experienced a dramatic decline in its manufacturing industries, which in 1977 were employing 150,000 people of whom the majority (over 95,000) were men (see Table 2). By June 1990 the total had fallen to just over 100,000, which included approximately 67,000 men. This decline in male manufacturing employment represented a loss of approximately one third of such jobs. A further 13,300 jobs were lost in the construction industry over the same period. As the manufacturing sector declined, the service sector experienced rapid growth. In 1977, 290,100 people were employed in that sector; by 1990 the number had risen to 371,200, representing a rise of 28%. As can be seen quite clearly in Table 2, the increase occurred in both men's and women's employment; however, the increase in female employment was 2.5 times the growth in male employment. The increasing dominance of the service sector in the economy of Northern Ireland can be seen clearly when one notes that in 1977 47% of all male employees and 73% of all female employees worked in that sector. By 1990 well over half (59%) of male employees and just over 8 out of 10 (82%) female employees depended upon the service industries for employment.

The data analysed so far represent a simple count of jobs; no distinction has been made between full-time and part-time employment. It is quite possible that there is an element of double counting whereby one person has, for example, two part-time jobs and hence counts as two in the official figures. Official data on the full-time/part-time breakdown of employment statistics appears every three years (Department of Economic Development, various dates). In 1981, part-time employees accounted for just under 17% of all employees and 35% of female employees in employment. The 1984 data showed that the overall proportion had risen to 22% and the female component had increased to 36%. The latest data available (1989) show a further increase, to 25% and 39% respectively. A breakdown of the 1984 data by industries reveals that 27% of all employees in the service industry were working part-time, with 41% of female employees classified as part-time. As would be expected, by

Table 2: Northern Ireland employees in employment by selected industry and sex*

Industry	1977 000s	1979 000s	1981 000s	1984 000s	1987 000s	1990 000s
Manufacturing:						
males	95.2	94.2	81.9	69.5	65.6	66.7
females	49.7	51.3	41.2	37.8	37.8	38.1
Services:						
males	137.6	148.2	150.1	149.8	154.2	161.1
females	152.5	172.0	175.0	183.5	192.9	210.1

* June each year, in thousands

Source: NIAAS No. 9, 1990; and Statistics Notices DED.

1989 the proportion of all employees who were working part-time in the service industry had increased to 30%, with 44% of females working part-time. By 1989, 92% of the 99,080 female part-time employees in the Northern Ireland economy worked in the service industry.

These official data on part-time employment provide a detailed insight into the changes in the total numbers of employees in employment; namely, the decline in the manufacturing sector and the rise in importance of the service sector which resulted in a loss of full-time "male" jobs and was accompanied by a rise in part-time "female" jobs. It will be shown later in this chapter that the type of work carried out by women has hardly changed since 1977, and that the structure of the Northern Ireland labour market remains highly segregated by sex. The majority of women continue to work in low paid, low status occupations, jobs which until the cold wind of economic depression blew would not have been considered acceptable by men.

The dramatic movements in the number of employees in employment have naturally been reflected in the unemployment figures. For men the relationship is quite clear and as expected. Specifically, a steady fall in the number of male employees in employment has been accompanied by an equally steady rise in male unemployment from the onset of the recession in 1979 until mid 1987. For women the relationship is more complex, insofar as the rise in female employment over the same period has also been matched by a rise in female unemployment (see Chapter 5 for a more detailed discussion). It is interesting to note that during the eight year period from 1979 to 1987 (Table 3), male unemployment increased by 120% compared to 89% for female unemployment (Trewsdale, 1990). However, the official data on unemployment of women must always be viewed with some scepticism due to the high incidence of under-recording (see Chapter 8).

Table 3: Northern Ireland unemployment as % of workforce* (including school leavers; not seasonally adjusted)

Unemployment	1979**	1981**	1985	1987	1988	1989	1990
Males:							
(000s)	41.6	69.1	87.6	91.5	84.4	76.9	71.9
(Rate %)	13	21	21	22	20	19	17
Females:							
(000s)	18.0	26.8	33.8	34.1	31.3	27.3	23.2
(Rate %)	7	11	13	12	11	10	8

*   Claimant Basis: June each year
**   Basis for calculating unemployment rate 1978-81; denominators excluded self-employed and HM Forces which are included from 1985-87.

Source: NIAAS No. 9, 1990

From 1987 there was an improvement in the economy of Northern Ireland. The number of employees in employment rose by 10,000, and there was a slight increase in the numbers employed in manufacturing as well as in the service industries. However, the growth in the Northern Ireland economy after 1984 was led by a continuing expansion in consumers' expenditure, particularly in durable goods, relatively few of which are produced in Northern Ireland. In the autumn of 1990 it was clear that the economy of the United Kingdom was entering yet another recession, the extent of which has been shown to be both sharp and deep. Unlike the recession of the early 1980s, which manifested itself in the dramatic collapse of the manufacturing sector, the present recession has also hit the service industries. The loss of jobs in the service sector has resulted in the South East of England experiencing an increase in unemployment for the first time for many years.

It is against this background of economic recession, followed by slow and short lived recovery, which in turn has been followed by a further if somewhat different recession, that we turn to a more detailed analysis of the work histories of the women who participated in the WWLS.

Industry and Occupation Change: 1940-1990

The WWLS provides, for the first time, retrospective longitudinal data on women's work histories in Northern Ireland. By its very nature, the information relies on the memory of the woman questioned, and is thus subject to all the inherent problems associated with that method of data collection (see Martin and Roberts, 1984; Dex, 1991). However, if the problems are recognised and understood when interpreting the resulting data, the data themselves can nevertheless provide an insight into the broad changes which have taken place in women's work patterns since the early 1940s.

In the WWLS the questions on work history were designed to account for all stages of women's lives from leaving school to the present time. In order to overcome some of the problems associated with cataloguing longitudinal data it was decided to capture this information in the form of periods, each delimited by a change of employment status. For example, if a respondent left school and proceeded to further education, the first period would be defined as education, after which the second period may have been full or part-time employment, unemployment, looking after children and so forth. Further questions were included to indicate precisely when the period began and ended and the reason for change (for example, promotion, marriage, sickness, pregnancy, redundancy, dismissal).

948 effective responses were available for analysis (see Note at end of chapter). Of the women interviewed, some had never worked, some worked continually whilst others did not work in their first period of economic activity or inactivity after leaving school. To accommodate these different experiences, the chapter reviews the data in different ways. On some occasions the industries, occupations and economic status of all women who have ever worked is considered whilst at other times only Period One of the respondents' career history is identified and particularly when looking at changes and trends over time.

An initial scan of the results shows that the majority (82%) of the women covered by the survey were economically active during the first period of their post secondary education lives (Period One), and that three quarters of them were working full-time with a further 13% continuing in full-time education (Table 4). The first industry in which women worked was either "Other manufacturing" (31%), "Distribution" (24%) or "Other services" (33%) (Table 5), and within those industrial sectors they worked as semi-skilled workers in "Material processing" (23%), "Selling" (14%), "Clerical" (29%) or "Catering/ Cleaning" (13%).

Within the industrial sector "Other manufacturing", 46% of women started work in leather, clothing and footwear with 24% in each of textiles and food drink and tobacco, thus confirming the historical importance of clothing and textiles as employers of female labour. The service industry "Distribution" was dominated (76%) by the retail industry, whereas in "Other services" there was no dominant industry; first time employees were fairly evenly spread between public administration, education, health and so forth.

These results refer to the aggregate data of the 948 women whose responses

Table 4: Employment status during Period One (i.e. after leaving school)

Employment status	%
Self-employed (alone)	0
Self-employed (with staff)	0
Full-time employee	75
·Part-time employee	1
YTP	2
Unemployed	3
Full-time education	13
Temporary sick	0
Permanently sick	0
Looking after children	1
Looking after other relative(s)	0
Looking after home	2
Total %	100
N	*948*

Table 5: First industry of all who have worked

Industry	%
Agriculture	2
Energy/water	-
Minerals	-
Metal goods	2
Other manufacturing	31
Total manufacturing	34
Construction	-
Distribution	24
Transport	1
Banking	7
Other services	33
Total %	100
N	*900*

to the career history section were accessible.   When the data are broken down by time, in the form of the decade in which a woman started work, a far more interesting yet also predictable pattern emerges (Table 6).   Of those women who entered the labour force in the 1940s and 1950s, the majority (over 60%) worked in the industrial sectors of either "Other manufacturing" or "Distribution" with "Other services" accounting for around 20%. By the 1960s the importance of "Other manufacturing" as the first time employer had started to wane, falling from a high of 49% in the 1950s to 34% in the 1960s of the relevant female employees covered by the WWLS. This decline continued until, by the 1980s, the proportion had fallen to 21%.

Table 6 : First industry by decade

Industry	Pre 1949 %	1950s %	1960s %	1970s %	Post 1980 %	All %
Agriculture	4	2	1	1	1	2
Energy	-	-	1	1	-	-
Minerals etc	-	1	1	1	-	-
Metal goods	2	2	3	4	-	2
Other manuf	44	49	34	29	21	35
Construction	-	1	1	1	-	-
Distribution	22	24	28	17	29	24
Transport	4	1	1	2	1	2
Banking	2	2	7	11	7	6
Other services	22	18	23	34	40	27
Total %	100	100	100	100	100	100
N	*111*	*160*	*162*	*164*	*136*	*733*

This well recorded decline in manufacturing as an employer of female labour is mirrored by the rise in the importance of "Other services". Of women entering employment in the 1950s just under one in five went into "Other services"; by the 1980s this proportion had doubled to two in five. The change in the occupational pattern reflects that of the industrial structure. Throughout the 1940s and 1950s over one third of the women surveyed went into "Material processing" as their first occupation; by the 1980s the proportion had fallen by one half and had been overtaken by "Selling", "Catering" and "Clerical and related" as first time occupations.

In order to see if women migrate through or across the occupational hierarchy it was decided to compare the occupations of those in their first period of activity after school with their current occupations. Of those women who were working at the time of the survey and who had worked after leaving school, the least likely to have stayed in their first occupation were those who started out in "Selling", closely followed by those who started out in semi-skilled jobs. In both cases the majority had moved out of employment altogether (Table 7).

Of those who remained in employment, 12% who started in "Selling" had moved to professional jobs in education, welfare and health, and 16% of those who started in semi-skilled jobs in material processing had moved into "Catering and cleaning". The most stable occupational grouping was that of

Table 7: Occupation in Period 1 by present occupation (selected occupations)

	Occupation in Period 1				
	Prof. (educ. welfare health)	Clerical and related	Selling	Catering and cleaning	Semi-skilled
Current occupation	%	%	%	%	%
Prof. (educ., etc.)	58	15	12	8	4
Clerical and related	-	43	9	2	3
Selling	-	2	9	1	4
Catering and cleaning	4	9	12	34	16
Semi-skilled	-	1	8	3	13
Not working	36	30	50	51	58
Total %	100	100	100	100	100
N	*55*	*208*	*116*	*86*	*230*

the "Professionals in education, welfare and health", where 58% of those who began their careers in this group were classified as having remained within the group. The "Clerical and related" occupational grouping also demonstrated a high level of stability with just over two in five women having remained from the first to the current period, with a further 15% having moved into "Professionals in education, health and welfare" by the current period. One third of women who started their working lives in "Catering and cleaning" were still in the same occupational grouping at the time of the survey.

The overall conclusion which can be drawn is that there would appear to be two extremes operating which are dependent on the qualifications required for, and the status of, the occupation under consideration. Professionals such as teachers, nurses, doctors are relatively immobile between occupations as, to a slightly lesser degree, are clerical and related staff. In contrast, the semi-skilled worker is more likely to move out of employment or to move into other similar occupations. Caterers and, more especially, cleaners, are also relatively less mobile, probably as a result of lack of opportunities rather than choice.

Analysis of the data by industrial base reflects upon the changing industrial structure, as discussed earlier. Overall women have tended to move from "Other manufacturing and distribution" into "Other services", with "Other services" itself being the only relatively static sector (Table 8).

When the data in Table 8 are examined in more detail within the three industrial sectors of "Other manufacturing", "Distribution" and "Other services" the pattern becomes easier to discern. Those women in "Other manufacturing" who started their working lives in textiles and clothing have moved into "Other

Table 8 : Industry in Period 1 by present industry (selected industries)

	Industry in Period 1			
	Other manufacturing	Distribution	Banking	Other
Current industry	%	%	%	%
Agriculture	1	1	2	-
Energy	1	-	2	1
Minerals	-	-	-	-
Metal	2	1	-	-
Other manufacturing	14	7	4	1
Construction	-	-	-	-
Distribution	5	18	10	7
Transport	-	1	4	-
Banking	2	-	28	2
Other services	20	25	26	52
Not working	55	47	24	37
Total %	100	100	100	100
N	*259*	*177*	*46*	*202*

services", as have those who began their careers in food, drink and tobacco. Relatively few (8% for textiles, 18% for clothing and 11% for food, drink and tobacco) have remained employed in the initial industry. The same pattern is true within "Distribution", with only 23% of those who began in the retail sector staying in retailing. Likewise, those who began in hotels and catering and wholesaling have moved into "Other services" leaving only 4% and 6% respectively still employed in their original industrial sector. A high proportion of those who commenced working in these three industrial sectors were currently not working. This is explicable to a large extent by the fact that 46% of all respondents to the WWLS were not in employment when the survey was undertaken.

The relatively static public sector has seen 68% of those who began in public administration, 51% of those who began in both education and health, and 44% of those who began in the "Other services", remaining employed in those same industrial classes in the current period.

The shift of female employment away from the traditional manufacturing sectors and towards the service sectors, and within the service sectors from "Distribution" to "Other services", is symptomatic of the general movement of the Northern Ireland labour force. However in the case of the female employee the status of her job has remained low or unskilled (Trewsdale, 1987).

Employment Record

The WWLS provides information on the number of employers the women in the survey had worked for as a function of the number of years worked (Table 9). Of all the women in the survey who had ever worked, just under 30% had worked for more than three employers. The average number of employers for whom women had worked was 2.9, with the average number of years worked per employer standing at exactly three years.

Table 9: Number of employers by total years worked

	Years in employment					
	< 5	6 - 10	11 - 15	16 - 20	>20	All
Number of employers	%	%	%	%	%	%
1	48	28	15	10	5	22
2	36	32	25	23	19	27
3	12	20	22	30	27	22
4	3	13	20	14	22	14
5 +	1	7	18	23	27	15
Total %	100	100	100	100	100	100
N	*194*	*191*	*156*	*114*	*238*	*893**
Ave. no. employers	1.7	2.4	3.1	3.3	3.8	2.9
Ave. no. yrs per employer	1.9	2.7	3.4	3.7	4.1	3.0

*There was a small number of respondents (6) for whom the number of employers and total years worked could not be computed from the available information.

As would be expected, the number of employers for whom the women have worked increased with the number of years worked. For those who had worked up to five years the vast majority (84%) had worked for a maximum of two employers, while for those who had worked for more than 20 years, the proportion fell to just under one quarter. However, even for these long term workers the average number of employers for whom they had worked was still only 3.8. It should be noted that the long term worker accounted for the highest proportion of the sample, representing 27% of the 893 women who answered the questions.

The analysis of the data which focused on the time the women spent in work naturally leads on to consideration of the time they spent out of work. The structure of Table 9 was replicated, this time to crosstabulate the number of breaks from work by the years out of work (Table 10).

Table 10: Number of breaks from work by total years out of work

	Years out of work					
	< 5	6-10	11-15	16-20	>20	All
Number of breaks	%	%	%	%	%	%
1	70	66	60	55	61	63
2	24	25	32	37	30	29
3	5	7	8	8	8	7
4	1	2	0	0	1	1
Total %	100	100	100	100	100	100
N	*163*	*149*	*96*	*80*	*158*	*646*
Average number	1.4	1.5	1.5	1.5	1.5	1.5
Average length	2.9	7.9	13.2	17.5	30.0	14.0

As can be seen from Table 10, the majority of women who took a break from work took only one or two such breaks, a fact which was true regardless of the total number of years spent away from work. The average number of breaks approximates 1.5 across all classes but the average length of the break moves closer to the upper limit of each class as the number of years out of work increases. This pattern is possibly a function of the age of the women concerned as the older the woman the more likely she was to have left work permanently, either on marriage or on the birth of a child. This hypothesis is supported to some extent by the reasons the women gave for changing their employment status. When asked why they had changed their employment status the women in the survey responded fairly consistently over the first three periods of their career history, by the end of which almost all of those who were ever employed had experienced employment. Two in five in each period had changed jobs in order to move to a better position, one in five had moved involuntarily (i.e. either declared redundant or dismissed) and approximately 15% had left due to pregnancy (Table 11). Those who stated that they changed for voluntary reasons mentioned factors such as "unhappy with work", "boredom", "gave up work", "personal reasons", and this did not necessarily imply that they then became unemployed. As explained previously, each period represents a new phase of economic activity/inactivity, and could thus include moving into employment or taking up a new post.

When the data were analysed according to decade of first starting work and reason for leaving job at the end of the first period of activity after leaving school, an interesting pattern emerged. The proportion leaving "involuntarily" rose from 17% for the pre-1949 group to 26% for the 1980s group, possibly a reflection of the changing economic climate. However, in stark contrast the number who left on marriage declined dramatically from 26% to 3% over the

Table 11: Reasons for change at end of employment period

Reason	Period 1 %	Period 2 %	Period 3 %
Involuntary move	20	20	23
Voluntary move	8	8	9
Better position	40	43	43
Further education	2	1	-
Marriage	13	8	6
Pregnancy	14	14	16
Stay at home	3	5	4
Total %	100	100	100
N	*843*	*673*	*489*

same period. The changing social attitudes to married women working and the change in employers' rules no doubt has had an effect on this trend (see Chapter 10). For example, up until the early 1970s the Northern Ireland Civil Service and the teaching profession required women to leave their jobs on marriage. The proportion leaving for a better position rose from 31% to 47% post-1980, an indication that women have become increasingly prepared to leave their jobs to move up the employment ladder (Table 12).

Table 12: Reasons for change at end of Period One by decade of leaving school

	Decade of leaving school					
Reason	Pre-1949 %	1950s %	1960s %	1970s %	Post-1980 %	All %
Involuntary move	17	16	16	23	26	20
Voluntary move	9	8	10	7	9	8
Better position	31	38	44	42	47	40
Education	0	2	3	-	3	2
Marriage	26	17	12	7	3	13
Pregnancy	12	13	12	18	11	14
Stay at home	5	5	2	3	1	3
Total %	100	100	100	100	100	100
N	*132*	*179*	*185*	*195*	*152*	*843*

Taken as a whole, these results refute the assumption that women workers are transient employees. Further research may be appropriate but assuming that the results reflect upon the female workforce in Northern Ireland, employers should be made aware that they have an under-utilised resource which could, with proper investment in the form of appropriate training and staff development, yield considerable long term benefits.

Promotion

The fact that the majority of working women are to be found in low paid, low status jobs is often excused by the argument that women do not seek advancement because they prefer jobs that carry little, if any, responsibility. In short, the assumption is that women in general are not interested in promotion. The WWLS contained a series of questions on the respondents attitudes to promotion, on their past experiences and on their future expectations. An occupational breakdown of these data revealed some interesting results, namely that 64% of the women who answered the relevant question would have liked to have been considered for promotion. However, the proportion varied widely from occupation to occupation. Of those working in the professional occupations, 91% were interested in promotion, as were 68% of those in "Clerical and related", but the proportion fell to only 45% of those working in "Catering and cleaning". These expectations were no doubt a function of past experience and based on a realistic assessment of future prospects. When asked whether promotion had already occurred within their occupation, 73% of the professionals answered "Yes", as did 45% of the "Clerical and related", however only 3% of those working as caterers or cleaners reported that they had been promoted. As far as future prospects were concerned, over 60% of the professionals said further promotion was possible compared to 52% of the clerical and related workers and 27% of those in "Catering and cleaning".

The industrial breakdown of the data revealed 54% of those working in "Banking" had been promoted compared to 23% of those working in "Other manufacturing" and 42% of those working in "Other services". This past experience was again reflected in the employees expectations with 69% of those in "Banking", 47% of "Other manufacturing" and 65% of those in "Other services" replying that they would like to be considered for promotion. A full-time/part-time breakdown produced predictable results, with 48% of full-time workers having been promoted compared to only 15% of part-timers, and 53% of full-time employees but only 34% of part-time employees replying that promotion was possible. At the same time, less than half of part-time women workers (45%) would have welcomed promotion, compared to 72% of full-timers.

It would seem that a fairly high proportion of the women in the WWLS survey had been promoted and were interested in further promotion should the opportunity arise, but in turn that opportunity depended on the occupation and the industry in which the individual was working. How women's prospects for advancement actually reflect in job changes is difficult to predict, although the lack of mobility, as demonstrated in Table 9, could equally reflect on lack of opportunity as on lack of ambition.

Age Profile

The age profile of the women in work in the survey shows quite clearly that over the decades, the proportion of working women in the youngest age groups (i.e. 15 - 19; 20 - 24) has consistently been over two thirds, and in some decades, the proportion of young women in work has been much higher (Table 13). After age 24, there is a fall in the proportions of women working and particularly for those aged between 25 and 34. The fall in each decade for these age groups follows a similar pattern to Great Britain, documented as the first part of the "M" profile of women's economic activity rates (Greenhalgh, 1977; Joseph, 1983). However, looking at the proportions of these women in employment over the decades, it is clear that, as in Great Britain, there has been a discernible change over time so that while only 47% of those aged 25 - 29 were in employment in 1959, this figure had risen to 60% in 1989. Similarly, the proportions of women in employment in the 30 - 34 age group had increased from 39% in 1959 to 57% by 1989. As a consequence, by 1989 the proportion of women in work during the child rearing years of 25 - 29 and 30 - 34 remained high at around 60%. In contrast to previous decades which showed a fall in the proportions of women in work in these age groups, followed by only a slight increase with age beyond these years, by 1989 this dip was no longer apparent. The reasons for this change may include shifting attitudes and increased opportunities for part-time employment, coupled with the impact of economic recession on the labour market. The effect of this change is to flatten out the centre of the "M" profile, leaving the initial rise, a plateau effect and the final fall, much more akin to a slide towards the retirement years than an "M".

Table 13 : Proportion of women working at different dates by age

	1949	1959	1969	1979	1989
Age at date	%	%	%	%	%
15-19 % Working	75	90	86	86	70
N	*65*	*87*	*69*	*84*	*47*
20-24 % Working	64	64	70	68	62
N	*70*	*92*	*110*	*99*	*111*
25-29 % Working		47	40	55	60
N		*72*	*109*	*101*	*123*
30-34 % Working		39	41	45	57
N		*71*	*92*	*111*	*101*
35-39 % Working			40	53	60
N			*72*	*110*	*98*
40-44 % Working			55	53	63
N			*71*	*91*	*112*
45-49 % Working				54	51
N				*72*	*110*
50-54 % Working				52	52
N				*71*	*91*
55-59 % Working					31
N					*71*
60-64 % Working					23
N					*70*
Total % working	70	62	55	58	54
N	*135*	*322*	*523*	*739*	*934*

Conclusion

In terms of general trends, the pattern of female employment in Northern Ireland over the decades has closely followed developments in the regional economy. In the early years of this century, women were to be found working in the manufacturing industries and in particular in the clothing and textile sectors. This pattern remained until the 1960s and 1970s when the industrial structure of the Province, in common with the rest of the United Kingdom, witnessed a dramatic change. The decline of the manufacturing sector and the expansion of the service industries resulted not only in a redistribution of the labour force but also in an increase in the number of part-time jobs. These new part-time jobs, predominantly in the service industries, tended to be low paid and of low status and were taken up by women. The longitudinal data from the WWLS show this general trend. The older women in the survey, who began their working lives in the 1940s and 50s, originally went into clothing and textiles but over their working lives have moved into the service sector, thereby joining the younger women in their first jobs. The type of work carried out by the women changed from weaving and stitching to catering and cleaning. Only the teachers, nurses and clerical workers tended to remain in the same occupation over their working lives.

The WWLS has shown that women, for whatever reason, tend to stay with the same employer for a reasonable length of time, thus contradicting the idea that women are a poor long term investment in terms of human capital. The most common reason given for leaving an employer was to move on to a better position. This was confirmed by the relatively poor promotion prospects many women experienced in their existing jobs. The argument that women do not wish to be promoted was clearly refuted, with 64% answering they would have liked to have been considered for promotion.

Looking at evidence of change over the decades it is quite clear that the traditional "M" profile of female economic rates is less and less accurate as a model of women's lives in the 1990s. The traditional pattern of women's employment habits has changed. The survey data have shown that the proportion of women who remained at work in the childrearing age range of 25 - 34 had increased to 60% by 1989. This result could be the first indicator that increased opportunities for part-time work, changing social attitudes and equality legislation are having an effect on women's working lives.

The WWLS longitudinal data have confirmed and refuted many of the hypotheses and myths which have been propounded on the working habits of women but as with all such surveys, the WWLS raises as many questions as it answers. The 1990s has been hailed as a decade of opportunity for women. As demographic trends predict a shortage of young people entering the labour market it is expected that women will be available to fill the void. It will be interesting to see whether this new phenomenon will result in a fundamental shift in women's employment prospects or whether part-time, low pay, low status jobs will remain the norm for women who have to cope with caring responsibilities.

References

Department of Economic Development (various dates). *Census of Employment*. Belfast: HMSO.

Dex, S. (1991). 'The reliability of recall data: A literature review.' *Occasional Papers of the ESRC Research Centre on Micro-social Change.* Occasional Paper 6, Colchester: University of Essex.

Greenhalgh, C. (1977). 'A labour supply function for married women in Great Britain.' *Economica, 44*, 249-65.

Harris, R.I.D., Jefferson, C.W. and Spencer, J.E. (eds.) (1990). *The Northern Ireland Economy. A Comparative Study in the Economic Development of a Peripheral Region.*

London: Longman.

Isles, K.S. and Cuthbert, N. (1957). *An Economic Survey of Northern Ireland.* Belfast: HMSO.

Joseph, G. (1983). *Women at Work.* Oxford: Philip Allan.

Martin, J. and Roberts, C. (1984). *Women and Employment: A Lifetime Perspective.* Department of Employment, Office of Population Censuses and Surveys. London: HMSO.

McEwen, A. et al. (1987). *Women in the Professions in Northern Ireland.* Belfast: Equal Opportunities Commission for Northern Ireland.

McWilliams, M. (1991). 'Women's paid work and the sexual division of labour.' In C. Davies and E. McLaughlin (eds.), *Women, Employment and Social Policy in Northern Ireland: A Problem Postponed.* Belfast: Policy Research Institute.

Trewsdale, J.M. (1987). *Womanpower No. 4: The Aftermath of Recession: Changing Patterns of Female Employment and Unemployment in Northern Ireland.* Belfast: Equal Opportunities Commission for Northern Ireland.

Trewsdale, J. M. (1990). 'Labour force characteristics.' In R.I.D.Harris, op. cit.

Trewsdale, J. M. and Trainor, M. (1981). *Womanpower No. 2: Recent Changes in the Female Labour Market in Northern Ireland.* Belfast: Equal Opportunities Commission for Northern Ireland.

Note

Data from pilot interviews were subsequently incorporated into the main data set given that no major problems arose during piloting. However, given different techniques used for gathering information on work histories during the pilot, it was not appropriate to analyse these returns. Hence effective respondents for the section on career history were reduced to 948.

Chapter 4

EDUCATION AND TRAINING

Carol Curry

Introduction

In Britain as elsewhere, increasing attention has become focused on women's education and training. There are two principal reasons why this has been the case. Firstly, a shortfall has been created by declining numbers of young people available to join the labour market (though this shortfall is not so pronounced in Northern Ireland as in other parts of the United Kingdom). Secondly, there have been fundamental shifts in employment patterns during the 1980s, shifts which have made "women's work" (seasonal, casual and part-time) increasingly prevalent (see Chapter 3). Recognition of the position of women in employment has been demonstrated recently by the launching of a major policy initiative, Opportunity 2000, this time with the explicit support of John Major as Prime Minister. The campaign aims for greater participation of women in the workforce, promoting the message that if companies come to recognise their pool of under-utilised, female employees they will eventually be rewarded with a more highly motivated staff, lower job turnover and bigger profits.

The principal concern of the chapter is not women's education per se but the relationship between women's educational qualifications and the labour market. As Cormack, Miller and Osborne (1987) have pointed out, "the problems women face are less in educational institutions and much more significantly in the labour market, in translating educational qualifications and credentials into quality employment with good career prospects". Even "educationally elite" women do not escape this problem. For example, in research which has compared the careers of female and male graduates, women fared less well on all indicators of job rewards. They were less likely to be in graduate level work and were more likely to be in routine non-manual work; they were paid less on average regardless of level of work, level of higher education attainment, subject of degree course, marital status or religion. In fact, being female was found to be the single most significant variable examined (Miller, Curry, Osborne and Cormack, 1991).

In order to deal systematically with the complexities of the relationship between formal education and employment, discussion will be framed around three concerns, namely access, process, and outcome, bearing in mind the considerable overlap and interplay between each. Whilst recognising the difficulties of distinguishing between education and training, here the two will be treated separately. While it is impossible to distinguish elements of training from educational courses, training is taken to refer to government and job-related training schemes specifically. The chapter concludes with a more general discussion of employment training to consider how government and employers have responded to the training needs and requirements of women. If the education system has failed to address the needs of the labour market, and has denied equal opportunities to all, then training becomes a vital link in the chain between the school and the workplace, and hence it offers a fitting conclusion to the chapter.

Education in Northern Ireland

The backcloth against which this analysis is conducted is Northern Ireland, a region where the education system is unique in several key respects. Looking at simple indices of success, as measured by average results, the number of pupils leaving school with good qualifications is impressive. The proportion of school leavers who obtained five or more GCE 'O' levels in Northern Ireland is greater than England and Wales, and, per head of population, a higher proportion of sixth form pupils continue into higher education (Cormack, Miller, Osborne and Curry, 1986). Unfortunately these figures only present one side of the coin. For all its merits, the system is also without question highly selective, some would say élitist, involving a two-tier structure of grammar and non-grammar schools within a framework where Protestant and Catholic children are, for the most part, educated separately. The consequence of a procedure based on selection is that the majority of children are screened out of the more academic grammar school places at 11 years of age. For the 70% and more of children who attend post-primary non-grammar or secondary schools, the profile of leaving qualifications is far from impressive. Compared to England and Wales, a higher proportion of those in non-grammar schools leave school with few or no qualifications. In fact it has been suggested that the proportion of children leaving school at the age of 16 without any qualifications is the highest in the United Kingdom (see Cormack, Miller and Osborne, 1987 for discussion).

In addition to selectivity, two features of the Northern Irish education system are worthy of note. Firstly, Northern Ireland has a significant proportion of post-primary schools which are single-sex, a percentage which is far higher than the rest of the United Kingdom. The pros and cons of single sex education have been much discussed with type of school emerging as one of the principal factors affecting girls' and boys' choices of subjects. For example, Dale (1969; 1971; 1974) showed that girls attending girls-only schools were more likely to take science subjects than those attending co-educational schools, and similar analyses have been proposed by Shaw (1980), Spender (1982) and Kelly (1982).

The evidence indicates that co-education has an inhibiting effect on girls' choice of science and mathematics subjects, in that girls tend to opt out of educational competition with boys in science subjects and suffer an apparent lack of self-confidence and self-esteem as a consequence of the "masculine" presentation of science (Kelly, 1982). However, the picture may be less clear-cut as there is evidence that the social class profile of girls attending single-sex schools is higher than that of girls in co-educational schools (Smithers and Collings, 1981; Bone, 1983). McEwen and Curry (1987) found that when factors of ability and social class were controlled for, there was no significant difference in the percentages of girls taking mathematics and the physical sciences in the different types of schools in Northern Ireland.

As well as considerations of single-sex versus co-educational schooling, a further strata appears when religion is taken into account. The majority of schools in Northern Ireland are segregated on the basis of religion, with most Protestant pupils attending state controlled schools wholly funded by the government and in which the church has a minority say in management. In contrast the majority of Catholic pupils attend maintained schools, still mostly funded by the government (apart from 15% of capital costs) but in which the government has a minority interest in school management. Differences between Catholic and Protestant pupils in terms of attainment at age 16 have been found, with pupils in Protestant schools achieving higher results (Gallagher, 1988). Osborne (1985) showed that more Protestant pupils left school with two or more GCE 'A' levels and these were more likely to be in science rather than arts subjects.

The education system in Northern Ireland is therefore unique; in many respects it is praiseworthy, in other respects it is far less meritorious. From a research perspective, this combination of structural factors offers considerable potential for gender research, and it is towards the position of girls and women within this system that we now turn. The WWLS surveyed women from the age of 18 to 65, therefore, although interviews were conducted at one point in time, the experience of the older women gives some insight as to how women have fared in the education system from the 1930s through to the 1990s.

Access to Education

Access to education starts with school attendance, and with this in mind it is noteworthy that nearly one-fifth of the women surveyed in the WWLS had no experience of secondary education. With the compulsory school leaving age set at 16 since 1972/73, it is also of note that more than two-thirds (69%) of the sample had left school by the age of 16, with just over a fifth (21%) having left at age 14 or younger. This point should not be ignored; too often research focuses on the educational élite and their experience whilst ignoring the stark fact that for the vast majority of the population, educational experience is limited to say the least.

Table 1 shows how these changing trends in compulsory schooling translate into the lives of the women in the survey. While nearly three-quarters of the over 60 group had left school at age 14 or earlier, nearly half of the younger age group had stayed at school after the compulsory school leaving age. Just over a quarter (26%) of the under 20 group had experience of full-time education at age 18 or older, as compared to only 3% of the over 60 group.

Table 1:   School-leaving age (from full-time education)

	Respondents' age						
	up to 20	21-30	31-40	41-50	51-60	61+	All
School leaving age	%	%	%	%	%	%	%
14-	-	-	2	18	61	73	21
15	-	6	25	39	9	5	18
16	51	54	35	18	9	8	30
17	24	17	18	13	10	11	15
18+	25	22	20	12	10	3	16
Total %	100	100	100	100	100	100	100
N	59*	245	217	231	173	73	998

* includes six still in full-time education

In relation to secondary education, the demographic stability of Northern Ireland (Compton, 1986) is revealed by the finding that almost nine out of ten women (88%) received their secondary education exclusively within Northern Ireland itself. As so many of the women living, working and mothering in Northern Ireland (and providing role models for their children) are the product of its education system, an examination of that system and the opportunities which it provides or denies becomes even more imperative. For example, regarding access to education, a stark illustration of the way in which discriminatory policy may directly deny equality of access from an early age was evident as recently as 1988. In that year, the Equal Opportunities Commission for Northern Ireland successfully brought litigation which ended the allocation of grammar school places on the basis of treating boys and girls as separate populations. Prior to this action, although girls performed better than boys, they were awarded the same percentage of places.

In terms of the WWLS, only 29% of the those who experienced secondary education attended a grammar school. Of those who went to a non-grammar school, the majority (81%) had attended a secondary (non-grammar) school,

12% attended a comprehensive (of which there are a small number in Northern Ireland), and 7% a further education or technical college. More girls than boys stay at school beyond the minimum leaving age in Northern Ireland. 57% of 17 year olds at school and 53% of 18-plus year olds are girls (Johnston and Rooney, 1987; see Montgomery and Davies, 1990, for further discussion). In terms of higher education, since 1963 when Robbins first highlighted the "wastage" of female ability, the participation of women in higher education has increased (Barry, 1992). In Northern Ireland, this increase has resulted in the proportion of female university entrants rising from 27% in 1966/67 to 48% female entry to degree level courses in the mid-80s to 51% by 1990/91, though part of this rise can be accounted for by the simultaneous contraction in places available in teacher training colleges. This increase in participation in higher education is encouraging but at the same time it should not be forgotten that still only 16% of the entire sample had received full-time education to the age of 18.

When dealing with the question of access, as well as describing structural constraints it is also important to take into account the factors which the individual identifies as facilitating or hindering her progress through the system. Those who had left school at primary level (N = 185) and those who had left at secondary level (N = 495) were asked to say why they had not continued their education. As Table 2 shows, almost three quarters of the women (74%) left to start work. Only 2% of the women said that they left school because they were needed at home. Looking beyond the data, it is impossible to tell from these responses if women actually left education voluntarily or if any pressure was exerted from families perhaps because of financial hardship or because girls were considered to have "had enough education".

Table 2: Reasons for leaving school

	%
Wanted to start work	74
Did not like school	10
Parents/relatives/friends advice to leave	6
Not aware of any other course	5
Needed at home	2
Nothing to go to	1
Don't know	2
Total %	100
N	*680*

As the opportunities now exist for those with few or no educational qualifications to take up courses as mature students, the WWLS asked those who had left school at either primary or secondary level whether they now regretted leaving school when they did, and whether they had any future plans for reviving their education. 60% of the women who did not continue with any further education had no regrets about leaving school when they did. Most of those who said they did have regrets felt that they had not achieved what they could have achieved at school (51%) or felt that their career prospects were now affected (37%).

Although three-quarters (75%) of those who had left school before or at secondary level had no plans to continue their education in the future, 132 women (19%) were planning further education, (definitely - 26%; probably - 18%; possibly - 55%).   The types of courses they hoped to take were very varied, with women often mentioning several possibilities. In addition to academic courses, (for example, GCSE [19%]; 'A' levels [9%]; degrees [7%]; other educational courses [18%]) other courses which were more related to employment were mentioned, (24% opting for some kind of clerical/secretarial course, 8% social work, 10% nursing, 9% childcare, 11% skills training and 2% planning to study for professional examinations). Although the courses are varied, what is of note is that almost all appear as very conventional, with no discernible shift towards non-traditional areas.

Women who were considering furthering their education were asked to give their reasons and, as Table 3 shows, 53% of women chose "Personal development". Although this reason was often only one of several, it would appear that women are selecting courses which they perceive to be beneficial in terms of their own needs. On the basis of their responses, it is clear that these women were taking a positive personal and career oriented action in returning to education.

Table 3: Reasons for planning future education *

Reasons	%
Personal development	53
Improve career	42
Help return to work	18
Boredom	15
Change of job	15
N	*132*

* Respondents may have replied to more than one item so %s do not sum to 100.

The majority of women who continued with some kind of post-secondary further education tended to do so immediately after leaving secondary school

(79%), while 12% did so within five years and the rest at some later stage (in discussing education after secondary level the term "further education" is used to cover all types of education including higher education, unless otherwise specified). In terms of full-time or part-time education, the majority went into full-time further education (77%), with the remainder studying part-time. Most of those who were studying part-time were also working, some for only a few hours per week but others showed evidence of greater commitment, with 61% working between 30 and 40 hours per week and 19% over 40 hours per week. There were few differences between those who had studied full-time and part-time in terms of the reasons given for opting for further education, with around a third of both groups citing personal development, a further third citing career improvement, and 36% of full-time and part-time students choosing both of these reasons. Altogether these reasons accounted for 94% of responses of full-time students and 80% of part-time students.

Given the proportion of women who attended non-grammar schools, it is perhaps not surprising that the majority of full-time and part-time students went on to take non-degree courses (Table 4).

Table 4: Choice of further/higher education courses

Course	Full-time %	Part-time %
GCSE or equivalent	3	19
Secretarial/business	27	41
C&G/HND/BTech	9	11
Skilled occupation	4	3
Degree courses	20	6
Teacher training	12	1
Nurse training	14	1
Professional exams	-	3
Other	11	14
Total %	100	100
N	225	64

For the full-time students, secretarial/business courses were the most popular. Although the survey does not provide details of the precise nature of the subjects taken, the "other" category included courses on cookery, hairdressing, dental therapy, which when taken with teaching, nursing and secretarial courses reflects the traditional orientation of women. Those who had taken or were taking part-time education showed quite a different pattern in their choice of courses, with the largest percentages taking GCSE (19%) or secretarial/business courses (41%). Half of those who studied part-time also worked part-time, and 15% worked full-time while they were studying. Most had studied either in the evenings and at week-ends (71%) or had day/block release (21%), with a further 6% doing both.

The different types of courses studied full and part-time are reflected in the types of institutions in which they were undertaken. Of those studying full-time, most had attended a college of further education (40%), 22% a university or polytechnic, 11% a teacher training college, 8% a school of nursing, and 10% a secretarial/business school.   Over three-quarters of part-timers were completing their courses in a college of further education. Only 6% had attended a university or polytechnic and a further 6% a secretarial/business school.

Educational Processes

Although the present survey was not able to look directly at the experiences which women gained through the course of their education, it is nevertheless possible to draw inferences from some of the findings. Given that a principal aim of the 1944 Education Act was to ensure that secondary education should be accessible to all, irrespective of social or financial circumstances, the assumption would surely follow that a fundamental principle would be equality for all children, whether male or female. As research over the years has indicated, what has been termed the "hidden curriculum" affects girls and boys differently. For example, in early primary classes, sex stereotypes are typified by different uses of the "Wendy House" (Whyte 1983), the sex-typed content of early school readers and the complex set of factors underlying different teacher-pupil interaction for girls and boys (Mullin, Morgan and Dunn, 1986).

Whilst the introduction of the common curriculum has been hailed as a means of introducing equality in subject provision for all pupils, Morgan (1991), who has recently considered the impact that the new common curriculum will have on equality issues, has questioned whether equality of access to school subjects will result in equality of outcomes for all pupils. If girls and boys are unable to take the same advantage of the curriculum offered, then underlying gender differences in school experience may not be overcome.

Two further factors which are of immense importance in Northern Ireland, and particularly in post-primary schools, are religion and school type, that is single-sex or mixed-sex. The interplay of both of these factors has been discussed earlier but one stark example of the effects of school type on opportunity has been revealed by Reid and Kremer (1990). As recently as 1988, they noted that no single-sex girls school in Northern Ireland offered craft, design and technology as a school subject, nor did they have the workshop facilities to begin to address this gap in provision. Within mixed schools, the numbers of girls taking these technically oriented subjects was very low - only 6% of GCSE candidates in 1989 were girls. The impact of this lack of provision on career development for women is immense. The biases which exist within schools are made more complex by the ethos which characterises both Catholic and Protestant school systems and the arguably different emphasis that have been placed on the arts/humanities and science subjects within the two traditions (Osborne, 1985).

Overall, a slightly greater proportion of women in the WWLS had attended a post primary mixed-sex school (56%). Of those who attended grammar schools, 64% were educated at single-sex schools. However, at non-grammar secondary schools the reverse was true, with the greater percentage (61%) attending mixed-sex schools. Almost three-quarters (74%) of the Catholic sample attended secondary non-grammar schools compared to 69% of Protestant women, and a much higher percentage of Catholic women attended single-sex schools, both grammar and non-grammar, as shown in Table 5. (These figures are based on the 96% of the sample who indicated a religious category.)

Table 5: Type of education

		Protestant		Catholic	
		%	N	%	N
Grammar:					
	Mixed-sex	15		3	
	Single-sex	16		22	
	Total	31	*145*	25	*79*
Non-grammar:					
	Mixed-sex	51		37	
	Single-sex	18		37	
	Total	69	*324*	74	*230*
Total		100	*469*	100	*309*

The experience of women in education in Northern Ireland is influenced by a more varied set of factors than applies in Great Britain. As elsewhere, a school may be good or bad, it may be geographically urban or rural, it may draw from predominantly working class or middle class families and it may be large or small. However, in Northern Ireland the school may also be either Protestant or Catholic, and at secondary level, either grammar or non-grammar and single-sex or mixed-sex. In their own way, each of these factors will influence the child's educational experience and ultimately his or her academic achievements.

Educational Outcomes

How do girls ultimately fare; what qualifications and experience do they derive from this system? Johnston and Rooney (1987) discuss gender differences in the uptake of subjects and qualifications and point out that fewer girls (19%) leave school unqualified than boys (29%) and, in terms of high achievers, 12% of girls gain two or more 'A' levels compared to 9% of boys. In fact examination results at secondary level have consistently revealed that girls do better than boys at both GCSE and 'A' level. However, it is in the subject choices which girls make that they are disadvantaged in terms of the labour market. Although from 1982 to 1986, the percentages of GCE 'A' level awards made to females studying mathematics increased (31% to 40%), similarly with physics (27% to 33%) and chemistry (40% to 47%), males still outnumber females in these subjects.

In terms of the qualifications of those surveyed for the WWLS, to reiterate, the most striking statistic is the number of women who left secondary education without obtaining any kind of qualifications, 38%. If those who did not have any secondary education are included, then half the sample (50%) left school with no certificates of any kind. Just over one third (35%) had achieved secondary certificates up to GCSE level or equivalent while less than 10% had achieved one or more GCE 'A' levels. The remainder (7%) had various vocational certificates including secretarial and catering.

To see how the position of women has changed in terms of school qualifications over the years, Table 6 gives a breakdown by age of respondent. As expected, more older women left school unqualified and more younger women gained higher qualifications. More than half of those who left school with no qualifications are in the 41 - 60 age category. Over three-quarters of the best qualified school leavers, that is those with 'A' levels, are younger women in the 21 to 40 age band. Various secondary certificates up to GCSE level or equivalent were obtained by the 21 to 50 group, and "other" qualifications were mostly obtained by the 31 to 50 age groups.

Table 6: Qualifications gained at primary/secondary level by age

Qualifications	up to 20 %	21-30 %	31-40 %	41-50 %	51-60 %	60+ %
None	21	29	44	59	74	65
< GCSE	66	51	33	27	23	15
'A' levels	11	16	15	5	0	6
Other	2	4	8	9	4	13
Total %	100	100	100	100	100	100
N	53	247	214	231	168	78

Table 7 gives the highest qualification gained by the women in the sample and compares their post secondary qualification with those gained at secondary level. Only 4% of those who left school with no qualifications have gone on to gain some kind of post-secondary school qualification, leaving 46% of the sample with no qualifications.

Table 7: Educational qualification achieved at secondary and post-secondary levels

Qualifications	Primary/secondary education %	Highest qualification achieved %
No qualifications	50	46
Up to GCSE or equivalent	35	19
A level or equivalent	9	9
Vocational	6	16
Professional/Academic	-	10
Total %	100	100
N	984	984

The WWLS clearly demonstrates the disadvantaged position of older women in the Northern Ireland labour market in terms of qualifications. In addition, the findings highlight that a high percentage of the pool of potential women returners, 44% of those aged 31 to 40 and 59% of those aged 41 to 50, are likely to have no formal qualifications. If women are to find their way into the labour market and are not to be confined to the low paid, low status jobs which have traditionally been the lot of women returners, then it is essential that education and training policy address this disadvantage. In recent years, with the expansion and encouragement of adult education, decisions made during secondary education may no longer be final, but for the older women in the sample, the qualifications which they left school with tend to cast the mould for the rest of their working lives. Indeed, overall only one quarter of the sample (26%) gained qualifications beyond secondary level schooling - 16% vocational and 10% professional or academic.

For women, much more so than for men, there is no straightforward relationship between qualifications and employment status. Irrespective of educational qualifications, for many women employment depends not only on the job market and availability of work but more critically on family and domestic considerations, especially when children are young (see Chapter 2). That said, the impact of lack of qualifications comes through clearly in an examination of the qualifications of part-time and full-time employees. Not surprisingly Table 8 shows that more part-time than full-time employees were unqualified, and that more full-time employees were represented in the vocational, professional and academic grades.

Table 8: Qualifications of full-time and part-time employees

	Employment status	
	Full-time	Part-time
Qualifications	%	%
No qualifications	27	45
Up to GCSE level	27	20
A level	12	11
Vocational	17	18
Professional/Academic	17	6
Total %	100	100
N	327	207

Even taking into account the difficulties associated with relating qualifications to pay for women, there are discernible patterns as regards earnings. For those in full-time work, the higher the qualification, the higher the earnings (Table 9). For example, while nearly half of those who were unqualified were earning between £100 and £150 per week, over half of those who had post-secondary qualifications (either vocational/professional or academic), were earning over £200 per week. Similarly, nearly nine in ten (89%) unqualified part-time workers earned less than £100 per week, compared to 60% of those who had post-secondary qualifications.

Table 9: Earnings by qualifications

	Employment status					
	Full-time			Part-time		
Gross earnings per week	No quals	School quals	Post-school	No quals	School quals	Post-school
	%	%	%	%	%	%
<£25-£50	3	2	2	47	35	27
£51-£100	23	23	9	42	39	33
£101-£150	49	31	22	8	17	18
£151-£200	13	25	16	2	5	18
£201-£300	8	12	28	1	3	-
>£301	3	7	23	-	-	4
Total %	100	100	100	100	100	100
N	86	124	103	89	57	45

In contrast with most educational research, the WWLS has turned attention away from school pupils and towards a broader spectrum of women between 18 and 65 years of age. Educational qualifications need not remain fixed at the level achieved at primary or secondary school, and there were women who were planning to restart their education, for their own personal development as well as to enhance their careers. On the more negative side, for many women, and particularly older women, education remained very much a thing of the past; nearly half (46%) of the sample were unqualified and less than 10% had professional or academic qualifications.

While there can be no satisfactory definition of where education ends and training begins, the analysis has concentrated on compulsory education, and further/higher education courses, either taken or planned. Clearly, given the percentage of women who remained unqualified on completion of their education, there is a problem which needs to be addressed. As technological change continues within all aspects of employment, the need for training (and re-training) of new skills becomes more acute. Therefore it is pertinent to examine the experience which women have had of government and job-related training to ask just how interested are women in training, what opportunities exist for training, how useful the training is felt to be, and whether women welcome the opportunity for further training. These are all questions which the WWLS is able to address.

Government Training Schemes

Increasingly, government is being forced to recognise the significance of women's training needs, in many respects to redress the imbalance of opportunity which has been afforded to girls and boys through the formal education process. Interest has turned to the development of skills which women may need in order to meet the needs or technological requirements of the labour market. In Northern Ireland, there are recent examples of policy statements from government which would appear to show concern for this issue. For example, the Department of Economic Development's Training and Employment Agency (NI) (1991) recently stated:

> *In seeking to achieve the Agency's overall aim of assisting economic growth in Northern Ireland by ensuring the provision and operation of training and employment services which contribute to firms becoming more competitive and to individuals obtaining the skills and competence required for increased competitiveness and for securing employment, the Board and Chief Executive are committed to the view that women here have an important role to play in helping to secure the achievement of this aim (Department of Economic Development, 1991).*

There are signs that women's training is being afforded a higher priority within government. Programmes to encourage women back into the labour market at management level have been piloted by the Training and Employment

Agency, and earlier criticisms of the Youth Training Programme (YTP) on the grounds of sexual inequality seem to have been taken on board, at least to some extent, by the publication of a Code of Practice on Sex Equality for the training organizations.

How policy initiatives actually translate into practice remains to be seen but one starting point is to monitor the number of women who were currently involved in government training schemes, and the types of courses which they were taking. Table 10 gives the percentages for female and male participation in the various programmes. The numbers involved are substantial - with over 20,000 people involved on YTP and the Action for Community Employment (ACE) programmes alone. Of the 13,115 young people on the YTP in the first quarter of 1991, just over one third were female. With regard to the craft apprenticeships run by the Training Centres, of the adults attending, only 12% of the 286 attending were female, and only 2% of the 1545 young people attending centres were women (DED, 1991).

Table 10: Male and female participation on government training programmes (quarter ending March 1991)

	Programmes			
	YTP (16-18)	*Training Centres	Job Training	ACE
Sex	%	%	%	%
Female	36	4	32	47
Male	64	96	69	54
Total %	100	100	100	100
N	13,115	1,831	3,011	10,265

*Figures for young people are included in the overall totals for YTP

Source: Department of Economic Development, 1991

Montgomery and Davies (1990) have drawn attention to the need to explore not only overall representation on training schemes but also the specific representation of males and females on particular courses within schemes. Using such an approach in assessing equality of opportunity in one government scheme, the YTP, they found a high degree of segregation by sex along traditional lines. They concluded that action for equality needed to be implemented at all levels of the programme, and found that just as girls are associated with traditional girls' subjects at school, they continue to be easily channelled into traditional courses on the YTP. Table 11 illustrates how the more traditional YTP courses are, for the most part, clearly identified with one sex or the other, while the newer courses, such as Recreation and Information Technology, show a more mixed participation.

Table 11: Full-time further education college vocational courses associated with YTP by gender, 1988-1989

	N	Number of females	% of females
Male-dominated schemes:			
Construction	188	-	0
Engineering	65	1	1
Engineering/Construction	58	-	0
Electronics	52	3	6
Agriculture/Horticulture	4	-	0
Soccer skills	25	-	0
Video/TV	11	-	0
Female-dominated schemes:			
Office/Clerical	164	141	86
Caring services	120	114	95
Catering/Caring	28	23	82
Personal services	60	55	92
Travel and Tourism	34	31	91
Mixed-sex schemes:			
Catering	113	43	38
Recreation	41	17	42
Information Technology	19	10	53
Distribution	21	9	43
Drama	20	11	55

Source: Cited in Montgomery and Davies (1990); original source DENI.

Problems encountered by young girls and women (especially those attending non-traditional courses) have been documented by recent research. These include difficulties such as the timing and venue of courses which mean that women with family responsibilities find it impossible to attend, a lack of effective information which would positively encourage women to participate, counter-signals such as leaflets showing only men doing particular jobs, and a lack of compensatory education and confidence building for women who have been out of work for long periods (McCorry, 1985). The effectiveness of any training scheme is not only dependent on the quality of the scheme but on the differing skills and motivations which the participants bring to such a scheme. It was not possible to take these factors into account in the WWLS, but rather to audit the extent of training offered and the women's perception of its usefulness.

It is perhaps significant that in total, less than 10% of the sample had participated in a government training scheme. As Table 12 shows, the most frequently taken courses were YTP courses (46%), with a further 7% citing other general courses such as "Youthways", "Youth Community Programme" and the "ACE" scheme, with 6% taking courses in childcare. 20% had taken a secretarial/clerical type course, 4% a hairdressing course and 4% a catering course. The remainder (12%) mentioned an assortment of courses with no more than one person in any of the categories.   Overall, these choices seem to reflect a continuing and strong traditional bias in terms of women's work. Exceptions were rare, for example one woman stated that she had been on a light electronics course.   In terms of perceived usefulness of the courses, however, more than three-quarters (79%) rated the course they had taken as very or quite useful in terms of work opportunities.

Table 12: Type of government course undertaken

Course	%
YTP	46
Clerical/secretarial	20
Youthways/Ace etc	7
Community care/visitor	6
Hairdressing	4
Catering	4
Other	12
Total %	100
N	*86*

Government training schemes do not seem to play a significant part in the lives of women, and when women do attend, the courses they take are very traditional. It is to be hoped that the aims of the Equality Monitoring Unit of the Training and Employment Agency will be effective - "the purpose is to identify programmes in which there are fewer applicants or participants than would be expected from particular sectors, groups or categories such as women." (DED, 1991, p 1.)

Job Related Training

A second type of training is that associated with a person's work. This may be either "on the job" or "in-house" training offered by the employer, or a combination of this and additional courses organized away from employment, for example, by day release to a course run at a further education college. The WWLS enquired about both these types of training in relation to the women's current occupation. For those in professional employment (e.g. teachers, managers, nurses, doctors) training for professional qualifications was included only where this was directly relevant to their present work and where training was given while they were in post. The data are based on the responses from 490 women who were working as employees, and are concerned with the duration and usefulness of training the women received in general. They are not offered as an assessment of the effectiveness of the training given.

Table 13 shows that half the women working as employees had not received any training and a further 18% had received less than one week's training. Only 9% had received training which lasted over six months. As expected, more part-timers than full-time employees had not received any training, and more full-time employees had received training in almost all the categories listed (with the exception of "2 days"). In comparing the amount of training reported here with that noted by Martin and Roberts (1984), half of the women in the WWLS received no training from their employer, compared to 42% reported by Martin and Roberts. They also found that part-timers were much more likely not to have had any training associated with their present job.

Table 13: Training associated with present employment

	Employment status		
	All	Full-time	Part-time
Duration of training	%	%	%
None	49	40	64
Half a day or less	3	3	3
One day	3	2	3
2 days but less than 1 week	13	14	11
1 week but less than 1 month	10	12	8
1 month but less than 6 months	13	20	3
Over 6 months	9	9	8
Total %	100	100	100
N	490	297	193

For those in full-time paid work, when training associated with current occupation is examined no clear-cut pattern emerges (Table 14). This is perhaps because training for current occupation may have been gained with a previous employer, or, in the case of those in professional occupations, training would be gained prior to starting work. Around half the women in clerical, selling and catering occupations received no training in their current employment.

At the other end of the scale, for those who received six months or more training, the professionals account for 63%, and those in catering 15%, while clerical, selling and processing account for very low levels of extended training.

Table 14:   Duration of training associated with full-time current occupation

	Current occupation				
	Professional	Clerical	Selling	Catering	Processing
Duration of training	%	%	%	%	%
None	32	46	55	56	19
half day to 1 week	22	20	22	10	13
1 week to 1 mth	12	11	7	13	12
1 mth to 6 months	14	20	15	10	53
Over 6 months	20	2	-	10	3
Total %	100	100	100	100	100
N	*86*	*98*	*27*	*39*	*32*

Of those who had received some kind of training, "On the job" training accounted for 40%, with "Courses at work" accounting for another 26%. Day and block release as well as a combination of courses and "On the job" training accounted for a further 24%. Only 4% of women had attended a residential training course. 7% had pursued professional qualifications. As Table 15 also shows, whether women work full-time or part-time, the rank order of the type of training given to women is the same for both groups, with "On the job" training and courses at work the most common, and residential courses least likely.

Table 15: Type of training associated with present job

	Employment status		
	All	Full-time	Part-time
Type of training	%	%	%
"On the job"	40	38	43
Courses at work	26	25	27
Day-block release	14	15	13
Courses and "on the job"	10	10	9
Professional qualifications	7	8	4
Residential courses	4	3	4
Total %	100	100	100
N	*246*	*177*	*68*

How does this apparently low level of training compare with that available to men employed in the same organisations? The women were asked about the level of training they received "In comparison with men at your place of work". The WWLS is only able to report the womens' perception of the situation, and as 70 women worked in single-sex environments, the responses are based on those 175 women who were currently working with men. As Table 16 shows, the majority of women (85%) thought that they were treated fairly in comparison with men as regards training.

Table 16: Women's perception of relative training opportunities for women and men

		Employment status	
	All	Full-time	Part-time
Women receive:	%	%	%
Much more training	1	1	0
More training	2	1	7
Similar training	85	87	77
Less training	5	3	10
Much less training	3	4	0
Don't Know	5	4	5
Total %	100	100	100
N	175	135	40

Over one-third (36%) felt that there would be no additional training associated with their present job. 62% of the women felt they would have opportunities for further training but of these nearly 27% said the training would only be for new or more complex jobs. In terms of whether women are interested in additional training, 60% of the 245 women in this survey who had already received some form of training would welcome the opportunity for more training. Almost all said they would prefer day release or in-house training with only 6% preferring residential courses away from home. This again most likely reflects womens' responsibilities towards home and children and the amount of effort involved in organizing families in order to be able to attend a residential course.

Conclusion

On the one hand this chapter has illustrated that the participation of women in education has increased over the years, but at the same time, the analysis has served to highlight the persistent problem of under-utilisation of women with the necessary skills, together with the number of women who have left school with few, if any, marketable qualifications. The WWLS suggests that, at the present time, half the population of women of working age in Northern Ireland do not possess any kind of educational qualifications. It is increasingly possible for women who have missed out on their education "first time around" to take up educational courses as adults, and almost one-fifth of those who left school at secondary level have at least an idea or a positive plan to take up an educational course in the future. However, there remains a large number of predominantly older women for whom education remains a closed book.

With regard to training, fewer women than has been found elsewhere in Britain had the opportunity for training associated with their current employment, and the numbers who have availed themselves of government training schemes is low. Part-time employees were less likely to be given any training than full-time employees. Over half of all working women stated they would welcome the chance of further training, but almost all of these women would prefer not to have training courses that took them away from home. While working women are keen to take up training opportunities, they would prefer that this training was not organized on a residential basis.

In order to address the needs of women and ultimately ensure that industry and commerce are provided with a resource which is kitted out with the necessary skills and experience, it is beholden to those involved in education and training to recognise the special requirements of women, and to identify and lower the barriers which have hindered progress and equality of opportunity in the past. To begin this process it is necessary to chart systematically the impediments to progress, and here the work of Boswell (1985) may be significant.

In examining the reasons why many girls are precluded specifically from entering mathematics and science-related fields, Boswell (1985) identified three sets of factors. These can easily be used to frame the relationship between womens' educational achievements and the labour market more generally. The first set of factors includes external structural barriers. Although various pieces of legislation and policy documents relating to education and employment have prescribed equality for all, it would be naïve to assume that discriminatory barriers no longer exist. The present chapter has identified many such barriers, including differential access to technological courses. Until the practice of equality of opportunity genuinely matches the policy, then these structural impediments will remain insurmountable obstacles for many women.

Secondly, there are social pressures. These derive from significant others, such as parents, teachers and peers, and they act to constantly remind girls what are acceptable social norms. While external structural barriers may no longer be immediately threatening, there is still little positive encouragement for many girls and women to consider non-traditional careers, for example in the more lucrative science and technological fields. In addition there is also strong social pressure reinforcing the role of women as child carers, especially when children are under five, and maintaining traditional attitudes against women with young children working outside the home. One indication of the strength of these pressures may be gauged by the low take-up rate of non-traditional courses on government training schemes.

Thirdly, there are internal barriers. These include lack of confidence, fear of success, and in general, negative attitudes towards careers that have traditionally been regarded as "male" preserves. The significance of these barriers is more difficult to quantify, but until the first two barriers have been removed then the opportunity for women to begin to realise their potential will be that much more difficult, and women's self-esteem will continue to suffer. The end result of this process is that many competent and able women may be setting their sights (in career terms) lower than is justified by their proven abilities.

References

Barry, R. (1992). 'Females in education: The statistical picture. Paper presented at the British Psychological Society (Northern Ireland Branch) Conference, *Girls and Women in Education.* Stranmillis College, Belfast.

Bone, A. (1983). *Girls and Girls Only Schools: A Review of the Evidence.* Manchester: Equal Opportunities Commission.

Boswell, S.L. (1985). 'The influence of sex-role stereotyping on women's attitudes and achievement in mathematics.' In S. Chipman, L. Brush and D. Wilson (eds.), *Women and Mathematics: Balancing the Equation.* Hillsdale, New Jersey: LEA.

Collins, E. (1989). *Girls in Education.* NICER Summary Series No. 8. Belfast: Northern Ireland Council for Educational Research.

Compton, P. (1986). *Demographic Trends in Northern Ireland.* Belfast: Northern Ireland Economic Council.

Cormack, R.J., Miller, R.L., Osborne, R.D. and Curry, C.A. (1986). *Higher Education Demand Survey, Interim Report.* Belfast: ELMS.

Cormack, R.J., Miller ,R.L. and Osborne, R.D. (1987). 'Introduction.' In R.D. Osborne, R.J. Cormack and R.L. Miller (eds.), *Education and Policy in Northern Ireland.* Belfast: Policy Research Institute.

Curry, C.A. and McEwen, A. (1989). 'The "Wendy house" syndrome: A teenage version.' *Research in Education, 41,* 53-60.

Dale, R.R. (1969). *Mixed or Single-Sex Schools, Vol. 1: Pupil Teacher Relationships.* London: Routledge and Kegan Paul.

Dale, R.R. (1971). *Mixed or Single-Sex Schools, Vol. 2: Some Social Aspects.* London: Routledge and Kegan Paul.

Dale, R.R. (1974). *Mixed or Single-Sex Schools, Vol. 3: Attainment, Attitudes and Overview.* London: Routledge and Kegan Paul.

Department of Economic Development Training and Employment Agency (1991). *Women's Training and Related Issues.* Belfast: TEA.

Egerton, E.A. (1987). 'Women in medicine.' In R.D. Osborne, R.J. Cormack and R.L. Miller (eds.), *Education and Policy in Northern Ireland.* Belfast: Policy Research Institute.

Gallagher, A.M. (1988). *Transfer Pupils at Sixteen.* NICER Summary Series No 4.

Belfast: Northern Ireland Council for Educational Research.

Hakim, C. (1979). *Occupational Segregation: A Comparative Study of the Degree and Pattern of the Differentiation between Men and Women's Work in Britain, the United States and Other Countries.* Department of Employment Research Paper No. 9. London: Department of Employment.

Johnston, J. and Rooney, E. (1987). 'Gender differences in education.' In R.D. Osborne, R.J. Cormack and R.L. Miller (eds.), *Education and Policy in Northern Ireland.* Belfast: Policy Research Institute.

Kelly, A. (1982). 'Gender roles at home and school.' *British Journal of Sociology of Education, 3, 3,* 281-285.

Kremer, J. and Curry, C. (1986). *Attitudes towards Women in Northern Ireland.* Belfast: Equal Opportunities Commission for Northern Ireland.

McCorry, M. (1985). *Women and the Need for Training.* Belfast: Women's Education Project.

McEwen, A., Curry, C.A. and Watson, J. (1986). 'Subject preferences at A-level in Northern Ireland.' *European Journal of Science Education, 8, 1,* 39-50.

McEwen, A. and Curry, C. (1987). 'Girls' access to science: single-sex versus co-educational schools.' In R.D. Osborne, R.J. Cormack and R.L. Miller (eds.), *Education and Policy in Northern Ireland.* Belfast: Policy Research Institute.

Martin J. and Roberts C. (1984). *Women and Employment: A Lifetime Perspective.* London: HMSO.

Miller, R.L., Curry, C.A., Osborne, R.D., and Cormack R.J. (1991). *The Labour Market Experiences of an Educational Elite: A Continuous Time Analysis of Recent Higher Education Graduates.* Centre for Policy Research, Research Paper No. 2. Jordanstown: The University of Ulster at Jordanstown.

Montgomery, P., and Davies, C (1990) *Sex Equality in the Youth Training Programme.* Belfast: Equal Opportunities Commission for Northern Ireland.

Morgan, V. (1991). *Common Curriculum - Equal Curriculum: Girls and Boys and the Northern Ireland Common Curriculum: Mathematics, Science and English.* Belfast: Equal Opportunities Commission for Northern Ireland.

Mullin, B., Morgan, V., and Dunn, S. (1986). *Gender Differentiation in Infant Classes.* Belfast: Equal Opportunities Commission for Northern Ireland.

Osborne, R.D. (1985). *Religion and Educational Qualifications in Northern Ireland.* Fair Employment Agency Research Paper No.8. Belfast: Fair Employment Agency.

Reid, C., and Kremer, J. (1990). *Craft Design and Technology: The Northern Ireland Experience.* NICER Summary Series No.13. Belfast: Northern Ireland Council for Educational Research.

Robbins Report (1963). *Higher Education.* London: HMSO.

Shaw, J. (1980). Education and the individual: schooling for girls or mixed schooling, a mixed blessing. In R. Deem (ed.), *Schooling for Women's Work.* London: Routledge and Kegan Paul.

Smithers, A. and Collings, J. (1981). 'Girls studying science in the VIth form.' In A. Kelly (ed.), *The Missing Half.* Manchester: Manchester University Press.

Spender, D. (1982). *Invisible Women, the Schooling Scandal.* London: Reader and Writer's Publishing.

Whyte, J. (1983). *Beyond the Wendy House: Sex role stereotyping in primary schools.* London: Longman.

Chapter 5

EMPLOYMENT

Janet Trewsdale and Ann Toman

Introduction

The European Community

Over recent years the European Community (EC) as a whole has experienced a growth in employment creation. Between 1985 and 1988 employment in Europe grew by 4%, representing a total of 4.8 million jobs (Commission of the European Communities, 1990). For women in particular, this has been a very significant period as they have filled the majority of these new jobs (2.8 million or 58%; Commission of the European Communities, 1990). It is also noteworthy that this increase in employment has not reflected in a similar decrease in female unemployment, as many of the jobs have been filled either by young people entering the employment market for the first time or by women who were not previously considered to be officially unemployed.

Whilst the EC in general experienced employment growth between 1985 and 1988, this growth was far from uniform, varying from 3% - 3.5% a year in Portugal and Spain, to under 2% in the United Kingdom (UK) and Denmark, less than 0.5% in France, and in Belgium employment actually fell during this time. However, in all member states, bar West Germany, female employment rates increased significantly more than male employment rates, with a related trend, in the majority of countries, for part-time employment to increase at a higher rate than full-time employment. Despite the widespread increase in women's employment, by 1988 the proportion of the population aged between 15 and 64 years who were in employment was still relatively low (approximately 60%), in comparison with over 70% amongst economic competitors such as the United States and Japan. The participation of women of working age in the labour force, based on 1988 figures, also varied throughout the EC, ranging from just over 30% in Spain and Ireland to just under 60% in Denmark. The UK participation rate of around 50% compared favourably with the EC average of 41%. The male participation rate average was just over 68% for the same period.

Looking towards the future, it is generally accepted that the potential for women to increase their labour force participation is favourable in the 1990s as the fuse on the so-called "demographic time-bomb" grows shorter. This time-bomb results from falling birth rates from the mid 1960s onwards, with smaller family sizes naturally resulting in a shortage of young persons entering the labour market in the late 1990s (Compton, 1989). This relatively smaller cohort of young persons will cause the age profile of the population to rise, and one of the countries which will experience this most acutely is West Germany given that the number of births has fallen by 40% since the 1960s. However, the effect of this decline has been cushioned by an influx of guest workers from countries such as Turkey, and since 1990 by the reunification of Germany. Spain, Portugal and Italy also experienced large falls in their birth rates during the 1960s, resulting inevitably in fewer school leavers during the 1980s and 1990s. The result of this demographic shift has been, and will be, that EC employers must rethink their recruitment policies and concentrate more attention on previously economically inactive persons such as women seeking to re-enter the labour market after an absence of several years, and women seeking to combine their jobs with family responsibilities which require absences or leaves of varying duration. With this in mind, it has been estimated that within the EC there are some 21 million economically inactive women in the 25-49 age group (Commission of the European Communities, 1990), that is, those who classify themselves as housewives or otherwise are unable to take up employment. Given that the labour force participation rate for women with children is around 50% in the EC as a whole, with substantial differences between member states, this group represents a significantly under-utilized resource.

The United Kingdom

The effects of the demographic time-bomb will also be evident in the UK where it is predicted that during the 1990s, all regions will witness a decline in the numbers of people under 25 years of age, varying from 9% in Northern Ireland to 29% in Scotland (Department of Employment, 1990). At the same time it is estimated that there is likely to be an overall increase of 3.7% in the total number of persons in the UK labour force by the year 2000. Given a shortage of young people and that most suitably qualified men will be employed, the single most obvious alternative supply of labour will be mature women, those between the ages of 25 and 55 who either will be returning to the labour market after raising their families or will be fresh recruits.

Comparing Britain with the rest of the EC in terms of employment creation and women's participation in the labour force, trends follow a similar course. In 1979 the economic activity rate for women of working age in Great Britain (16 - 59) was 63%. Although this increased substantially to 71% by 1989, it was still some way below the comparable figure of 88% for men. Over this same period the number of women in employment in Great Britain grew by 19% from nine million to 10.7 million and this growth is expected to continue (Department of Employment, 1990). Most of the growth in employment in the decade to 1989 was in the services sector, where many of the jobs which were created were part-time and subsequently more appealing to women who have to combine the conflicting demands of work and family (see Chapter 2). The growth in the services sector was fuelled by the expansion of credit in the 1980s and occurred in sectors such as retailing, catering and financial services where the patterns of working depend on demand, examples of this being late night and lunchtime opening. On the other hand, traditional manufacturing industries such as heavy engineering, steel and shipbuilding continued to shed labour and factories closed throughout the decade, thus providing few job opportunities for women or men. It is expected that the trend towards job creation in the services sector will continue through the 1990s in the UK and other Western industrialised nations.

At present, women account for over 40% of the UK workforce and are forecast to make up over 80% of the increase in the labour force to 1995. The UK government began issuing advice in the late 1980s which was directed towards employers and which encouraged them to think carefully about their recruitment and selection policies. The Employment Secretary commented that the 1990s would be "the decade of the working woman", and in 1991 the Department of Employment issued a guide to employers on the benefits of a flexible approach to working arrangements (Department of Employment, 1991). Employers hoping to tap into the female labour market have had to adjust to the fact that many women are unable to follow the traditional "male" pattern of employment and that women may only be able to work if they can dovetail employment with domestic responsibilities and in particular the care of children and other dependants. In practice, this will mean the introduction of more flexible working conditions in the form of part-time working, term-time working, job sharing, flexible working hours, homeworking, teleworking, career break schemes and an improvement of childcare facilities. In the area of childcare the government has recently introduced tax relief for employers to establish workplace nurseries for the children of employees. Many of these employment arrangements have already been adopted by the Civil Service and the major banks. In a study undertaken to examine effective methods to improve the recruitment and retention of women, it was reported that the most popular measure was the introduction of such flexible working provisions (Industrial Relations Services, 1990).

During the 1980s, organizations were being told to prepare themselves for a reduction in the number of school leavers, at a time when the UK economy was expanding rapidly and when employers in South East England were having difficulty in recruiting and retaining employees. However, by 1990 the UK economy had moved into recession and the demand for employees has receded, although this may only be a short-term fall. For those far sighted employers who have encouraged women to return to the labour market there are more likely to be long-term benefits when an upturn occurs in the economy as they will be in a better position to retain their employees. Employers have been under pressure from the labour supply side to change their recruitment and retention strategies in order to attract women. However, employers have also benefited from the demand side in that it has suited them to introduce more flexible patterns of work. Service sector employers often require different patterns of working such as shifts and shorter core periods to cope with extended opening hours and peak business hours. Taking the examples of retailing and banking, two sectors where women form the majority of employees, it is to the employers advantage to take on part-time, temporary and casual staff whose hours are accordingly more flexible. For some women the introduction of more flexible work patterns may make it easier for them to participate in the labour force. On the other hand, part-time, temporary and casual forms of employment carry disadvantages where the contractual terms and conditions attached to these forms of employment are less favourable than the contractual terms and conditions for full-time employees (Martin and Roberts, 1984).

Northern Ireland

As a part of the UK, many of the trends which are evident in Great Britain are generally paralleled in Northern Ireland, but with certain notable exceptions. One such exception is that during the 1990s Northern Ireland will be less acutely affected by declining birth rates. The fall of 9% in the proportion of under 25 year olds is the smallest of all the UK regions, while the birth rate of 16.5 per thousand is the highest (Central Statistical Office, 1991). Northern Ireland also has the highest long term unemployment rate of any region in the UK and has traditionally had to cope with the problem of creating sufficient jobs to match the expanding population of working age. As a consequence, many workers have migrated to other areas of the UK in search of employment (Eversley, 1989; Gudgin and Roper, 1990). Although the Northern Ireland economy is closely linked to that of Great Britain, it does tend to expand more slowly in periods of growth, such as that experienced in the 1980s, and it recovers more slowly from times of recession. Part of the reason for this pattern of economic progression is due to the greater concentration of employment in the public sector in Northern Ireland. In 1990, approximately 42% of all jobs in Northern Ireland were in the public sector, compared to 30% in Great Britain. Whereas private sector employment, especially in the services industries, can fluctuate widely depending on the state of the economy, the public sector is traditionally more stable. Therefore, there has been less pressure on bringing women into the labour market to counteract shortages of other entrants, as in the other regions of the UK. Indeed, a recent press release on a Northern Ireland salary survey confirmed that employers in the private sector were doing little to attract or retain women (Coopers, Lybrand and Deloitte, 1991).

In common with Great Britain and other Western industrial societies, employment trends in Northern Ireland in recent years have shown a movement away from traditional manufacturing and towards the service industries. In many instances the shift of jobs into sectors such as health and education services, retailing and financial services has created part-time employment opportunities. This has been associated with an increased activity rate for women of working age in Northern Ireland, although the region still lags approximately 10% behind the UK as a whole in terms of female participation and this trend could well continue into the 1990s and beyond. Projections for the year 2000 (Employment Gazette, January 1990), indicate that activity rates for women of working age in Northern Ireland may be 62.1%, while for the UK they may be as high as 73.7%. Northern Ireland has the second lowest female activity rate of any of the UK regions, which implies an under-utilisation of a potential pool of human capital.

As discussed earlier, public sector employment accounted for 42% of all employees in employment in Northern Ireland in 1990 and 62% of those employees in the public sector were women (Northern Ireland Annual Abstract of Statistics, 1990). The Conservative government's policy has been to privatise public sector services, especially ancillary services, and it has been predicted that as a result of privatisation the terms and conditions under which many women are employed could deteriorate since a large proportion, approximately 32%, of public sector jobs are part-time. It is claimed that the only way in which private organisations can take over the public sector services is by cutting costs, for example, reducing hours of work so that they fall below the threshold required for National Insurance related benefits such as sick pay and maternity pay. In addition, increasing demands from employers in the private services sector for more flexible patterns of working (for example, extended opening hours) are resulting in more "atypical" forms of employment such as contract, temporary, casual, seasonal and part-time working. These developments are more likely to affect women who predominate in the service sectors where these changes are occurring and they will be discussed in more detail in the main body of the chapter.

The WWLS was therefore carried out against a background of changing employment patterns not only in Northern Ireland but also in the UK and throughout the EC. Focusing on employment, this chapter explores a number of themes. Firstly, using the WWLS and other sources, the chapter considers how many women are actually in paid employment, and how many other women could, in theory, work. The chapter then goes on to identify the kind of work undertaken by women in the labour market, looking at the different industrial areas where women are found and at the types of occupations they enter. Related to the kind of work women do is whether women work full or part-time and the next section considers the growth of part-time employment and whether it is prevalent in particular occupations or industries. The number of hours worked in different occupations and industries, the terms and conditions under which women are employed and women's earnings are also explored. Finally, a discussion of women's employment prospects in the 1990s is offered and whether, post 1992 and the completion of the Internal Market in Europe, there will be an improvement in women's position in the labour market in Northern Ireland.

Defining Economic Activity: How Many Women Are in the Work Place?

The economic activity rate for any group is defined as the economic participation of that group within a particular economy, and it is measured as the ratio of employed plus the unemployed (defined as those actively seeking work) to the total population, classified by age and/or sex. The actual economic activity rate for any group of people may vary according to the working definition used in its calculation. Hence rates can differ by as much as ten percentage points depending on the age range specified or the definition of unemployment used. For example, the Northern Ireland Social Attitudes Survey (1990) estimated that the female economic activity rate for 18 to 59 year olds was as high as 55%, with 28% in full-time employment, 18% in part-time employment, and 9% unemployed (Montgomery and Davies, 1991). The female economic activity rate for those aged 16 or older, as recorded by the 1981 Labour Force Survey (LFS) at 43.2%, was slightly higher than that for females aged 16 or older as recorded by the Census of Population for that year, namely 41.6%. The 1.6% difference was due to the fact that the LFS included women who classified themselves as unemployed but who did not necessarily appear in the official statistics which are based on a claimant count. By 1985, the LFS estimated that the female activity rate in Northern Ireland had remained at just over 43%, made up of 37.9% in employment and 5.3% unemployed. Of the 37.9% in employment it was estimated that 23.5% were married, resulting in an economic activity rate for married women of 44.8%, approximately 7% lower than the equivalent Great Britain rate. The latest data available from the LFS are for 1990 when a female activity rate for Northern Ireland of 48% was recorded, including 44% in employment and the remaining 4% being unemployed.

The WWLS returned an economic activity rate for 18 to 65 year olds of 59%, which was made up of 33% in full-time employment, 21% in part-time employment and 5% unemployed (Table 1). The differing rates are attributable to the precise age groups included, and each in turn must be viewed in the context of its precise definition.

Table 1: Age distribution by economic activity

	Economic activity						
Age	Working full-time %	Working part-time %	Total working %	Unemp- loyed %	Econo- mically inactive %	Full- time student %	All women %
<20	10	2	7	12	1	52	6
21 - 30	35	15	28	32	19	44	25
31 - 40	21	32	25	20	18	0	22
41 - 50	21	32	25	14	22	4	23
51 - 60	11	16	13	22	25	0	17
>60	2	3	2	0	15	0	7
Total %	100	100	100	100	100	100	100
N	329	207	536	50	391	23	1000

Irrespective of definition, one finding which is common to all estimates is that historically the female economic activity rate in Northern Ireland has been one of the lowest of any region in the UK (Trewsdale, 1987). The reasons for this low female activity rate are numerous and complex but the main factor is likely to be the persistent shortage of job opportunities, coupled, or so it is argued, with traditional attitudes to women, work and the family (Ward and McGivern, 1980; Roulston, 1989). On the other hand, women in the categories "economically inactive" may actually be available for work in certain circumstances (McWilliams, 1991), but may not register as unemployed and seeking work because of their perception that no jobs are available or because of changes in eligibility for social security benefits.

The relative lack of job opportunities affects all women of working age but nowhere is the social and cultural difference between Northern Ireland and Great Britain more apparent than among married women. The LFS estimated that in 1985, of those married women who were not seeking work, 43% classified themselves as both housewives and "retired", although they were under the statutory retirement age of 60. The WWLS results show that 71% of the non-working women were married and of the total, 85% were under the age of 60. Unlike their counterparts in Great Britain, women in Northern Ireland traditionally have had a tendency to leave the labour force permanently (see

Chapter 3). In more recent years, there has been a noticable change in this behaviour, brought on by a combination of economic necessity, employment legislation and perceptible shifts in social attitudes (See Chapters 2,3 and 10 for further analysis).

The WWLS results allow a detailed insight into this change in female economic behaviour, in that the women were questioned on their family responsibilities and their employment position. The economic activity rate for women with no children under the age of 16 was ten percentage points higher than that of women with children under 16; 65% compared to 55%. The difference was even more marked when the actual number of children under 16 was considered (Table 2). The rate dropped from 59% for those with two children, 52% for those with three children and 43% for those with four or more. As would be expected the proportion of women working full-time fell markedly from 31% for those with just one child to 13% for those with four or more. Thus, what at first sight may seem a relatively high overall economic activity rate in fact masks a situation where the importance of part-time employment overtakes that of full-time employment as the number of dependent children increases.

Table 2: Current economic activity by number of children under 16*

	Number of children under 16				All women with children under 16	No children under 16	All women
	1	2	3	4 +			
Economic activity	%	%	%	%	%	%	%
Working full-time	31	24	16	13	23	46	34
Working part-time	23	33	33	25	28	13	21
Total working	54	57	49	38	51	59	55
Total "unemployed"	6	2	3	5	4	6	5
Total economically active	60	59	52	43	55	65	60
Total economically inactive	40	41	48	57	45	35	40
Total %	100	100	100	100	100	100	100
N	176	172	102	77	527	450	977

*All women except full-time students

The age of the youngest child is significant with regard to type of employment. Whereas 61% of all working women were in full-time employment, only 35% of those whose youngest child was aged between five and ten years were working full-time, compared to 54% for those whose youngest child was aged between zero and four (Table 3). This result may at first sight seem surprising, however, it is relatively more easy and more common to obtain childcare

Table 3: Proportions of full and part-time workers by age of youngest child (working women)

	Childless women	Age of youngest child			All ages		All working women
		0-4	5-10	11-15	0-15	16+	
Employment status	%	%	%	%	%	%	%
Full-time	89	54	35	47	46	52	61
Part-time	11	46	65	53	54	48	39
Total	100	100	100	100	100	100	100
N	173	102	78	61	241	120	534

facilities for pre-school children through the extended family system in Northern Ireland than to make arrangements for children to be collected after school and also cared for during the school holidays (see Chapter 8). This thesis was indirectly supported by the response of women who had switched from full-time to part-time working; they cited childcare as the single most important reason for their move.

As noted at the beginning of this section the unemployed are included in the calculation of economic activity as they form part of the potential labour pool. Therefore economic activity is not simply a measure of those in work but rather a measure of the existing and potential labour supply. The non-working women in the WWLS are considered in detail in Chapter 7, in this chapter the emphasis is on the economic concept of unemployment and its effect on the economic activity rate for women. The question of who is actually unemployed is of particular importance when attempting to calculate an economic activity rate for women and especially as many women who consider themselves to be unemployed and actively seeking work are not included in official unemployment statistics. The reason for this is twofold. Firstly, in order to qualify for claimant status (the basis for the official unemployment count) a person must be seeking full-time employment. As will be shown later, a relatively high proportion of women are seeking part-time work and hence are not eligible. Secondly, after receiving unemployment benefit for twelve months a claimant is transferred to income support and is automatically and officially defined as moving into the long-term unemployed category. This, of course, applies to all unemployed persons. However, a married woman living with her husband is not entitled to claim income support unless the family circumstances are such that she is regarded as the head of household. Therefore, unless she chooses to register for National Insurance credits (to ensure her state pension rights), she will disappear from official statistics.

The total number of unemployed persons cannot be considered in isolation but must be viewed within the context of the whole labour force, both employed and unemployed. The normal expectation would be that assuming the potential workforce remained constant, a reduction in the number of persons employed would result in an increase in the number claiming unemployment benefit. A detailed examination of the male labour market in Northern Ireland does reflect this pattern, which is not surprising, although it does suggest that much of the natural increase in the male component of the Northern Ireland labour force has been "exported" in the form of migration.

However a similar examination of female labour market data reveals a completely different picture. The overall trend with regard to both female employees in employment and female unemployment from 1981 to 1987 was upwards. There had been a net increase of 6000 in the number of female employees in employment alongside a net increase of approximately 7000 in the number of women claiming unemployment benefit. On a quarter-to-quarter basis (that is, in the short term) some inverse relationship between the two series can be seen but the overall trend in both sets of data was positive.

The explanation for this difference between the labour market for men and for women requires careful consideration. A simple explanation could be drawn from the female economic activity rate, an increase in which would be the result of a relative increase in the numbers employed and/or unemployed. However, the female economic activity rate for those aged 16 or over in Northern Ireland remained relatively stable at around 43% between 1981 and 1987 (Trewsdale, 1990). A more likely explanation may lie in the existence of two female labour forces, one looking for full-time employment and another seeking part-time employment (Trewsdale, 1990). The economic climate in Northern Ireland over the past 20 years has resulted in a substantial increase in female part-time employment accompanied by only a small increase in full-time jobs. Official figures show that of the 28,200 increase in total female employees in employment between 1981 and 1989, 20,900 or 74% were part-time (Department of Economic Development, 1981; 1989), and since 1989 there is no reason to believe that this trend has not continued. As regards unemployment, the rules for claiming benefit state quite clearly that a person must be seeking full-time employment (and, since 1988, must be over 18 years, see below) in order to qualify for unemployment benefit, and as a result warrant inclusion in official statistics. The majority of unemployed women who appear in these statistics are in the younger age groups, and hence are seeking full-time employment. It follows that it is unlikely that the women who take up the part-time jobs flow directly from the "count" (the official unemployment measure) into employment, and hence the resulting mismatch of the two sets of data. What is more likely is that the "new" part-time employees, who tend to be in an older age group, take up a job locally when it becomes available and when it is convenient with regard to their domestic circumstances. In other words, they are not necessarily actively seeking work in the official sense nor are they eligible to claim benefit but they are nevertheless prepared to take on part-time employment should the opportunity arise. Therefore from 1981 to 1987 the female labour market consisted of a dual system in which potential employees moved into employment from either the official count (as in the case of males) or from an unofficial pool of potential workers who were primarily interested in part-time employment. The increase in both the numbers of female employees and the number of women who were unemployed over this period would seem to be an inevitable result of the workings of this labour market.

From 1987 to 1990 it would seem at first sight that there has been an important change in this pattern, in that official data show an increase in female employees in employment, accompanied by a fall in the number of women claiming unemployment benefit. The rise of 18,900 in the number of female employees in employment was complemented by a fall of 10,900 in the number of women claiming unemployment benefit. However the true explanation for this apparent reversal of the previous trend is probably due to the change in the rules for claiming unemployment benefit which took place in 1988. Specifically, any person under the age of 18 is not eligible to claim unemployment benefit, that is any person aged 16 or 17 and who is not a full-time student must be registered on a government training scheme and hence is considered to be in employment. As stated earlier the majority of females who appear in the official statistics are in the younger age group so it would seem safe to conclude that the decrease in the female unemployment numbers is in large part the result of a change in qualification rules.

What Kind of Work Do Women Do?

To return to the employed and the types of work which they do, as can be seen from Table 4 there has been little change over time. In 1971 the Census of Population recorded that just over 60% of employed females were to be found in jobs in the "Clerical and related" field, in "Education, welfare and health", in "Catering and cleaning" and in "Other services". The WWLS data support the 1990 LFS data, with these three occupational groups accounting for just under three-quarters of the employed female workforce.

A more detailed analysis of the data shows that even within the professional and related group of education, welfare and health, women are found in the relatively low status occupations. School principals and heads of department are likely to be men, primary school teachers women; nurses are likely to be

Table 4:   **Northern Ireland occupational analysis by selected occupations**
(females)

Occupation	1977 %	1979 %	1981 %	1985 %	1990 %	WWLS %
Professional in education welfare and health	14	15	18	18	20	22
Clerical and related	24	26	28	25	29	29
Selling	8	8	9	10	9	7
Catering, cleaning, hairdressing etc.	26	24	24	25	23	24
Material processing (ex. metal)	4	13	10	8	6	8
Other	23	15	11	15	13	10
Total %	100	100	100	100	100	100

Source: Labour Force Surveys 1977; 1979; 1981; 1985; 1990; and WWLS

women whereas the more senior administrative posts in health are held by men; home-helps are invariably women, as are school "dinner ladies" and ward orderlies (Trewsdale, 1987). Within the catering, cleaning and hairdressing group the existing low status jobs are made more precarious in that over two-thirds of those employed are employed as part-timers, a point which will be taken up in the next section.

The industries in which women work reflect the change in the structure of the Northern Ireland economy which has taken place over the previous two decades (see Chapter 3). The movement of employment away from the manufacturing industries and towards the service industries has resulted in the majority of women working in the service sector (Table 5).

Table 5: **Northern Ireland industrial analysis by selected industries**
(females)

Industry	1977 %	1979 %	1981 %	1985 %	1990 %
Total manufacturing	25	25	21	17	14
Distributive trades	19	17	18	22	21
Other services	40	39	50	50	51
Others	16	18	10	11	14
Total %	100	100	100	100	100

Source: Labour Force Surveys 1977; 1979; 1981; 1985; 1990

In 1977, 25% of female employees were employed in manufacturing; by 1990 the proportion had fallen to 14%. In contrast, the proportion in the two main service groups of "Distributive trades" and "Other services" had risen from 59% in 1977 to 72% in 1990, a figure which had remained static since 1985 (Trewsdale, 1987).

The WWLS reflects these data with 15% of the women in employment in the manufacturing sector and 75% in "Distribution" and "Other services". The category "Other services" is an increasingly important group which comprises such public services as health, education and public administration. The importance of the public sector as a major employer in Northern Ireland is apparent when one recognises that around 42% (or 220100, NIAAS, 1990) of all employees are employed in that sector, representing just under one-third of all male employees and just over one-half of all female employees, the highest figures for any region in the UK. The rise in the relative importance of education and health services, as well as distribution, is clearly seen in Table 6.

Table 6: Northern Ireland industrial breakdown of employees in employment, in thousands (females)

	1977	1979	1984	1987	1990
Industry	(000s)	(000s)	(000s)	(000s)	(000s)
Total manufacturing	49.7	51.4	37.5	37.8	38.1
Wholesale distribution, retailing, hotels and catering	34.2	38.8	40.3	45.4	50.1
Transport and communications	3.3	3.5	3.7	3.8	4.4
Banking, insurance and business services	10.5	12.2	13.9	15.1	18.3
Public administration and defence	15.1	16.6	17.5	18.4	19.5
Sanitary services	1.2	1.4	1.5	2.7	4.0
Education	34.4	36.5	38.6	37.9	38.6
Health Services	29.6	33.7	36.3	37.1	39.0
Other Services not elsewhere specified	24.4	29.6	31.9	32.7	36.2
All industries and services*	209.4	230.8	227.6	236.7	255.5

* Columns do not sum to totals due to the omission of agriculture, energy and construction.

Source: NIASS No 9, 1990; Statistics Notices, DED

Whereas in 1977 total manufacturing employed just under 50,000 women, compared to 34,200 in distribution, 34,400 in education and just under 30,000 in health services, by 1990, distribution, education and health each employed more women than total manufacturing. Over the same period a marked rise in the numbers employed in banking, insurance and other business services was recorded which, although in absolute terms accounted for only 7800, in percentage terms represented the highest growth of any of the major sectors, 74%.

In summary it is clear that the industries in which women work in Northern Ireland are predominantly service oriented and are likely to be service industries operating under the auspices of the public sector. However, within those industries women are not necessarily employed full-time. In fact, a high proportion of women, especially those in "Other services", work fewer than 30 hours a week and as a result are officially classified as part-time workers.

The Growth of Part-Time Employment

Perhaps the most fundamental change in the nature of the UK labour market has been the degree to which women participate in the labour force and the extent to which they do so on a part-time basis. The Northern Ireland labour market is no exception to this general trend. In 1971 just under 19% of all female employees in employment worked part-time; by 1977 the proportion had risen to 31%; by 1984 the figure had reached 36%; and by 1989 (the latest date for which official figures are available, based on those working less than 30 hours per week) this had risen to 39%. This trend is confirmed by the WWLS with 39% of women in employment classifying themselves as working part-time (Table 7).

Table 7: Breakdown of Northern Ireland female labour force by full-time/ part-time working

Employment status	1979 %	1981 %	1985 %	WWLS %
Full-time	69	68	62	61
	50	*50*	*53*	*54*
Part-time	30	30	37	39
	89	*86*	*84*	*88*
Not stated	2	2	1	0
Total %	100	100	100	100

(Figures in italics refer to the proportion of married women in each category.)
Source: Labour Force Surveys 1979, 1981, 1985; and WWLS.

The WWLS provides data which allow for a more detailed analysis of part-time women workers in Northern Ireland. First and foremost, and as would be expected, the majority (over 88%) were married. However, this proportion represents almost no change from the 89% recorded in 1979 by the LFS but a four percentage point increase from the 1985 figure of just under 84%, which, like the WWLS, is based on self-classification..

Although it has long been recognised by researchers in the field that women do not work for "pin-money" but rather from economic necessity (see Montgomery and Davies, 1991), the myth is still propounded. The results of the WWLS showed that the main reason given by women in the survey for working, whether full-time or part-time, was that they needed the money, the fact that they liked to work was the second most popular reason, with having something useful to do a distant third (see Chapter 10 for further analysis).

The age breakdown of the female part-time workforce reflects, indirectly, the predominance of the married employee, in that the proportion working part-time showed a marked increase in the older age groups. The WWLS revealed that 64% of part-time workers were aged between 31 and 50 years. As can be seen in Table 8, part-time employment increased in importance for women aged over 30, with just under half of all women employees working part-time, compared to 22% of those aged 21 to 30.

Table 8: Proportions of full and part-time workers by age (working women)

Employment status	<20 %	21 - 30 %	31 - 40 %	41 - 50 %	51 - 60 %	>60 %	All %
Full-time	89	78	51	51	52	54	61
Part-time	11	22	49	49	48	46	39
Total %	100	100	100	100	100	100	100
N	35	144	135	136	71	13	534

Having established the extent of female part-time employment and identified the characteristics of the women involved, we turn now to the occupational breakdown of the workforce in an attempt to analyse the types of jobs carried out by women part-time workers. It was noted earlier that over two-thirds of female employees in employment are to be found in three occupational groups ("Clerical and related"; "Education, welfare and health"; and "Catering, cleaning and hairdressing"). Hence it would seem appropriate to concentrate our attention on these groups. By including the occupational grouping "Selling", coverage is extended to over three-quarters of all female employees in Northern Ireland. It is upon these four groups that the occupational structure of the female part-time labour force will be based. Within each of these groups the proportion of part-time employees was calculated and is set out in Table 9.

Between 1981 and 1985 each group recorded a substantial increase in the proportion of part-time employees; the seven percentage point increase in the "Selling" group resulted in just over 50% of the employees working part-time. The group with the largest proportion of part-time employees, just under 69% in 1985, was "Catering, cleaning etc.", which by the very nature of the employment offered, is part-time oriented. The WWLS has confirmed this trend towards part-time working overall but at the same time there has been a decrease in the proportion of part-timers in selling and catering occupations.

Table 9: Proportion of part-time employees in employment by selected occupations

Occupation	1981 %	1985 %	WWLS %
Professional and related in education welfare and health	20	26	33
Clerical and related	18	26	33
Selling	44	52	46
Catering, cleaning hairdressing and other personal services	63	69	66
All industries	30	37	39

Source: Labour Force Surveys 1981, 1985: and WWLS

The industrial structure of female part-time employment mirrors the occupational structure in that the majority of the workers, over 84% in 1985, are to be found in the service sector (Table 10). Within the service sector, the category "Other services" included over one half of all female part-time employees. In contrast, the importance of the manufacturing industries as employers of female part-time workers has declined from 13% in 1977 to 7% in 1985. The LFS indicates that the proportion of part-time workers in manufacturing has remained fairly constant since 1981, at around 8%, while the proportion in the distributive trades has fallen to less than one in five currently employed in that sector in 1990. The WWLS showed that over 91% of part-time female workers were employed in the service sector with 67% working in "Other services". Thus the decline in the importance of the manufacturing sector and the rise of the service sector in the economy as a whole is directly reflected in the changing pattern of female part-time employment.

As stated earlier, the official definition of part-time work is based on someone contracted to work fewer than 30 hours a week. However, the results of the 1985 LFS showed that the majority of women (71%) who classified themselves as working part-time reported that they worked fewer than 21 hours a week

(Trewsdale, 1987). This result represented little change from the 70% who fell into this category in 1977 (Trewsdale and Trainor, 1979). There was, however, an increase in 1985 in the proportion working between eight and 21 hours at the expense of those working fewer than eight hours.

Table 10: Breakdown of part-time employees in employment by industry (females)

Industry	1977 %	1979 %	1981 %	1985 %	WWLS %
Total manufacturing	13	13	8	7	8
Distributive trades	17	18	26	29	18
Other services	54	58	59	55	67
Others	16	11	7	9	7
Total %	100	100	100	100	100

Source: Labour Force Surveys 1977, 1979, 1981, 1985; and WWLS

The WWLS allowed an exploration of the contracted weekly hours of 475 women (Table 11). The majority, 61%, worked between 30 and 44 contracted hours per week, with only 13% working fewer than 16 hours per week and a mere 4% working fewer than eight hours per week. Thus only 4% of the working women in the sample qualified for minimum statutory employment rights, whereas 87% of the working women qualified, at least using the criterion of hours worked, for all statutory employment rights (see next section).

Table 11: Contracted hours by employment status

	Employment status		
Hours	Full-time %	Part-time %	All %
< 8 hrs	0	10	4
8 - 15 hrs	0	24	9
16 - 29 hrs	2	57	24
30 - 44 hrs	95	9	61
45+ hrs	3	0	2
Total %	100	100	100
N	290	185	475

When the data on contracted hours are broken down by full-time and part-time employees, the distribution changes, with 98% of full-time employees working 30 or more hours per week and 91% of part-time employees working fewer than 30 hours per week. Just over one half (57%) of part-time workers stated that they were contracted to work between 16 and 29 hours per week with an additional 9% working 30 hours or more. As would be expected, the 4% of the total who were working fewer than eight hours were all part-timers, representing 10% of the part-time total.

Over 98% of the women providing information on their contracted hours worked in the four industrial sectors of "Other manufacturing", "Distribution", "Banking" and "Other services". The latter accounted for 59% of the total and included all the women working fewer than eight hours per week. However the majority (56%) of women working in "Other services" worked between 30 and 44 hours per week with the remaining 37% working from eight to 29 hours per week. The industrial sector with the second highest proportion (17%) of female workers was "Distribution", where 43% worked from eight to 29 hours per week and 52% between 30 and 44 hours.

The occupational breakdown as shown in Table 4 indicates that 29% of female employees worked in the "Clerical and related" group, with a further 24% in "Catering". The majority (68%) of those working in "Catering" worked fewer than 30 hours per week which, applying the official definition, would result in them being classified as part-time employees. A similar pattern was observed in "Selling", where 48% worked fewer than 30 hours. The professionals employed in "Education, health and welfare", on the other hand, worked longer hours with 70% working between 30 and 44 hours per week. Hence they would be officially classified as full-time employees. Overall, the results certainly confirm the expected pattern of relatively low and varied hours being worked in the "Catering" and "Selling" occupations and especially in comparison with "Education, Health and Welfare". In addition, the results also demonstrate how misleading the self-defined labels of full-time and part-time work may be unless they are cross-referenced with actual hours worked per week.

Terms and Conditions of Work of Part-time and Full-time Workers

The continued rise in the relative importance of female part-time employment, as outlined above, leads directly on to the terms and conditions of that employment. It is noteworthy that two-fifths of female employees in Northern Ireland work part-time, compared to 11% of male employees and that of every ten part-time employees, eight are women (Department of Economic Development, 1989). Statutory and contractual employment rights are geared primarily to full-time workers in that they are based on total pay and on hours worked per week, hence immediately placing the part-time worker at a disadvantage. The rules governing National Insurance contributions, which in turn affect eligibility for state benefits, are based on total pay. Given her smaller pay packet, the part-time worker who becomes unemployed is usually denied unemployment benefit and, as there is a strong probability that a part-time woman worker will be married and living with her husband, income support will also be denied. In addition, trade unions have been reluctant to recruit part-time workers of either sex. Indeed union density for part-time employees is over 50% for only two industries in Great Britain, national government and hospitals (Department of Employment, 1991). Thus the part-time worker is far more vulnerable at work than his or her full-time counterpart.

In addition, both statutory and contractual employment rights such as pension provision, maternity leave, sick pay and holiday entitlement are also currently geared to the permanent full-time worker rather than the part-time worker. Not only do part-time employees tend to have lower hourly rates of pay than full-time workers in similar jobs, many of them are also excluded from a number of statutory employment rights including protection from unfair dismissal and qualifying for statutory redundancy payments.

The actual entitlement to qualify for many statutory employment rights is determined by the number of hours worked per week. A part-time employee who works for 16 or more hours per week is entitled to the same statutory employment rights as a full-time employee. An employee who works for fewer than 16 but more than eight hours per week has the same statutory rights as a full-time employee but only after five years continuous service with the same employer. Those working fewer than eight hours have very few statutory rights. Those that they do have include protection under the equality legislation, statutory maternity pay at the lower rate (subject to service and earnings qualification) and statutory sick pay (providing they have earned more than the National Insurance lower earnings threshold). They have no rights covering a written statement of terms of employment, guaranteed pay, unfair dismissal or redundancy pay. Under existing domestic legislation, it also appears that part-time workers falling into this category have no rights to maternity leave. However, following decisions of the European Court of Justice, in the cases of Dekker v Stichting Vormingscentrum Voor Jonge Volwassenen (VJR v Centrum) Plus, (1991) IRLR 27 and Hertz v Aldi Marked K/S (sub nom Handels Og Kontorfunktionaererernes Forband i Danmark v Dansk Arbejdsgiverforening) (1991) IRLR 37, it appears that the exclusion of those working fewer than eight hours per week may be contrary to EC law.

In relation to contractual pension schemes, many schemes currently require that an employee works a minimum number of hours in order to qualify for access to the scheme. Thus large numbers of part-time workers are currently excluded. However, again following the recent decisions of the European Court of Justice, Bilka-Kaufhaus v Weber Von Hartz (1986) IRLR 317 and

Barber v Guardian Royal Exchange Assurance Group (1990) IRLR 240, it appears that such exclusions may be contrary to Community law.

The WWLS provides a detailed insight into the contractual and statutory terms and conditions of female workers in Northern Ireland. Bearing in mind Table 11 and the fact that only 13% of either full-time or part-time working women included in the WWLS were contracted to work for fewer than 16 hours per week, those women in work were asked a series of questions on their contracts and on the employment rights provided by their employer (Table 12).

Table 12:   Contractual terms and conditions of employment*

	Full-time work		Part-time work		All	
	Yes	No	Yes	No	Yes	No
Conditions	%	%	%	%	%	%
Written contract	68	24	62	30	66	26
Entitlement to sick pay from employer	88	11	57	40	76	23
Membership of pension scheme (where available)	79	21	55	45	72	27

*Where yes/no %s do not add to 100, the difference is accounted for by "Don't know" responses.

The majority of women in work (66%) had a written contract of employment. When this figure was disaggregated, 68% of full-time workers and 62% of part-time workers had such a contract. Of those who had no written contract of employment, 47% of part-time workers answered that either they were not eligible because they were part-time or that such a contract was simply not available. 34% answered they did not know why they were without a written contract. The majority of full-time workers (87%) stated that either a written contract was not available or like the part-time workers, they did not know the reason.

76% of all women workers answered that they were entitled to contractual sick pay from their employers but there was a marked difference between full-time and part-time workers. 88% of full-time employees said they would receive sick pay, compared to 57% of part-timers (see Table 12). In reality, and significantly, all would have been entitled to statutory sick pay. When those who had stated they were not entitled to sick pay were asked why, 77% of full-time employees answered either that there was no sick pay scheme provided by their employer, or that they did not know. The majority of part-timers answered that it was because they were working part-time or they were only temporary workers. An analysis of the occupational grouping of the employees who were entitled to receive sick pay from their employer revealed 72% to be working in either "Professional, teaching and welfare", "Clerical" or "Catering".

When questioned as to the availability of an employer's pension scheme, just over half the women in employment (52%) replied that their employer did not offer a scheme, with a further 27% stating that they did not belong. Approximately eight out of ten of the full-time workers belonged to a scheme compared to just over five out of ten of the part-time employees. When asked why they did not belong to their employer's pension scheme, 28% of part-time employees answered that it was because they were working part-time and 35% stated that they had not worked long enough for their employer. Of the full-time employees who did not belong to a scheme, 26% said it was because their job disqualified them, 24% were either too young or too old and a surprising 24% did not know the reason why. These results were very similar to those obtained by Martin and Roberts (1984).

When asked whether their employer provided a maternity leave scheme 64% of all employees replied "Yes". Of these, 59% were entitled to full pay, 36% to part pay and 5% to unpaid leave . As with the previous questions on the terms and conditions of their employment, a relatively high proportion, 25%, said that they did not know. The full-time workers fared better than the part-time workers in that 74%, as compared to 49%, worked for employers who provided some form of maternity leave scheme. As would be expected, the proportion of full-time workers who stated that they were eligible for maternity leave, be it contractual or statutory, was nearly twice that of part-time workers (68% compared to 35%).

The information provided on the provision of nursery or crèche facilities by employers was most enlightening. 96% of the women in work stated that there were no such provisions and only 3% stated that facilities were available. However, none of these women had actually used the childcare facilities.

When asked about entitlement to paid holidays, 25% of all working women answered that they did not know what their entitlements were. However, fewer than 64% were entitled to between three and ten weeks paid holiday and of these, 36% received six to ten weeks a year. As would be expected the full-time workers fared slightly better than part-timers with 44% receiving six to ten weeks compared to 24% of part-timers. In total, 71% of full-time workers were entitled to between three and ten weeks whereas the comparable figure for part-timers was 53%. (Table 13).

Earnings

Women in employment were asked to provide information on both their gross and net weekly earnings. This section concentrates on gross earnings as they are regarded as the more standard measure by which to compare various categories (Trewsdale, 1983). Gross earnings were subsequently analysed by employment status, age, industry and occupation.

Table 13: Number of weeks paid holiday by employment status

	Employment status		
	Full-time	Part-time	All
Weeks	%	%	%
None	0	10	4
1 - 2	0	5	2
3 - 5	27	29	28
6 - 10	44	24	36
11 - 15	6	3	5
Not known	23	29	25
Total %	100	100	100
N	*298*	*193*	*491*

Of all the women who answered the question over two-thirds (68%) were earning less than £150 per week and only 7% were earning more than £300 per week. As expected, the part-time workers earned less than those working full-time with 91%, compared to 54%, falling below the £150 per week line. When the median or mid-point wage was calculated the absolute difference was £80 per week, £144.73 compared to £64.60.

Gross hourly earnings were calculated for all those women who answered the question on earnings. This information is presented in terms of gross hourly earnings for part-time and full-time employees (Table 14). The results show quite clearly that full-time employees are better paid on an hourly basis than part-time employees. The average gross hourly wage of a full-time worker was £4.00, compared to £3.47 for a part-timer. 51% of part-time workers earned less than £3.00 an hour while just over 39% of full-time workers fell into this category. The observed earnings gap may be even more inequitable than appears at first glance given that research into women's part-time earnings in Northern Ireland has highlighted the possibility that part-time workers may actually be relatively more productive than full-time workers. (Harris, 1991).

The optimal age in terms of earning power was between 21 and 40 years where 40% earned more the £150 per week, compared to an average of 24% for older workers. No-one in the under 20 age group earned more than £150 per week. At first sight, it may be that the relative prosperity of the 21-40 year olds is explicable with reference to the full-time/part-time breakdown by age. Whereas this factor is certainly relevant for the 21-30 age group, as just over

21% were working part-time, it is not true of the 31-40 age group, where 49% stated they were part-time workers, exactly the same percentage as in the 41-50 age group. From this it can be deduced that the part-time worker in her thirties was earning substantially more than her counterpart in her forties.

Table 14: Estimated minimum gross hourly earnings by employment status

	Employment status		
	Full-time	Part-time	All
Hourly pay	%	%	%
£1 - £1.99	16	15	16
£2 - £2.99	24	36	28
£3 - £3.99	20	20	20
£4 - £4.99	15	8	12
£5 - £5.99	10	8	10
£6 - £6.99	6	5	5
£7 - £7.99	3	4	3
£8+	8	3	6
Total %	100	100	100
N	*302*	*156*	*458*

The two highest paid industries were "Banking" and "Other services", with 43% and 40% respectively earning more than £150 per week. At the other end of the scale, only 12% of those working in "Distribution" reported such high earnings. Once again a full-time/part-time analysis by industry reveals some interesting anomalies. As would be expected, the proportion of part-time workers in "Banking" was relatively low, at just under 29%, however the proportion in "Other services" was as high as 44%, indeed higher than that in "Distribution" (40%). This leads to the conclusion that part-time women workers in "Other services" are relatively higher paid than those in other industrial sectors. This fact is borne out when one considers the occupational breakdown of the earnings data. Of those working as professionals in "Health, education and welfare", 71% were found to be earning more than £150 per week, yet within this group nearly one third (35%) were working part-time. Predictably the occupational group "Catering" included the lowest paid workers, with 45% earning less than £50 per week and 83% earning less than £100 per week; two-thirds of those in "Catering" were working part-time. The occupational category which contained the largest number of workers, of which 33% were working part-time, was "Clerical and related". The distribution of earning in this category was the least skewed, with the most frequently occurring weekly pay being £127.50 which compared with the most frequently occurring weekly earnings of less than £50 for "Catering".

Prospects for Women in Employment in Northern Ireland in the 1990s

While it is impossible to predict exactly what will happen throughout the 1990s, there are certain trends which were evident in the 1980s and which are useful indicators for the coming decade. The demographic trend of falling number of school leavers forcing employers to look for alternative sources of labour will continue, and Northern Ireland should benefit in terms of increased labour force participation for women, albeit more modestly than the rest of the UK. This should ensure that women will continue to be in demand as employees in years to come, although in times of recession women may also increase the numbers of unemployed, where service industries such as retailing tend to contract and make staff redundant.

Another trend which is likely to continue is that new employment creation will be in the services sector rather than in manufacturing, a long term trend in Western industrialised nations. Taking into account recent trends, a high proportion of service jobs are likely to be taken by women rather than men. However, if the recession continues and unemployment rises then more of these jobs may be undertaken by men (Gudgin and Roper, 1991). Northern Ireland already has a substantial proportion of employment in the services sector and the question for the 1990s is whether service jobs will remain in the public sector or transfer to the private sector.

Changes affecting the position of women in employment in Northern Ireland are increasingly influenced by events further afield, both in the UK and elsewhere in the EC. The end of 1992 may yet be a watershed for the EC, marking the completion of the internal market. This major economic event should stimulate further labour force participation given the expectation that employment opportunities will arise when trade barriers fall (Jackson, 1990). However, while it is estimated that the effect of the internal market is positive, there is no guarantee that the gains will be automatically distributed equally across the EC (Meulders and Plasman, 1991). Imbalances may occur at different levels, either sectoral, regional or between different groups. For example, the proportion of women in those industrial sectors which have been identified as most sensitive to the completion of the internal market varies from less than 10% in heavy industries such as shipbuilding to more than 75% in sectors such as textiles. In total, 40 sensitive industries have been identified (Jackson, 1990) and in Northern Ireland, the textile sector which includes clothing would appear to be the most vulnerable industry employing a large number of women. This sector has already experienced extensive restructuring and incurred significant job losses in recent years and this trend is likely to continue since the textile sector is faced with external competition from low cost producers. A recent report by Meulders and Plasman (1991) was pessimistic about prospects for the textile industry throughout the EC, arguing that employment in this sector will continue to fall during the 1990s.

The EC may also have a major effect on terms and conditions of employment through its Directives. Currently, draft Directives in relation to maternity provision and the treatment of atypical workers are under consideration at Community level. If these Directives are adopted then they may result in an improvement in the treatment of part-timers in relation to maternity provision and other employment rights. Looking further ahead, the implications of Maastricht on women's employment prospects requires some consideration. At this summit the UK objected to the proposal to extend the "Social Charter" in the Treaty of Rome, to allow greater scope for action and more qualified majority voting on social policy which includes measures covering working conditions and equal rights for men and women (CREW, 1992). The result is that the other 11 Member States agreed to adopt the proposed extensions to the "Social Charter" as a separate protocol, which may mean that working conditions in the UK will be poorer than those in the rest of the EC. The full and detailed implications of the Maastricht Summit, however, are not yet clear as the Maastricht Treaty itself, if ratified, will not come into effect until 1993, and opposition to the Treaty within Member States continues.

While the above mentioned trends, namely demographic changes, the growth of service industries, and the influence of EC membership, all have long term effects on the Northern Ireland economy, there are other less predictable factors which also need to be considered. The economy, which is closely linked to that of Great Britain, is currently in a period of recession. This means that new job creation is more difficult at a time when many organisations are making staff redundant. Northern Ireland also has the highest unemployment rate for men of all UK regions and efforts in job creation tend to be towards cutting male unemployment. Against this trend, many of the recently announced job creation schemes have been in "back office" jobs, establishing new government agencies or relocating office jobs from other areas of the UK. These jobs are more likely to be filled by women as they will be clerical in nature and may also be suited to part-time working; as the WWLS confirmed, almost 30% of women are already concentrated in clerical occupations.

Overall, there has been little change in the occupational structure vis-à-vis women in the last two decades. As already discussed over 66% of women are concentrated in the three main groupings of "Professional and related in education, welfare and health", "Catering, cleaning and hairdressing" and "Clerical and related", and it is unlikely that this concentration will shift in the 1990s. These are the occupational groupings where jobs are likely to occur and increasingly they are likely to be part-time jobs. Traditionally employers have used women in part-time positions to provide cover at peak times but in the

1990s employers are becoming increasingly aware that to retain valued employees, part-time working arrangements can also be made for higher status jobs, including those at managerial level.

The 1990s are likely to prove a golden opportunity for the few women whose skills are in demand, such as those in professional occupations and industries where employment status and equal pay are the norm for women and men (Evans, 1990). For most women however, the prospects are not so positive as many of the jobs on offer require few skills, have low pay and low status and are more precarious in terms of job security. Northern Ireland is a very small regional economy on the periphery of the UK which is on the periphery of the EC and thus has little direct control over its economy. Much of the job creation is through government expenditure and while those employed in public sector jobs may have the same terms and conditions and rates of pay as their Great Britain counterparts, this situation may change in response to shifts in government policy. For working women in particular these shifts will be significant.

References

Central Statistical Office (1981). *Indexes to the Standard Industrial Classification Revised 1980.* London: HMSO.

Central Statistical Office (1991). *Regional Trends.* London: HMSO.

Compton, P.A. (1989). Northern Ireland: *Demography and Manpower Prospects.* Unpublished Manuscript, Queen's University of Belfast.

Coopers and Lybrand Deloitte Ltd. (1991). *Northern Ireland Salary Survey.* Belfast: Coopers and Lybrand Deloitte Ltd.

CREW (1992). 'Maastricht: UK isolated in slow lane of Social Europe as EC leaders agree on European Union.' *CREW Reports, 12, 1,* 13 - 14.

Department of Employment (1990). *Employment Gazette: Regional Labour Force Outlook to the Year 2000.* London: HMSO.

Department of Employment (1991). *Employment Gazette: Membership of Trade Unions in 1989.* London: HMSO.

Department of Employment (1991). *The Best of Both Worlds: A Guide for Employers.* London: Central Office of Information.

Department of Economic Development (1981). *Census of Employment.* Belfast: HMSO.

Department of Economic Development (1989). *Census of Employment.* Belfast: HMSO.

Directorate General (Employment, Industrial Relations and Social Affairs) (1990). *Employment in Europe 1990.* Luxembourg: Commission for the European Communities.

Evans, L. (1990). 'The 'Demographic-Dip': A golden opportunity for women in the labour market.' *National Westminster Branch Quarterly Review, February,* 48 - 69.

Eversley, D. (1989). *Religion and Employment in Northern Ireland.* London: Sage.

Gudgin, G. and Roper, S. (1990). *The Northern Ireland Economy, Review and Forecasts to 1995.* Belfast: Northern Ireland Economic Research Centre.

Gudgin, G. and Roper, S. (1991). *The Northern Ireland Economy, Review and Forecasts to 2000.* Belfast: Northern Ireland Economic Research Centre.

Harris, R. I. D. (1991). *Part-time Female Earnings: An Analysis using N.I. NES Data.*

Unpublished manuscript, University of Waikato, New Zealand.

Industrial Relations Services (1990). *Effective Ways of Recruiting and Retaining Women.* London: IRS Publications.

Jackson, P.C. (1990). *The Impact of the Completion of the Internal Market on Women in the European Community.* Luxembourg: Commission of the European Communities.

McWilliams, M. (1991). 'Women's paid work and the sexual division of labour.' In C. Davies and E. Mclaughlin (eds.), *Women, Employment and Social Policy in Northern Ireland: A Problem Postponed.* Belfast: Policy Research Institute.

Martin, J. and Roberts, C. (1984). *Women and Employment: A Lifetime Perspective.* London: HMSO.

Meulders, D. and Plasman, O. (1991). *The Impact of the Single Market on Women's Employment in the Textile and Clothing Industry.* Luxembourg: CEC.

Montgomery, P. and Davies C. (1990). *Women's Lives in Northern Ireland Today.* Coleraine: Centre for Research on Women, University of Ulster at Coleraine.

Montgomery, P. and Davies, C. (1991). 'A woman's place in Northern Ireland.' In P. Stringer and G. Robinson (eds), *Social Attitudes in Northern Ireland: 1990-91 Edition.* Belfast: Blackstaff Press.

Morrissey, H. (1991). 'Different shares: Women, employment and eanings.' In C. Davies and E. Mclaughlin (eds.), *Women, Employment and Social Policy in Northern Ireland: A Problem Postponed.* Belfast: Policy Research Institute.

Northern Ireland Annual Abstract of Statistics (NIAAS) (various dates). Belfast: HMSO.

Northern Ireland Economic Council. (1991). *Economic Strategy in Northern Ireland: Report 88.* Belfast: NIEC.

Roulston, C. (1989). 'Women on the margin: The women's movement in Northern Ireland 1973-1988.' *Science and Society,* 53, 219-36.

Trewsdale, J.M. (1987). *Womanpower No. 4: The Aftermath of Recession: Changing Patterns of Female Employment and Unemployment in Northern Ireland.* Belfast: Equal Opportunities Commission for Northern Ireland.

Trewsdale, J.M. (1990). 'Labour force characteristics.' In R.I.D. Harris, C.W. Jefferson and J.E. Spencer (eds.), *The Northern Ireland Economy: A Comparative Study in the Economic Development of a Peripheral Region.* London: Longman.

Trewsdale, J.M. and Trainor, M. (1979). *Womanpower No. 1: A Statistical Survey of Women and Work in Northern Ireland.* Belfast: Equal Opportunities Commission for Northern Ireland.

Trewsdale, J.M. and Trainor, M. (1981). *Womanpower No. 2: Recent Changes in the Female Labour Market in Northern Ireland.* Belfast: Equal Opportunities Commission for Northern Ireland.

Trewsdale, J.M. and Trainor, M. (1983). *Womanpower No. 3: The Impact of Recession on Female Employment and Earnings in Northern Ireland.* Belfast: Equal Opportunities Commission for Northern Ireland.

Ward, M. and McGivern, M. (1980). 'Images of women in Northern Ireland.' *Cranebag Book of Irish Studies,* 4, 579-85.

Chapter 6

TRADE UNION INVOLVEMENT

Robert Miller and Donal McDade

Introduction

Women's involvement with the trade union movement has had a long but chequered history. In theory at least, as trade unions constitute a progressive movement for the protection of all workers' rights and levels of pay, by right women should be able to share in this protection and enjoy these benefits. In practice, traditionally the trade union movement has been dominated by men and has placed the needs and rights of male workers above those of women. For example, in the nineteenth century, unions were instrumental in first the exclusion and later the segregation of women into those parts of the industrial structure that were, or came to be, typified by lower-paid, semi-skilled and unskilled work (Walby, 1986; Spitze, 1988). During and after the two world wars, trade unions lobbied for the removal of women from industries where they had replaced male workers during wartime, often against the opposition of employers (Walby, 1986). Until recent decades, pay campaigns were directed more at preserving men's pay rates rather than achieving parity between the sexes, and unions championed the "ideal" of the so-called "family wage" as a rationale justifying differential rates of pay that disadvantaged women (see, for example, Meehan, 1987). In the late nineteenth and early twentieth centuries women reacted by forming women-only unions. The later incorporation of many of these into their male counterparts has been seen by some as a measure of their success (Jones, 1988). Simultaneously, others have argued that, ironically, incorporation often also led to the loss of a distinct voice representing women workers and to the eclipse of demands associated particularly with "women's issues" such as childcare provision (Beechey, 1986; Bradley, 1989).

Not surprisingly, unions came to be seen by many women workers and trade unionists as a "male preserve" (Purcell, 1984). Trade unionists refer to each other as brothers, rarely, however, as sisters. Throughout the British Isles, activists and officials are predominantly male, even in those unions whose rank-and-file membership is mainly female (Randall, 1987). The under-representation of women is even more extreme at more senior levels. In Britain the extent of this under-representation did not change over the three decades from 1951 to 1981 (Ellis, 1988), and Evason (1985) and Clancy and MacKeogh (1987) have both argued that the position of women as "second class citizens" in the trade union movement applies equally to Northern Ireland and the Irish

Republic respectively.

The explanations for women's lower participation in trade union activism broadly parallel those given to explain their lower rates of participation in paid employment and in the upper reaches of bureaucratic organizations generally. Mirroring the obstacles to full-time working for married women, everyday family demands such as minding children, shopping and generally running a household are seen as constituting more of a barrier to trade union activism for married women than for married men. Similarly, married women are assumed to find it more difficult to attend residential courses or conferences.

> *Without malice or design, but also without concern, men have shaped trade union life to suit those who have no childcare or other domestic responsiblities and on an expectation that every trade union activist has endless evening hours to devote to union work.... To be on the union executive, you need to prepare yourself at weekend schools, on residential training courses and as a delegate to week-long congresses at the seaside resorts (Gill and Whitty, 1983; cited in Ellis, 1988, p.140).*

Women trade union activists are described as shouldering a "triple burden" of work, family responsibilities and union duties. For instance, Anne Cook, cited in Bakker (1988), comments:

> *When a woman tries to better her lot through collective action, she faces a second issue: union participation becomes a burden to be added to family and paid work. Even women who can overcome such barriers find that union activity is neither immediately accessible to them nor easy to manage. Moreover, the few women who are able to carry this triple burden very rarely rise to positions of power, even in those unions where women make up a substantial part of the membership (Bakker, 1988, p.34).*

Received opinion within the trade union movement often sterotypes women as more conservative, difficult to organize and generally less commited to the goals of trade unionism. These views, however, do not take account of domestic demands that fall unequally on women (see Chapter 2) nor the segregation of many women into part-time work and sectors of industry where organization is difficult for workers regardless of gender. They also ignore the many instances of women undertaking militant action (McCarthy, 1977). Once these factors are controlled for, research comparing women's and men's commitment to work, willingness to join unions, levels of militancy or propensity towards industrial action has not shown sex differences (Siltanen and Stanworth, 1984; Clancy and MacKeogh, 1987; O'Farrell, 1988). Most workers, regardless of their sex, are not militant trade unionists and the stereotype of the uncommitted trade unionist is no more accurate for women than it is for men (Meehan, 1987).

> *A considerable minority of women, who are committed to the principles of unionism, refuse to join a trade union or allow their membership to lapse. This may be regarded by some as a sign of inconsistency between belief and action. However, if women's accounts are taken seriously, the explanation is often to be found in disenchantment with trade union branches that are ineffectual and*

indifferent to the women's struggle. In the few studies which explore women's relation to trade unions, women often complain not because the union is too radical, but because it is not stalwart enough in defence of jobs, or too much in the pocket of management (Siltanen and Stanworth, 1984, pp.190-1).

In terms of gross numbers and proportions unionised and (arguably) in terms of participation in office-holding, women's involvement in the trade union movement has increased in recent decades. This may be partially attributable to present-wave feminism which has succeeded in placing women's concerns higher in the public consciousness, and particularly in the area of employment rights (Hagen and Jenson, 1988; Bakker, 1988). Activism in the women's movement may cross-fertilize with trade union activism, however the most significant cause of the higher profile of women and women's issues within the trade union movement undoubtedly stems from the increased participation of women in paid employment. As women have come to represent a growing proportion of the labour force, unions have been forced to recognise (belatedly) that the organization of women must be a priority. Throughout the 1970s and 1980s the proportion of women in the trade union movement rose steadily in both Great Britain and Northern Ireland, with increased female membership as the single most important factor countering an overall decline in trade union membership (Purcell, 1984,; Steinberg and Cook, 1988). Eileen Evason effectively summarizes the situation for Northern Ireland in the mid-1980s:

In 1953 (in Northern Ireland) 40,000 women were trade union members. By 1983 the figure was 107,300. In 1953 under a quarter of women in employment were unionised. By 1983 the figure was 44%. In crude terms, therefore, the increase in total trade union membership of 76,900 in this period is almost matched by the 67,000 additional female members. Indeed between 1974/75 and 1983 the number of women members rose by 21,300 whilst the number of male trade unionists actually fell by 6,600. In short in the post-war period women have been the major source of new recruits, they have played a major role in sustaining total trade union membership in Northern Ireland and now account for 38% of total membership as opposed to 19% in 1953.

[Of] unions with more than one thousand members here women are in the majority in twelve of these. Two thirds of these unions are in the public sector.

Nor are the unions that are dominated by women numerically of minor importance in terms of general trade union membership. The twelve unions where women are in the majority are in fact of slightly disproportionate significance within [the rest of unions with 1000+ membership] inasmuch as they contain 42% of the total membership - male and female - and unions in which women are the majority contain 38% of all trade union members in Northern Ireland (Evason, 1985, pp.4-7)

These trends have continued through the end of the decade. For example, women trade unionists make up 44% of those included in Table 1. Women are in a majority in ten of the 23 unions included in the table (NIPSA, COHSE, NUPE, RCN, INTO, NAS-UWT, UTU, NUTGW, IBOA and, USDAW).

Table 1: Male and female membership of ICTU unions with 1000+ members in Northern Ireland

	% membership female	N.I. members
General Unions		
ATGWU (Amalgamated Transport and General Workers' U.)	24.2	50,000
GMB (General Municipal Boilermakers and Allied Trade Us.)	24.3	19,001
SIPTU*** (Services Industrial Professional Technical U.)	33.3	9,001
SUBTOTAL*	25.3	78,002
Public Service Unions		
NIPSA (Northern Ireland Public Service Alliance)	59.0	32,800
COHSE (Confederation of Health Service Employees)	63.2	20,005
NUPE (National Union of Public Employees)	87.1	12,100
RCN (Royal College of Nursing)	88.9	10,000
NAS-UWT (Nat'l Assoc. of Schoolmasters - U. of Women Teachers)	53.3	7,266
UTU (Ulster Teachers' U.)	60.0	5,500
INTO (Irish Nat'l Teachers' Organization)	70.7	5,173
NATFHE (Nat'l Assoc. of Teachers in Further and Higher Education)	41.1	1,989
AUT (Assoc. of University Teachers)	15.1	1,260
FBU (Fire Brigades U.)	2.9	1,200
SUBTOTAL*	64.5	99,847
Engineering, Electrical etc. Unions		
AEU (Amalgamated Engineering U.)	10.0	12,000
EEPTU (Electrical, Electronic, Telecomms. and Plumbing U.)	7.4**	8,000
SUBTOTAL*	9.0	20,000
Other Industry Unions		
NUTGW (National U. of Tailors and Garment Workers)	88.4	10,678
UCATT (Union of Construction, Allied Trades and Technicians)	0.5	5,500
NGA (National Graphical Association)	7.6	1,650
SOGAT (Society of Graphical and Allied Trades)	40.1	1,502
BFWAU (Bakery and Food Workers Amalgamated U.)	NA	1,006
SUBTOTAL*	48.5	21,819
Postal and Telecommunications Unions		
UCW (Union of Communication Workers)	21.5	3,713
NCU (National Communication U.)	14.5	2,956
SUBTOTAL*	18.5	6,993
Other Professional/White Collar Unions		
MSF (Manufacturing Science and Finance)	35.0	9,701
IBOA (Irish Bank Officials' Assoc.)	54.7	4,739
NIMA (N.I. Musicians' Association)	11.0	1,003
SUBTOTAL*	38.3	16,952
Distribution and Transport Unions		
USDAW (Union of Shop Distributive and Allied Workers)	57.7	6,635
SUBTOTAL*	52.9	7,508
TOTAL	**43.7**	**250,529**

*   Subtotal includes unions with memberships of less than 1,000.
**   Number of women members is unavailable for 1991, based upon 1983 percentage given in Evason (1985).
***   SIPTU is a merger of ITGWU (Irish Transport and General Workers' Union) and FWI (Federated Working Union of Ireland).

NOTE: The ICTU union membership figures are as of 31 December 1991. Four unions not affiliated with the ICTU (RCN, NAS-UWT, UTU and IBOA) are included in the table. The figures for the first three of these unions came from the Equal Opportunities Commission for Northern Ireland (1990) and IBOA figures were obtained directly from the union.

Seven of these unions are located in the public sector, a sector where women make up almost two-thirds of all union members. These ten large unions, in which women form the majority, contain 46% of the total male and female membership. Most of the women are concentrated in a relatively small number of unions; the seven unions with the largest numbers of women members (ATGWU, NIPSA, COHSE, NUPE, RCN, NAS-UWT and NUTGW) contain 71% of all women trade unionists. The same is true for men, though for a rather different list of seven unions. These unions (ATGWU, GMB, NIPSA, COHSE, AEU, EEPTU and MSF) contain 71% of all male trade unionists but here, unlike for women, the concentration in public sector unions is not marked.

The rise in female membership has inexorably led to improvements in how trade unions deal with the concerns of women. The most significant changes, at least in terms of official recognition, have been the publication of the TUC Charter on "Equality for Women within Trade Unions" in 1979, the 1981 TUC resolution rejecting the idea of a "family wage" and commitments on issues such as day care and abortion. In recent years, the setting up of women's committees has been a positive development which has come to the fore, creating a framework in which women may gain the confidence to become actively involved in the trade union movement. Women's committees have been instrumental, through workshops and seminars, in encouraging women to become more involved as active members of trade unions. Women's committees may also function as "vehicles of explanation" with regard to the dissemination of information on recruitment and nomination to committees and full-time representative posts. As such, the committees help women to gain an understanding of the rules, procedures and mechanisms which govern progression from basic membership to full-time trade union office-holding. These changes, while for the better, cannot be seen as complete. The primary role of women in trade union activities still can be seen as one of championing issues of gender equality while male trade unionists deal with a broader variety of issues and have relatively little involvement with equality issues, "Women have not secured the visibility, level of participation, power and influence commensurate with their numbers within the trade union movement itself" (Evason, 1985, p.11). Gaps remain between the official policies of unions as promulgated "from the top" and the attitudes and activities of the unions at the grassroots level. In common with Britain, trade union leadership in Northern Ireland appears to be remaining disproportionately male with little change in the pipeline. As Ellis notes:

> *The vigour with which trade unions pursue or, at the very least, do not impede the improvement of opportunities for women will to some extent depend on the amount of effective pressure which women themselves bring to bear through trade union action at the workplace and the influence they can exert within the power structure of individual unions, the Trade Union Congress (TUC) and other formal or informal inter-union groupings (Ellis, 1988, p.136).*

Without question, unions in Northern Ireland, as elsewhere,   remain a "male affair". Within this context, let us examine the results of the WWLS.

Women In and Out of Trade Unions

Over half of women included in the WWLS (55%) have been in a trade union at some time in their lives (Table 2). 58% of those currently in work have a union available that they could join.   Of those with a union available, union membership is high; over three-quarters (76%) are in a union. The proportion of the total sample in work who report themselves to be currently in a union, 45%, corresponds closely with a figure of 46% union density for full-time and part-time employees available from the 1989 Northern Ireland Labour Force Survey. Both the figures for union availability and union membership are higher than those for Britain found by the WES a decade ago (Martin and Roberts, 1984).

Table 2: Union experience of WWLS respondents.

Union experience	%	N
% of sample ever in a union	55	549
% of sample who have ever left a union	30	302
% of sample currently in work	53	534
% in work with union available	58	312
% in work currently in union	45	239
% in work with a union available who are currently in a union	76	238

Just under a third of respondents, 30%, were no longer in a union. Rather than being an expression of dissatisfaction with the union, however, Table 3 shows that the majority of reasons for leaving unions reflect patterns of labour mobility: moving out of work (61%); moving to a new place of work where no union is available (18%); moving into part-time work where no union is available (4%); or to a senior position (2%). The reasons given for leaving unions that could reflect dissatisfaction with the trade union movement make up less than 15% of all responses.

The lack of dissatisfaction with the trade union movement among former members, however, should not be misconstrued as unqualified support. Of those former members of unions who were still in work but who were working in a place where no union was available, only 14% said that they would like to be in a union at the present time. Similarly, those former members who would like to rejoin unions gave reasons for wanting to rejoin that were often more instrumental than principled. 50% said they wanted to rejoin a union in

Table 3: Reasons no longer in union*

Reasons	%
Not in work	61
Union not available in current job	19
Cannot see point in joining	8
Part-time workers not eligible	4
Reason of principle	2
Senior/Staff position now	2
Union subscription too high	1
Other reasons/unknown	5
Don't know	3
N	*302*

*Respondents may have replied to more than one item so %s do not sum to 100.

order to improve working conditions, 43% mentioned pay, and 36% mentioned job security as a reason for rejoining. At the same time, 36% did say "working people should belong to a union" and 29% stated that they wanted to rejoin a union "as a matter of principle".

Among those who have never been in a trade union, the reasons given by respondents for having never been in a union appear to display a similar pattern in that most women reported that they had not had the opportunity of joining due to labour market circumstances rather than reluctance to join a union *per se*. In Table 4, fewer than 20% of the reasons for never having been in a union (for example, "cannot see point in joining" (12%); "reason of principle" (3%); "union subscription too high" (less than 1%)) reflect negative feelings about union membership.

Taking the results from Tables 2 through 4 as a whole, one may conclude that the main barrier to a larger proportion of working women being in unions was the fact that they worked in non-unionised enterprises. The majority of women working in locales where unions were available were members, and those opposed to joining were in a clear minority. At the same time, however, the lack of a principled opposition to union membership runs in parallel with a distinct lack of enthusiasm for full-time union membership among those for whom no union was currently available. Few of those who were no longer in unions missed them and many of those who were no longer members displayed only an instrumental enthusiasm for rejoining. A high proportion of working women did not enjoy union protection. If unions wish to continue to exploit their major source of growth in numbers in recent years, women, they will need to mount recruitment drives in non-unionised firms and these drives will need to be directed at concrete issues of concern to women.

Table 4: Reasons never in union*

Reasons	%
Never a union available	57
Not currently in work	21
Cannot see point in joining	8
Part-time workers not eligible	5
On principle	3
No mention made of joining	1
Union subscription too high	0
Other reasons/unknown	4
Don't know	11
N	*451*

* Respondents may have replied to more than one item so %s do not sum to 100.

Level of Involvement in Unions

Of the 239 women who were currently members of unions at the time of the survey, 19 had held some sort of office, and as regards the 549 who had ever been in a union, 41 (8%) had held office at some time or another. Table 5 shows the level of union involvement amongst those who were currently in work.

Table 5: Level of union involvement

Union involvement	%
Office holder	4
Member	41
Non-member but union available at work	14
Previous member, union not currently available	13
Never member, union not currently available	24
Do not know if union available	4
Total %	100
N	*534*

Table 6 shows that work status was associated positively and significantly with union membership. The most common work status category, full-time professional, made up a disproportionately large number of union members, 28%. While the full-time professionals were scattered across many unions,

Table 6: Work status by union membership

Work status	Member %	Non-member, but union available %	No union available %
Full-time work:			
professional	28	14	17
nonmanual	21	22	23
skilled manual	13	12	11
unskilled	7	1	7
Part-time work:			
professional	10	8	5
nonmanual	8	18	16
skilled manual	3	6	10
unskilled	10	19	11
Total %	100	100	100
N*	229	73	195

* Base figures may vary due to not applicable/unknown responses.

approximately a third were either in nursing or other health-related unions, teaching unions and the public sector union, the Northern Ireland Public Service Alliance (NIPSA). Outside of the full-time professional group, the single largest concentration of union membership was among full-time non-manual workers, with approximately a third in NIPSA. In accord with British results (Martin and Roberts, 1984; Beechey and Perkins, 1987), the categories of part-time workers, both non-manual and skilled manual, show disproportionately low levels of union membership. For all other work status categories, including the second largest category of union members (full-time non-manual workers), the proportion of union membership is equivalent to that which would be expected by chance.

Looking at work categories in relation to "no union available" reveals a negative image of that obtained from union membership. In particular, part-time skilled manual workers were less likely to have a union at their place of work. Unskilled workers in part-time work were the group most likely not to have joined unions when they were available. Reflecting their high levels of membership, full-time professionals were the group least likely not to have taken up the opportunity to join a union.

As one would expect, older respondents tended to have been in unions longer (Table 7). Full-time professionals were the category of employee who had been in unions significantly longer than any other.

Those women currently in a union reported very poor attendance at union meetings (Table 8). Over half never attended and three-quarters of the remainder only attended meetings occasionally. There was no relationship between the length of time respondents had been in unions and their frequency of attendance at meetings.

Table 7: Length of time in union

Time in union	%
Less than 5 years	33
5 to 10 years	33
11 to 20 years	24
21+ years	7
Don't know	3
Total %	100
N	549

Table 8: Frequency of attendance at union meetings

Attendance	%
Always	7
Often	5
Occasionally	37
Never	51
Total %	100
N	238

The most common reason for not attending meetings was lack of interest (28%) (Table 9). Almost as many cited "Inconvenient times" (26%) and a few (1%) mentioned "Distance to travel" as the single most important reason for not attending. These latter reasons would seem to be a specific instance of the difficulties women have in integrating family demands with work, union and other public activities, difficulties that are widely cited in the literature. One would expect mothers with young children to be the group who would find it most difficult to attend union meetings, however, this was not borne out by an analysis of union attendance by presence or absence of children under school age. Interestingly, the results suggest that there may be more fundamental problems in how unions are organized at the grassroots level in that 16% reported that either no union meetings were held, or that they did not know of union meetings. Only two women gave "Do not believe in unions" as a reason for not attending. Except for the very small number in Northern Ireland who "Do not believe in unions", these figures correspond closely to British figures (Martin and Roberts, 1984).

Table 9:   Reason union meetings not attended

Reason	%
Not interested/Find them boring	28
Inconvenient times	26
No meetings/Don't know of meetings	16
Staff not always notified	3
Distance to travel	2
Do not believe in unions	1
Other reasons	9
Unknown	15
Total	100
N	*238*

The intensity of union involvement may be affected by a multiplicity of factors and, furthermore, these factors may act in concert. That is, the level of involvement in union activity is unlikely to be the simple effect of one or two personal characteristics. In order to go some way towards disentangling such multiple effects, analyses utilising multivariate modelling techniques were used. To this end, a multiple analysis of variance of the effects of the age of respondents, their religion (Catholic or non-Catholic), level of education, work status (using the categories as shown in Table 6) and level of union involvement was carried out with respondent's total number of children as the dependent variable. While all of the other variables were found to be related to the total number of children, when the effects of these other variables were controlled, level of union involvement itself was not related to how many children were in the family. A similar multiple analysis of variance confined to mothers of children under school age also found no significant effects relating to level of union involvement. Likewise, a third analysis of variance looking at the amount of assistance the women received from their spouse or partner with five domestic tasks (washing, ironing, cooking, cleaning/vacuuming and shopping) again found no significant differences that could be attributed to level of union involvement. Crosstabulations of level of union involvement with marital status and, for married respondents, with the self-reported equality of distribution of household tasks between respondent and spouse also found no significant association (except that divorced/separated women were more likely than married/cohabiting women to be union office holders).

Taken together, the above analyses indicate that childcare and domestic concerns may not be the barrier to union involvement for women that the literature often suggests is the case (Crompton and Jones, 1984; Walby, 1988). Rather, these results confirm Evason's finding that, "The presence of dependent children did not appear to constitute the bar to active trade unionism that might have been expected." (Evason, 1985). One should note that activists, by any measure, constitute only a small minority of those in trade unions and are exceptional by their involvement (only about 10% of union members in the sample were office holders or attended union meetings regularly). This exceptionality may go a long way towards explaining the lack of evidence here for domestic duties limiting trade union activism. The assumption that women in particular will be limited in their public activities by domestic concerns can be seen, in a perverse way, as yet another extension of "malestream" social science views of women. Rather than a passive model of involvement in which activists are just those with the spare time to be active, perhaps women activists are those who, through capability, desire or sheer bloodyminded determination, shoulder a "triple" burden of work, domestic responsibility and union duties.

Union Involvement and Respondents' Attitudes

It may be expected that union membership and activity relates to women's attitudes to their work and employers. In order to investigate this, a series of analyses of respondents' attitudes in a number of work-related areas were carried out. Once a number of other "control" factors were taken into account (the age of respondents, their religion (Catholic or non-Catholic), their level of education and work status), the effects of union involvement were largely nil. Level of union involvement had no significant effect upon measures of either attitudes to women working, the respondent's commitment to her work, attitudes regarding the adequacy of pay in the respondent's own job, respondents' opinions on the likelihood of their promotion, attitudes towards the respondent's immediate superior or boss and respondent's opinions about her job generally. The only significant effect of level of union involvement was found in an analysis of variance of a scale measuring the attitudes of respondents to the organization they work for. In this instance, union members, and union office holders in particular, have significantly lower opinions of their work organization than those in the non-union categories.

Do Union Members Benefit from Membership?

The consideration of movement into and out of unions, and levels of involvement, indicate that membership was determined more by practical, instrumental considerations than by reasons of principle or commitment to trade union ideals. Given this practical orientation of union members, it is reasonable to query the extent to which union membership actually confers concrete benefits. First, and perhaps most importantly, was union membership associated with a better level of pay? With reference to Table 10, there was a positive relationship between union membership and take-home pay. Union members were less likely to be in the two lowest pay categories (none in the lowest category of less than £25 per week), and more likely to be in the four top pay level categories; that is, those earning more than £150 per week. Working women for whom no union was available were more likely to be in the three lowest pay categories, those earning £75 per week or less, and were less likely than the others to be in the top four categories. Women who did have a union available but who were not members were generally better off than those for whom no union was available, but worse off than union members. With the exception of 12% in the lowest pay category, their distribution across pay levels was as one would expect.

Table 10: Weekly pay levels by union membership

Weekly pay	Member	Non-member, but union available	No union available
	%	%	%
Less than £25	0	10	7
£25 to £50	5	18	22
£51 to £75	13	12	22
£76 to £100	19	22	25
£101 to £125	14	10	13
£126 to £150	12	12	6
£151 to £175	11	6	2
£176 to £200	7	1	1
£201 to £250	12	5	2
More than £250	7	4	1
Total %	100	100	100
N*	233	73	188

* Base figures may vary due to not applicable/unknown responses.

Type of work performed and whether the work was full-time or part-time obviously will also affect the amount of pay received, and the link between union membership and pay could be only a reflection, or statistical artefact, of this. Again, a multivariate analysis was undertaken in order to disentangle the combined associations of union membership and type of work upon pay levels. In this case, a loglinear analysis of pay level with work status and category of union membership was carried out to establish if the apparent association between union membership and pay level was real or merely a reflection of the type of work and/or whether the work was done on a full-time or part-time basis. Work status was significantly linked to level of pay as expected, but an independent association between category of union membership and pay level remained. In other words, the pay advantages for women of union membership and the presence of a union appear to be real advantages and exist independent from the type of work performed.

As well as pay, those in employment may benefit in other ways from their jobs. Table 11 shows how union membership related to a variety of job-related benefits, amenities and "perks".

Table 11: % in each union membership category receiving job-related amenities and "perks"*

Amenities and Perks	Member	Non-member, but union available	No union available
	%	%	%
Written employment contract	85	72	46
Specified salary or wage rate	94	97	92
Full sick pay	74	57	48
Paid holiday	92	86	81
Pension scheme	71	59	25
Maternity leave:			
at full salary	52	45	18
at part salary	31	12	18
don't know	12	32	33
Childcare provided at work	4	-	1
Rest breaks	74	57	60
Unsocial hours payments	32	22	10
"Flexitime"	21	25	17
Training opps. full-time at work	73	69	45
Training opps. similar or better than men**	88	93	84
Promotion opportunities	59	53	27
Bonus/merit scheme/payment in kind	19	17	15
Mortgage scheme	3	1	0
Loan scheme	5	3	3
Profit sharing	5	3	2
Career break scheme	12	14	2
Travel allowance	15	16	7
Company car	1	3	2
Other	3	0	1

*Respondents may have replied to more than one item so %s do not sum to 100.
**Only answered by those who said they did have training opportunities at work.

The general pattern to emerge is that, as with pay level, the union members did best, those with no union available were the worst off, and those not in a union but with one available at the place of work fell midstream. Significantly more union members had a written contract of employment, full sick pay, paid holidays and full pension schemes. Maternity leave, either at full or part salary, was also available to a significantly larger proportion of union members. Non-members of unions at places where a union was available were the group most likely not to know if maternity leave was available at their place of work. The three categories did not differ significantly in terms of the availability of childcare provision; in all cases, access to childcare was abysmal. Significantly more of the union members and significantly fewer of the non-members reported training and promotion opportunities associated with their jobs.

Among those with access to training, however, union membership did not influence their perception of gender inequality in training opportunities. In the main, if training opportunities were available, they were equally available to both sexes. Union membership did not affect the low percentages who had the opportunity to participate in flexitime arrangements.

As with pay level, it may have been possible that the significant differences between union membership categories were merely a reflection of differences in work status. Loglinear analyses equivalent to that described for pay level were carried out for all of the above items in which a significant association with union membership had been established. In all cases, while work status was significant, the association with union membership was not eclipsed.

Across the remaining benefits and "perks", union members continue to show an advantage in comparison to the other membership categories. Somewhat larger numbers of union members received bonuses or payments in kind, had the opportunity to participate in a merit scheme, received payments for unsocial hours of work, had regular rest breaks, travel allowances or had access to mortgage, loan or profit sharing schemes.

As a further test of the number of work-related benefits received by union members and non-members, both with a union available and not available for joining, the number of amenities and "perks" received by each working respondent was calculated (Table 12). An analysis of the number of benefits by union membership and work status found that union members on average enjoyed the largest number of benefits and those with no union available for joining the least. Taking into account work status, part-time non-manual workers who were in unions received a significantly greater number of work-related benefits than part-time manual workers. Also, full-time professionals who were not in a union when one was available received a higher number of benefits than part-timers.

Table 12: Mean number of job-related amenities and "perks" by union membership category and work status

Union membership	Mean
Member	8.1
Non-member but union available	6.9
No union available	5.0

Employment status	
Full-time work:	
Professional/Intermediate	8.6
Skilled non-manual	7.4
Skilled manual	6.3
Part skilled/Unskilled	6.5
Part-time work:	
Professional/Intermediate	7.1
Skilled non-manual	6.3
Skilled manual	3.9
Part skilled/Unskilled	4.9

Conclusion

In sum, union members enjoy higher levels of pay and work-related benefits and, amongst the non-members, those women who work in firms where a union is available seem to benefit indirectly from the presence of a union. The advantages associated with union membership appear to be additional to, and at least partially independent of, job status and whether working full-time or part-time. It is still possible of course that there may be other features of the women's employment that were the underlying cause of union membership, better pay levels and the broad spectrum of work-related benefits covered above (for instance, the type of industry that a person is employed in or a more detailed occupational breakdown than that used here). Similarly, having a union available to join could itself be seen as one of the "perks" of having a good job or a benevolent employer, like a pension scheme, training opportunities or a system of maternity benefits. Cross-sectional data such as these coming from the WWLS cannot establish definitively whether unions are a cause of the benefits received by their members. Case studies of the role of unions in securing better pay levels or benefits for their members that extended across time would be required to resolve the issue. However, the general pattern of union members doing consistently better than their non-union colleagues, after the effects of work status are allowed for, does imply strongly that there are concrete benefits accruing specifically to union membership itself.

As Martin and Roberts conclude after examining cross-sectional survey data for Britain:

> *Union representation is associated with better pay, job benefits and opportunities. Whether this is a direct effect of a union presence or because jobs which are likely to be unionised are independently likely to have better conditions of employment is impossible to say (Martin and Roberts, 1984).*

Nevertheless, in the absence of convincing counter results and despite much criticism, unions in Northern Ireland do seem to benefit women workers across a variety of dimensions.

References

Bakker, I. (1988). 'Women's employment in comparative perspective.' In J. Jenson, E. Hagen, and C. Reddy (eds.), *Feminization of the Labour Force.* Cambridge: Polity Press.

Beechey, V. (1986). 'Women's employment in contemporary Britain.' In V. Beechey and E. Whitelegg (eds.), *Women in Britain Today.* Milton Keynes: Open University Press.

Beechey, V. and Perkins, T. (1987). *A Matter of Hours: Women, Part-time Work and the Labour Market.* Cambridge: Polity Press.

Bradley, H. (1989). *Men's Work, Women's Work: A Sociological History of the Sexual Division of Labour in Employment.* Cambridge: Polity Press.

Clancy, P. and Mackeogh, K. (1987). 'Gender and trade union participation.' In C. Curtin, P. Jackson and B. O'Connor (eds.), *Gender in Irish Society.* Galway: Galway University Press.

Crompton, R. and Jones, G. (1984). *White-Collar Proletariat: Deskilling and Gender in Clerical Work.* London: Macmillan Press.

Ellis, V. (1988). 'Currrent trade union attempts to remove occupational segregation in the employment of women.' In S. Walby (ed.), *Gender Segregation at Work.* Milton Keynes: Open University Press.

Equal Opportunities Commission for Northern Ireland (1990). *Where Do Women Figure?* Belfast: Equal Opportunities Commission for Northern Ireland.

Evason, E. (1985). *Right Brothers! A Study of Women and Trade Unions in Northern Ireland.* Unpublished Manuscript, University of Ulster at Coleraine.

Godwin, A. (1977). 'Early years in the trade unions.' In L. Middleton (ed.), *Women in the Labour Movement.* London: Croom Helm.

Hagen, E. and Jenson, J. (1988). 'Paradoxes and promises: Work and politics in the postwar years.' In J. Jenson, E. Hagen and C. Reddy (eds.), *Feminization of the Labour Force.* Cambridge: Polity Press.

Martin, J. and Roberts, C. (1984). *Women and Employment: A Lifetime Perspective.* London: HMSO.

McCarthy, M. (1977). 'Women in trade unions today.' In L. Middleton (ed.), *Women in the Labour Movement.* London: Croom Helm.

Meehan, E. (1985). *Women's Rights at Work. Campaigns and Policy in Britain and the United States.* London: Macmillan.

O'Farrell, B. (1988). 'Women in blue-collar occupations: Traditional and non-traditional.' In A.H. Stromberg, and S. Harkess (eds.), *Women Working: Theories and facts in perspective.* Mountain View, California: Mayfield Publishing Company.

Purcell, K. (1984). 'Militancy and acquiescence among women workers.' In J. Siltanen, and M. Stanworth (eds.), *Women and the Public Sphere.* London: Hutchinson.

Randall, V. (1987). *Women and Politics.* Basingstoke, Hampshire: Macmillan

Siltanen, J. and Stanworth, M. (1984). 'The politics of private woman and public man.' In J. Siltanen and M. Stanworth (eds.), *Women and the Public Sphere.* London: Hutchinson.

Spitze, G. (1988). 'The data on women's labor force participation.' In A.H. Stromberg, and S. Harkess (eds.), *Women Working: Theories and Facts in Perspective.* Mountain View, California: Mayfield Publishing Company.

Steinberg, R.J. and Cook, A. (1988). 'Policies affecting women's employment in industrial countries.' In A.H. Stromberg, and S. Harkess (eds.), *Women Working: Theories and Facts in Perspective.* Mountain View, California: Mayfield Publishing Company.

Walby, S. (1986). *Patriarchy at Work: Patriarchal and Capitalist Relations in Employment.* Cambridge: Polity Press.

Chapter 7

UNEMPLOYMENT

Eithne McLaughlin

Introduction

Despite the research endeavours stimulated by mass unemployment in the 1930s and the late 1970s and early 1980s in the United Kingdom, until recently the implications of unemployment for women have been largely ignored. Typically, unemployment featured in both academic and policy debates as a phenomenon that predominantly affected men and was discussed as an essentially individual experience. Official employment statistics, being based on a simple count of those individuals who are registered as unemployed and claiming benefit, give a poor indication of the number of people who are experiencing the effects of unemployment, and tell us little of how that experience is distributed (Pissarides and Wadsworth, 1992). For example, they tell us nothing of the numbers of children whose parents are unemployed. Furthermore, women in general are undercounted in the official statistics because they are less likely than men to be entitled to benefits when unemployed, while the unemployed wives of unemployed men are even less visible.

A number of factors have contributed to the diversion of attention away from female unemployment. The undervaluation of women's participation in paid work, the different nature of their employment patterns compared with those of men and, in the case of many women, responsibility for children and other dependents, have all been assumed to mean that women's experience of their own unemployment is unimportant. This view has been challenged, however, by recent research exploring the relationships between paid work, unpaid work and non-work for women (see, for example, Brown and Harris, 1978; Warr and Parry, 1982; Coyle, 1984; Martin and Roberts, 1984).

As a result of this handful of studies on women and unemployment, a much broader perspective on unemployment in relation to both men and women is emerging (see Dex, 1985, for a comprehensive review). Although job loss clearly does happen to an individual, the costs borne by members of that individual's household and indeed by the larger community, are increasingly being acknowledged (Jackson and Walsh, 1987). This development forms part of the growth of a focus on "home economics" (Levy-Garboua, 1979) and "family and economy" (Close and Collins, 1985) which examines the interrelationship between economic and technological change, the struggle for livelihood at the level of the household, and the interaction of practices and ideologies of class, gender and kinship within this changing labour process (Redclift and Mingione, 1985).

The intentions of this chapter are to locate recent material on unemployment in Northern Ireland within this developing perspective (see Popay, 1985, for similar analysis in Britain), and in particular to present cross-sectional data from the WWLS relevant to women's experience of unemployment. The first part of the chapter considers women's unemployment, that is, unemployment where it is the woman herself who is unemployed. Assessment here is made difficult by gaps in official statistics (for instance, even the numbers of unemployed women) and the consequent ambiguity felt by many jobless women as to whether or not they are "unemployed". Under the heading "Her unemployment - nobody's problem?" both the extent and the effects of women's unemployment are discussed. Male unemployment has profound ramifications for other family members and in particular for the wives of unemployed men. Indeed male unemployment has been aptly described by McKee and Bell (1985) as men's loss but women's problem. The second part of this chapter accordingly explores three aspects of this theme of "His unemployment - her problem". Firstly, the employment status of the wives of unemployed men is discussed, then the issue of the burden of family poverty is explored, and finally, responsibility for domestic work is considered.

Her Unemployment: Nobody's Problem?

The Extent of Women's Unemployment

Undercounting of womens' unemployment is inherent in official unemployment statistics. Who is counted as unemployed clearly rests on the definition of what constitutes unemployment. That definition has always been linked to eligibility for National Insurance benefits and the criteria for eligibility have:

> *discriminated albeit indirectly against women and have thus acted as a disincentive for women to be registered, to register themselves or to think of themselves as "unemployed" (Dex, 1985, p.60).*

Indeed, recent changes have increased rather than decreased this bias against women. Official statistics of unemployment since 1982 include only those who are both registered as unemployed and who receive benefit by virtue of their unemployment. Statistics based on benefit receipt will inevitably not include many married women because women in two-parent families have no independent entitlement to income support, while their entitlement to unemployment benefit is often adversely affected by their previous patterns of employment (for example, low-paid part-time work and interruptions for childbearing and rearing). A woman's right to register as unemployed and to claim unemployment benefit has also been adversely affected by more stringent definitions of "availability for work" introduced in the late 1980s, and which now require that an unemployed mother has childcare arrangements which can be set in motion within 24 hours if she is to be considered "available for work".

Estimation of the extent of women's unemployment thus remains as much an art as a science (Trewsdale, 1983). Trewsdale (1988) found that in the 1985 Labour Force Survey in Northern Ireland, 55% of unemployed married women were not claiming benefit and therefore were not included as officially unemployed. The comparable figure for all men and women was 16%. The Labour Force Survey's definition of unemployment includes all those who classify themselves as unemployed and those temporarily sick. Using a similar definition (but excluding the sick), a survey of households in Derry City (McLaughlin, 1987) yielded surprisingly similar figures; 53% of unemployed women in Derry City in 1983 were not registered as such.

The problem of women's under-representation on the unemployment register is well known. What is given less attention are the consequences of that undercounting, an omission which has undoubtedly contributed to the low priority which politicians and policy-makers give to women's unemployment. Undercounting of women in the official unemployment statistics has the effect of not only making women's unemployment appear unimportant but also causing the overall unemployment rate to appear lower since the latter includes the figures for both men and women. For example in McLaughlin's survey of Derry City in 1987, the registered unemployment rate for men in the sample was 47% and that for women was 14%, giving an overall rate of 31%. Inclusion of unregistered unemployed women raised the overall unemployment rate from 31% to 39%. Clearly the undercounting of women's unemployment has political implications for both men and women.

That unemployed women are largely ignored by a system which does not even consider them important enough to count is not lost on women themselves. Trewsdale (1988) found that in 1981, before the adoption of the claimant-based system of recording unemployment, 59% of unemployed women registered at their local Jobmarket to find work. By 1985 this figure had fallen to just 17%. Instead, twice as many women as in 1981 used newspapers or personal contacts to find work. Beyond the obvious ramifications there are other more insidious effects of being marginalised in this way; "unemployment" is a concept which many women hesitate to apply to themselves even though they are either looking for work or would be interested in a suitable job if one became available. McLaughlin (1987) found that women were more likely to describe themselves as unemployed while they were receiving unemployment benefit, thus mirroring state definitions of unemployment. As Popay has pointed out :

These barriers to married women registering as unemployed effectively create a self-fulfilling prophecy. Women are actively discouraged from registering since unemployment is deemed to be less important for them than it is for men. Yet when they do not register it is seen as a reflection of own view of its unimportance (Popay, 1985, p.188).

All of these issues bearing on the relationship between women and definitions of unemployment were present in findings derived from the WWLS. Only 9% of women described themselves as unemployed, including literally only a handful of women with two or more children (that is, those with the most broken and part-time employment records, Table 1), a disproportionately small proportion of married women (Table 2), and few women in the middle age groups (Table 3). This pattern of response was entirely predictable given the way that benefit regulations structure who are permitted to call themselves unemployed. As regards the overall unemployment rate of women in the WWLS, it is important to note that the survey excluded young women under 18 who generally have a higher unemployment rate than women aged 18 and over.

Table 1: Number of children under 16 years old by woman's employment status

	No of children under 16					
	0	1	2	3	4+	All
Employment status	%	%	%	%	%	%
*Full-time employed	42	36	22	13	15	34
Part-time employed	15	24	33	33	22	21
Unemployed	9	11	3	9	10	9
**Caring	20	27	38	43	53	28
Retired/sick	10	2	4	1	-	6
YTP/Full-time educ.	4	1	-	1	-	2
Total %	100	100	100	100	100	100
N	535	171	148	86	60	1000

* Full-time employed in this and subsequent tables includes those waiting to take up work and the temporarily sick.
** Caring in this and subsequent tables includes those women not employed who were looking after children and/or adult dependants and those "keeping house".

Of the 86 women who described themselves as unemployed, 42% (38 cases) were not registered as unemployed. A very large majority of non-employed women in the WWLS were well aware that they were not entitled to benefit when they were not in employment (Table 4), but only this small minority (38 women) described themselves as unemployed.

Table 2: Woman's employment status by marital status

Employment status	Single %	Married %	Ex-married %	All %
Full-time employed	57	28	26	34
Part-time employed	6	27	12	21
Unemployed	15	7	9	9
Caring	7	33	38	28
Retired/sick	5	5	15	6
YTP/Full-time educ.	10	-	-	2
Total %	100	100	100	100
N	223	668	109	1000

Table 3: Age by employment status

Employment status	20 - %	21-30 %	31-40 %	41-50 %	51-60 %	60+ %	All %
Full-time employed	53	47	34	33	23	10	34
Part-time employed	7	13	31	29	20	8	21
Unemployed	15	9	7	7	10	8	9
Caring	3	26	25	27	35	44	28
Retired/Sick	-	1	3	4	12	30	6
YTP/Full-time educ.	22	4	-	-	-	-	2
Total %	100	100	100	100	100	100	100
N	59	246	217	231	174	73	1000

Table 4: Reasons for not registering as unemployed

Reasons	%
Know not eligible for benefit	69
Think not eligible for benefit	15
Think not worth it	6
Can't be bothered	4
Illness/Disability	3
Retired	1
Total %	100
N	378

In addition to the 48 women who described themselves as unemployed and were registered as such, and the 38 women describing themselves as unemployed but who were not registered as such, there were a further 33 women who were registered as either sick (nine cases) or caring for children and the home (24 cases). It may be the case that women, with young children in particular, feel a reluctance to label themselves as unemployed since this implies that they are "doing nothing". Many women in McLaughlin's research in Derry City responded to questions about their employment status in a classically ambiguous way, typically, "Well, I'm unemployed [or I haven't got a job] but I'm working - working in the house". To describe themselves as "unemployed" meant saying that they were "not working", and that was something many women were reluctant to do, not least because they recognised the domestic labour and childcare labour they were involved in as "work".

It is also the case that unemployment registration among women varies widely between localities within Northern Ireland, at least to some extent reflecting differential levels of employment opportunities (Table 5). In the WWLS, there were above average rates of female unemployment in Derry, Limavady, Strabane, Belfast, Down and Larne. While most of these areas are also those where male unemployment rates are high, the last is not. There were well below average rates in Coleraine, Ballymoney, Antrim, Newtownabbey, Carrickfergus, North Down, Castlereagh, Magherafelt and Cookstown. While most of these areas are also those where male unemployment rates are low, the last two are relatively high unemployment areas. Similarly low unemployment rates for women may go hand in hand with low employment rates for men (for example, Coleraine and Newtownabbey) while high employment rates may go hand in hand with high unemployment rates for men (for example, Strabane). This suggests that rates of registered unemployment for women are related not only to the presence or absence of employment opportunities but also to differences in the propensity of women in different localities to think of themselves as being in the labour market (whether employed or unemployed).

A number of dimensions may be important here, including an urban/rural divide, the degree of industrialization of medium sized towns, the specific history of women's employment and participation in each locality, fertility rates and demographic structures, religion, and, for married women, their partner's employment status (discussed further in the second half of the chapter). As regards religion, half of the difference in employment rates between Catholic and Protestant women is accounted for by the higher registered unemployment rate of Catholic women (Table 6). No doubt a good part of the remaining differential could be explained by higher levels of unregistered unemployment among Catholic than Protestant women, related to the higher unemployment rates of Catholic women's partners (see later section).

Table 5: Local government district by employment status*

District	Employed %	Unemployed %	Caring %	Ret/ sick %	F-t educ/ YTP %	Total %	N
Derry	54	15	26	2	4	100	(54)
Limavady	59	18	18	6	-	100	(17)
Coleraine	48	6	36	9	-	100	(33)
Ballymoney	38	6	56	-	-	100	(16)
Moyle	60	10	20	10	-	100	(10)
Larne	53	26	16	-	5	100	(19)
Ballymena	53	8	26	11	3	100	(38)
Magherafelt	43	5	48	5	-	100	(21)
Cookstown	53	6	29	6	6	100	(17)
Strabane	57	17	22	4	-	100	(23)
Omagh	46	7	46	-	-	100	(28)
Fermanagh	57	-	23	14	6	100	(35)
Dungannon	66	7	21	-	7	100	(29)
Craigavon	52	9	18	9	6	100	(46)
Armagh	59	9	18	9	6	100	(34)
Newry and Mourne	37	7	52	2	2	100	(52)
Banbridge	32	9	50	9	-	100	(22)
Down	53	14	28	-	6	100	(36)
Lisburn	58	7	23	11	2	100	(57)
Antrim	70	-	30	-	-	100	(27)
Newtownabbey	40	4	49	2	4	100	(45)
Carrickfergus	48	5	38	10	-	100	(21)
North Down	69	4	23	2	·2	100	(48)
Ards	60	9	23	5	2	100	(43)
Castlereagh	77	5	12	7	-	100	(43)
Belfast	58	11	20	8	3	100	(186)
N	550	86	279	60	25		1000

*Employed category includes full-time work, part-time work and temporarily sick.

Table 6: Employment status by religion

Employment status	Protestant %	Catholic %	None %	Other/refused/ missing %	All %
Full-time employed	36	31	37	50	34
Part-time employed	23	18	18	14	21
Unemployed	7	11	5	9	9
Caring	26	31	36	27	28
Retired/sick	6	6	4	-	6
YTP/Full-time educ.	2	3	-	-	2
Total %	100	100	100	100	100
N	563	393	22	22	1000

The Effects of Women's Unemployment

How did women's own unemployment affect them and their families? Not surprisingly, given that the current definition of unemployment is so male-oriented, research on the social, psychological and material consequences of unemployment has largely concentrated on men. The few studies which have explored the consequences of unemployment for women indicate that there are differences between single and married women's experiences of unemployment, with that of single women more closely paralleling that of men. However, there are more similarities than there are differences in the social and psychological consequences of unemployment for both men and women, married or unmarried:

> These studies [of women's unemployment] begin to show that a similar set of variables influence both women's and men's unemployment experiences; these include their age, their position in the lifecycle, the local labour market conditions, their level of resources, their health and their attitudes towards work (Dex, 1985, p.58).

The material consequences of female unemployment can be both immediate and more long-term. Clearly for single women unemployment means total reliance on benefits. At the same time, an assumption that married women have their partner's income to rely on should not be allowed to obscure the material importance of married women's earnings and hence the significance of their unemployment, registered or otherwise. Without a wife's earned income, the number of households in Britain in poverty would increase threefold (Morris, 1987). The economic hardship consequent upon the loss of female earnings has been documented by a number of British studies (for example, Coyle, 1984). The WWLS shows that both registered unemployment and non-employment among married women were associated with higher levels of financial stress in Northern Ireland (Tables 7 and 8).

Table 7: Married women's employment status by how managing financially

Employment status	Manage well	Manage	Often difficult	Do not manage*	All
	%	%	%	[N]	%
Full-time employed	36	19	12	[2]	28
Part-time employed	31	24	20	[1]	27
Unemployed	5	9	9	[2]	6
Caring	25	39	53	[9]	34
Retired/sick	2	9	6	[2]	5
YTP/full-time educ.	1	-	-	[-]	-
Total %	100	100	100		100
N	403	158	89	[16]	666

* Presented as raw data given N < 20

Table 8: Married women's employment status by whether worry about money

	Almost all the time	Quite often	Sometimes	Almost never	All
Employment status	%	%	%	%	%
Full-time employed	21	22	27	35	28
Part-time employed	15	19	32	28	27
Unemployed	16	12	4	5	6
Caring	44	44	33	26	34
Retired/sick	4	3	4	6	5
YTP/full-time educ.	-	-	-	-	-
Total %	100	100	100	100	100
N	*68*	*86*	*286*	*226*	*666*

Table 9 also examines the material impact of women's unemployment and non-employment. Whilst a minority of non-employed women had high earning husbands, Table 9 shows clearly that, across all household sizes, both non-employment and registered unemployment of wives/mothers was normally associated with below and well below average joint incomes. For example, in households with couples who were either married, with one primary school age child or with two pre-school children, 92 out of 108 couples (85%) had average or above average incomes when the woman was employed full-time (where average income is taken to be between £201 and £250 net per week). When the woman was unemployed, only five out of 20 had average or above average incomes and when the woman was engaged in childcare and/or housekeeping full-time, only 19 out of 87 (22%) had average or above incomes. In larger households (for example, those with three adults or couples with three or more primary school age children or two or more secondary school age children), the contrast between couples where the woman was employed full-time and those where the woman was registered as unemployed is even greater (25 out of 31 [81%] couples with the woman employed full-time had average or above average incomes compared with two of the 13 couples where the woman was unemployed).

His Unemployment: Her Problem

Married or cohabiting women are affected not only by their own unemployment but also by that of their partners. There are several reasons why "his unemployment" may be "her problem". One is that the task of handling the burden of poverty is normally taken on by the wife/mother rather than the husband/father. This will be discussed later. "His unemployment" can be

Table 9: Effect of woman's employment status on joint net weekly income, by weighted household size*

		Net joint weekly income									
Weighted household size >1, <2	<50	<75	<100	<150	<200	<250	<300	<350	<400	<500	501+
F-t. empl.	1	-	-	8	7	16	18	11	20	16	11
P-t. empl.	-	1	5	7	16	15	12	9	5	5	4
Unemployed	1	4	4	5	1	1	1	1	1	1	-
Caring	2	10	22	16	19	5	3	5	1	2	3
Ret/sick	1	1	5	6	5	4	2	3	2	1	-
N	*5*	*16*	*36*	*42*	*48*	*41*	*36*	*29*	*29*	*25*	*18*
Weighted household size >2,>3	<50	<75	<100	<150	<200	<250	<300	<350	<400	<500	501+
F-t. empl.	-	-	-	4	2	5	7	6	3	-	4
P-t. empl.	-	1	5	2	8	7	4	4	6	3	5
Unemployed	-	2	-	4	5	-	-	1	-	-	1
Caring	2	6	15	22	12	4	6	3	1	2	4
Ret/sick	-	1	1	1	-	1	1	-	-	-	-
N	*2*	*10*	*21*	*33*	*27*	*17*	*18*	*14*	*10*	*5*	*14*
Weighted household size >3,<4	<50	<75	<100	<150	<200	<250	<300	<350	<400	<500	501+
F-t. empl.	-	-	-	-	-	1	-	-	-	-	1
P-t. empl.	-	-	-	-	-	-	-	-	-	-	-
Unempl.	-	-	-	-	-	-	-	-	-	-	-
Caring	-	1	1	-	1	1	-	1	-	-	-
Ret/sick	-	-	-	-	-	-	-	-	-	-	-
N	*-*	*1*	*1*	*-*	*1*	*2*	*-*	*1*	*-*	*-*	*1*

* See Appendix 1 for description and derivation of weighted household size

"her problem" in quite another sense; unemployment is concentrated in some families at least partly because of the effect that a husband's unemployment has on a wife's employment status.

Labour Force Participation of the Wives of Unemployed Men

Survey evidence from Britain (Greenhalgh, 1977; McNabb, 1977; Layard, Piachaud and Stewart, 1978; Greenhalgh, 1980; Joshi, 1984; Moylan, Millar and Davies, 1984; Warr and Jackson, 1984) has confirmed that there is a net flow of women out of employment when their husbands are unemployed and thus a process of polarisation between couples where both are employed and those where neither are. Recent evidence from Northern Ireland shows the same phenomenon. In the WWLS, 14% of couples had neither partner employed, a higher level than was the case in Britain in 1985. Although the figures for Northern Ireland in 1985 and 1990 show the same trends (the minority role of the male breadwinner/female homemaker type of couple, the very low proportion of sole female breadwinners, the majority pattern of two-earner couples), an interesting difference may be the considerably smaller proportion of sole male breadwinners in the WWLS (Table 10).

Table 10: Couples' economic activity, Northern Ireland (1985 and 1990), and Great Britain (1985)*

	Northern Ireland				Great Britain
	1985 CHS**	1985 HES**	1985 LFS**	1990 WWLS	1985 GHS
Status:	%	%	%	%	%
Male breadwinner	40	38	33	29	31
Female breadwinner	3	5	3	6	4
Dual earners	43	39	55	51	55
Both unemployed	14	18	9	14	10
Total %	100	100	100	100	100
N	1,554	14,256	1,918	602	4,813

*excluding couples where both partners were over state retirement pension age

**Source: derived from McWilliams, 1991

The effect of male unemployment on female employment in Britain is also indicated by the low employment rates of women married to unemployed men. Where the husband was unemployed about a third of wives were in paid work compared with two-thirds where the husband was employed (Cooke, 1987). In the WWLS, 63% of the wives of employed men were themselves employed whereas only 29% of the wives of non-employed men and 19% of the wives of unemployed men were employed (Table 11).

Whilst it is true that unemployment could cluster because partners may share characteristics which afford a high risk of unemployment (for example, the area they live in, their level of educational qualifications, ethnicity or religion), substantial evidence now exists which shows that an important contributory factor is the operation of the social security benefit system, in

Table 11: Married/cohabiting womens' employment status by partner's employment status

	Partner employed	Partner unemployed*	Partner non-employed**	All
Employment Status	%	%	%	%
Full-time employed	31	9	16	27
Part-time employed	32	10	13	27
Unemployed	5	14	7	6
Caring	26	64	51	33
Retired/sick	6	3	13	7
Total %	100	100	100	100
N	505	69	92	666

* In this and subsequent tables, men counted as unemployed are those seeking work and those waiting to take up a job
** In this and subsequent tables, men counted as non-employed are those temporarily and permanently sick and the retired.

conjunction with a gendered and segmented labour market which offers most women low-paid jobs. McLaughlin, Millar and Cooke (1989) found that in both Coleraine (Northern Ireland) and West Yorkshire the wives of unemployed men were deterred from taking up (or staying in) part-time work by the low amount that they could earn before pound for pound deductions were made from households' unemployment benefit or more usually, income support. In addition there was the problem of the "hassle" that can arise from trying to combine earnings with unemployment benefit or income support. Declaring part-time earnings may result in delays in benefit payment, errors in the calculation of benefit, and other complications. The net financial return (£4 per individual per week in 1987, £15 per couple per week since 1988 [if the husband has been unemployed for more than two years, otherwise £5 per individual per week] under income support regulations) was very low compared with the risks to one's regular income from obtaining and declaring part-time work. Taking up (or staying in) full-time work while their husbands were unemployed was regarded as not financially viable because of the poor wages available to most women. Thus the unemployment of the husband had the effect of deterring wives from rejoining the labour market after time out to care for children, or from remaining in work if they were already in the labour market, when their husbands became unemployed (see also Dilnot and Kell, 1989).

Loss of the primary earner thus makes the employment of the secondary earner more difficult to sustain. The result is the concentration of paid work in certain households and the exclusion of other households from the whole realm of paid employment. This polarisation into no-earner and two-earner households (Morris, 1987) is obviously of particular importance in Northern Ireland where levels of male unemployment have always been high and where there remain very great differences between Catholic and Protestant male unemployment rates. As Table 12 shows, the discouraging effect of male unemployment on female employment is a phenomemon potentially affecting nearly four times as many Catholic women as Protestant women in the WWLS.

Table 12: Catholic and Protestant couples' employment status, excluding couples where male was sick/disabled/retired*

Status:	Catholic %	Protestant %
Male breadwinner	33	32
Dual earners	45	62
Female breadwinner	5	1
Both unemployed	18	5
Total %	100	100
N	217	335

* 16% of Catholic women's partners and 13% of Protestant women's partners were sick, disabled or retired.

The Burden of Family Poverty

When married men are unemployed there are several consequences which are either shared with, or borne by, their wives. As discussed above, one is that wives of unemployed men are less likely than other women to be employed themselves. This compounds another of the most significant consequences of unemployment - financial hardship. In Britain fewer than 3% of employed men would receive even 90% of their earnings if they became unemployed (Dilnot and Kell, 1987). In Northern Ireland, larger families and lower wages may mean that a rather higher proportion of unemployed men face similar levels of income in and out of work (although low take-up of in-work benefits, such as family credit, would affect this). Nonetheless, it is clear that for the majority of households affected, male unemployment involves a drop in income. Table 13 shows this in relation to the WWLS. The joint incomes of couples where the man was unemployed were very low - less than £100 a week in households containing, for example, a couple with one or two young children, and less than £150 in larger households (for example, couples with two or more older children). Table 13 also shows how the low employment rates of women married to unemployed men, discussed in the last section, greatly contributes to this impoverishment of households.

Table 13: Effect of man's employment status on joint net weekly income, by weighted household size

Net joint weekly income

Weighted household size >1, <2	<50 %	<75 %	<100 %	<150 %	<200 %	<250 %	<300 %	<350 %	<400 %	<500 %	501+ %
Man:											
employed	1	-	4	26	40	39	34	27	29	24	18
unemployed	4	5	14	4	1	-	-	-	-	-	-
ret/sick	-	11	18	12	7	2	2	2	-	1	-
Couples' employment:											
man only	1	-	4	17	20	10	6	7	4	4	3
woman only	1	1	5	6	3	2	2	-	-	1	-
both	-	-	-	9	20	29	28	20	25	20	13
neither	3	15	27	10	5	-	-	2	-	-	-
All	5	16	36	42	48	41	36	29	29	25	18

Weighted household size >2,>3	<50 %	<75 %	<100 %	<150 %	<200 %	<250 %	<300 %	<350 %	<400 %	<500 %	501+ %
Man:											
employed	-	1	4	13	22	17	18	14	10	5	14
unemployed	1	3	12	11	3	-	-	-	-	-	-
ret/sick	1	6	5	9	2	-	-	-	-	-	-
Couples' employment:											
man only	-	1	2	12	15	5	7	4	1	2	5
woman only	-	1	3	5	3	-	-	-	-	-	-
both	-	-	2	1	7	12	11	10	9	3	9
neither	2	8	14	15	2	-	-	-	-	-	-
All	2	10	21	33	27	17	18	14	10	5	14

Weighted household size >3,<4	<50 %	<75 %	<100 %	<150 %	<200 %	<250 %	<300 %	<350 %	<400 %	<500 %	501+ %
Man:											
employed	-	-	-	-	1	2	-	1	-	-	1
unemployed	-	1	-	-	-	-	-	-	-	-	-
ret/sick	-	-	1	-	-	-	-	-	-	-	-
Couples' employment status:											
man only	-	-	-	-	1	1	-	1	-	-	-
woman only	-	-	-	-	-	-	-	-	-	-	-
both	-	-	-	-	-	1	-	-	-	-	1
neither	-	1	1	-	-	-	-	-	-	-	-
All	-	1	1	-	1	2	-	1	-	-	1

The consequences of this drop in income have been found to be borne primarily by women. Work with both employed and unemployed families in Derry (McLaughlin, 1987) and unemployed couples in Coleraine (McLaughlin, Millar and Cooke, 1989) has documented this. In both areas, women were the financial managers in the majority of unemployed households as they are in the majority of low-income families (see Whitehead, 1981; Pahl, 1982, 1983, 1988, 1989; Burns, 1984; Charles and Kerr, 1986; Wilson, 1987, for British evidence). That is, it was typically the woman who had responsibility for meeting the family's collective consumption needs, that is paying for food, fuel, rent and clothing. Since it tends to be the woman who is responsible for making ends meet, when a drop in income occurs, such as that caused by male unemployment, it is the woman who has to bear the brunt of increased financial strain and carry a heavier "managerial" role.

In the WWLS, nearly half the wives of unemployed men (47%) said they either often found it difficult to manage or could not manage at all financially, compared with a quarter of the wives of other non-employed men and just 10% of the wives of employed men (Table 14). The majority of wives of unemployed men worried about money all the time or often (60%) compared with a quarter (27%) of the wives of other non-employed men and just 17% of the wives of employed men (Table 15).

Table 14: Partner's employment status by how managing financially

How managing?	Employed	Non-employed	Unemployed	All
	%	%	%	%
Manage well	70	43	14	61
Manage	20	30	39	24
Often difficult	9	23	36	13
Do not manage	1	2	11	2
Total %	100	100	100	100
N	505	91	70	666

Table 15: Partner's employment status by worry about money

Worry about money	Employed	Non-employed	Unemployed	All
	%	%	%	%
Almost all the time	7	12	30	10
Quite often	10	15	30	13
Sometimes	47	34	27	43
Almost never	36	37	13	34
Total %	100	100	100	100
N	505	91	70	666

It is important to note that when women have to pull the purse strings tighter because of male unemployment, the result is added responsibility not additional power. When money is short, managing and budgeting become burdens rather than sources of power. Pahl (1983) has pointed out that the ability to offload certain decisions and money-handling chores on to the other spouse can itself be a sign of power and Murcott has expressed much the same point, "The delegate may be responsible for execution of tasks, but they are answerable to the person in whom the power to delegate is originally vested." (Murcott, 1983, p.89).

The Domestic Division of Labour

Against this somewhat bleak picture of the ways in which men's unemployment becomes women's problem, some have speculated that as male unemployment has increased, men may be taking a greater share of domestic responsibilities and work. British studies (for example, Pahl, 1984; Morris, 1985) have found no evidence of greatly increased male participation in housework and childcare and what changes there have been do not seem to be particularly associated with male unemployment. In Northern Ireland, despite the long history of very high male unemployment in Derry City, McLaughlin (1987) found no evidence of greater levels of shared domestic responsibility than that reported from other areas. Whilst some men carried out both housework and childcare tasks (though more often the latter than the former) this seemed to have more to do with the nature and health of the marital relationship than it did with either women's or men's employment status. Trew and Kilpatrick (1984) in their study of unemployed men in Belfast also noted that unemployed men devoted very small amounts of time to domestic work.

In the WWLS, 56% of wives of unemployed men said they did all or almost all of the household work, compared with 58% of wives of other non-employed men and 75% of wives of employed men (Table 16), suggesting a limited shift towards more male involvement in household work in unemployment. Against that it has to be noted that only 34% of wives of unemployed men said their partners shared the work equally. Similarly in relation to childcare, 53% of the wives of unemployed men said they did all or almost all of the childcare compared with 65% of the wives of other non-employed men and 62% of the wives of employed men (Table 17). More positively, nearly half (48%) of the wives of unemployed men said their partners shared or had shared childcare equally, compared with a third of wives of employed men (39%). Overall, however, there is little evidence from the available data to support speculation that male unemployment fundamentally alters the domestic division of labour. To use Morris's (1984) phrase, it would appear that male unemployment is not a sufficient condition for such a renegotiation to take place.

Table 16: Partner's employment status by household work sharing

Household work	Employed	Non-employed	Unemployed	All
	%	%	%	%
Woman all	21	24	19	21
Woman most	54	34	37	50
Shared equally	23	37	34	26
Man most	1	4	10	3
Total %	100	100	100	100
N	505	91	70	666

Table 17: Partner's employment status by sharing of childcare

Childcare	Employed	Non-employed	Unemployed	All
	%	%	%	%
Woman all	9	24	5	10
Woman most	53	41	48	50
Shared equally	39	38	48	39
Man most	-	-	-	-
Total %	100	100	100	100
N	449	79	65	593

Conclusion

This chapter has attempted to demonstrate that, on the one hand, women are affected by male unemployment and, on the other hand, that female unemployment (and/or non-employment) is as much a "problem" as male unemployment. Policy measures targeted at alleviating unemployment and increasing employment should address the effects of both male and female unemployment and particularly the interaction between both. The norm of the male breadwinner (that is sole earner) which informs policy provision in these areas appears increasingly inadequate in the light of both the changing nature of employment (with the increase in part-time and casual employment) and increasing research evidence that the assumption is a myth rather than a reality for the majority of working class households (Morgan, 1985).

In addition to any unemployment they themselves experience directly, women carry a further burden of family poverty when other household members are unemployed. Policy measures and reforms targeted at alleviating poverty would do well to consider the way in which many women seem to be locked into poverty by a social security system which treats the needs of women and children as synonymous with those of men. The employment and unemployment statuses of husbands and wives are linked together by a social security system which treats households, rather than individuals, as the relevant income units. The outcome of this is the process of polarisation into two-earner and no-earner households which we have noted to be a result of the inhibiting effect of male unemployment on female employment. Given the relatively low employment rates of women in Northern Ireland and the high levels of male unemployment, particularly amongst Catholics, together with the low levels of out-of-work benefits, and a generally low wage economy, the management of poverty would seem to be the fate of the majority of Northern Irish women for the foreseeable future.

References

Brown, G. and Harris, T. (1978). *Social Origins of Depression: A Study of Psychiatric Disorder in Women.* London: Tavistock.

Burns, R. (1984). *Financial Management and the Allocation of Resources within Households: A Research Review.* EOC Research Bulletin No. 8. Manchester: EOC.

Charles, N. and Kerr, M. (1986). 'Eating properly, the family and state benefit.' *Sociology, 20,* 3, 412-29.

Close, P. and Collins, R. (eds.) (1985). *Family and Economy in Modern Society.* London: Macmillan.

Cooke, K. (1987). 'The withdrawal from paid work of the wives of unemployed men: A review of research.' *Journal of Social Policy, 16,* 3, 371-382

Coyle, A. (1984). *Redundant Women.* London: Womens Press.

Dex, S. (1985). *The Sexual Division of Work.* Brighton: Wheatsheaf.

Dilnot, A. and Kell, M. (1987). 'How women suffer.' *New Society, 21,* 22-23.

Dilnot, A. and Kell, M. (1989). 'Male unemployment and women's work.' In A. Dilnot and I. Walker (eds.), *The Economics of Social Security.* Oxford: Oxford University Press.

Greenhalgh, C. (1977). 'A labour supply function for married women in Great Britain.' *Economica, 44,* 249-65.

Greenhalgh, C. (1980). 'Participation and hours of work for married women.' *Oxford Economic Papers, 32,* 296-318.

Jackson, P. and Walsh, S. (1987). 'Unemployment and the family.' In D. Fryer, and P. Ullah (eds.), *Unemployed People: Social and Psychological Perspectives.* Milton Keynes: Open University Press.

Joshi, H. (1984). *Womens Participation in Paid Work: Further analysis of the Women in Employment Survey.* Department of Employment Research Paper 45. London: Department of Employment.

Layard, R., Piachaud, D., and Stewart, M. (1978).*The Causes of Poverty.* London: HMSO.

Levy-Garboua, L. (1979). *Sociological Economics.* London: Sage.

McKee, L. and Bell, C. (1985). 'His unemployment, her problem.' In S. Allen, K. Purcell, A. Watson, and S. Woods (eds.), *The Experience of Unemployment.* London: Macmillan.

McLaughlin, E. (1987). *Maiden City Blues: Employment and Unemployment in Derry City.* Unpublished Ph.D. Thesis, Queens University of Belfast

McLaughlin, E., Millar, J. and Cooke, K. (1989). *Work and Welfare Benefits.* Aldershot:

Avebury.

McNabb, R. (1977). 'Labour force particpation of married women.' *Manchester School of Economic and Social Studies, 45,3,* 221-235.

McWilliams, M. (1991). "Women's paid work and the sexual division of labour.' In C. Davies and E. McLaughlin (eds.), *Women, Employment and Social Policy in Northern Ireland.* Belfast: Policy Research Institute.

Martin, J. and Roberts, C. (1984).*Women and Employment: A Lifetime Perspective.* London: HMSO.

Morgan, D. (1985). 'Foreword.' In P. Close, and R. Collins (eds.), *Family and Economy in Modern Society.* London: Macmillan.

Morris, L. (1985). 'Renegotiation of the domestic division of labour.' *Sociology, 18,* 339-52.

Morris, L. (1987). 'Constraints on gender: The family wage, social security and the labour market; reflections on research in Hartlepool.' *Work, Employment and Society, 1, 1,* 85-106.

Moylan, S., Millar, J. and Davies, R. (1984). *For Richer, For Poorer? DHSS Cohort Study of Unemployed Men.* London: HMSO.

Murcott, A. (1983). 'It's a pleasure to cook for him: Food, mealtimes and gender in some South Wales households.' In E. Garmarnikow, D. Morgan, J. Purvis, and D. Taylorson (eds.), *The Public and the Private.* London: Heinemann.

Pahl, J. (1982). *The Allocation of Money and the Structuring of Inequality within Marriage.* Canterbury: Health Services Research Unit, University of Kent at Canterbury.

Pahl, J. (1983). 'The allocation of money and the structuring of inequality within marriage.' *Sociological Review, 31,* 237-62.

Pahl, J. (1988). 'Earning, sharing, spending: married couples and their money.' In R. Walker and G. Parker (eds.), *Money Matters.* London: Sage.

Pahl, J. (1989). *Money and Marriage.* London: Macmillan.

Pahl, R. (1984). *Divisions of Labour.* Oxford: Basil Blackwell.

Pissarides, C. and Wadsworth, J. (1992). 'Unemployment risks'. In E. McLaughlin (ed.), *Understanding Unemployment.* London: Routledge.

Popay, J. (1985). 'Women, the family and unemployment.' In P. Close and R. Collins (eds.), *Family and Economy in Modern Society.* London: Macmillan.

Redclift, N. and Mingione, E. (eds.) (1985). *Beyond Employment: Household, Gender and Subsistence.* Oxford: Basil Blackwell.

Trew, K. and Kilpatrick, R. (1984). *The Daily Life of the Unemployed.* Belfast: Department of Psychology, The Queen's University of Belfast.

Trewsdale, J. (1983). *Womanpower No 3: The Impact of Recession on Female Employment and Earnings in Northern Ireland.* Belfast: Equal Opportunities Commission for Northern Ireland.

Trewsdale, J. (1988). *Womanpower No 4: The Aftermath of Recession - Changing Patterns of Employment and Unemployment in Northern Ireland.* Belfast: Equal Opportunities Commission for Northern Ireland.

Warr, P., and Jackson, P. (1984). 'Men without jobs: some correlates of age and length of unemployment.' *Journal of Occupational Psychology, 57,* 77-85.

Whitehead, A. (1981). ' "I'm hungry, Mum": The politics of domestic budgeting.' In K. Young, C. Wolkowitz, and R. McCullagh (eds.), *Of Marriage and the Market.* London: CSE Books.

Wilson, G. (1987). 'Money: Patterns of responsibility and irresponsibility in marriage.' In J. Brannen, and G. Wilson (eds.), *Give and Take in Families.* London: Allen and Unwin.

Chapter 8

CHILDCARE

Irené Turner

Introduction

This chapter focuses on the two aspects of childcare which are of particular importance both to working mothers and to women who are considering remaining in work, or returning to work, after the birth of a child. Firstly, the chapter examines the extent to which husbands/partners participate in the care of their children. This support has been identified as crucial to the well-being of dual-earner families (Gilbert, 1988) and is also important in moderating the stresses experienced by working mothers (Pleck, 1985; Anderson-Kulman and Paludi, 1986). Secondly, the chapter considers the arrangements which mothers make for the care of their children while they are working because the availability, flexibility and cost of suitable care is necessarily a factor in decisions to remain, or to become, economically active.

How is Childcare Shared between Parents/Partners?

Studies in the United States and in Great Britain have shown that fathers undertake less practical childcare than mothers (for example, Lamb, 1976; Clarke-Stewart, 1980). Brannen and Moss (1988) point out that women are constantly reminded, by the media and other social influences, that being a "good mother" entails taking primary responsibility for the home and for the children. Perhaps this is why a sizeable minority of fathers almost never look after children on their own, and why in many families, mothers have to arrange for friends or relatives to provide childcare during any brief absences from home (Hill, 1987).

Although it is frequently asserted that marital roles are more clearly distinguishable in working class than in middle class families (see, for example, Newson and Newson, 1970), this does not hold true for childcare. Irrespective of social class, for all fathers participation most often takes the form of playing with the children or taking them out to give the mother a break, a reason which carries the implicit message that it is the mother who is regarded as the primary carer. Studies continue to endorse this hierarchy of father involvement, a hierarchy described more than thirty years ago by Herbst (1960). In its simplest terms, fathers' participation is most likely in the more pleasurable childcare activities with mothers taking far more responsibility for day-to-day routines and chores.

The extent to which fathers share in the care of children has been examined with reference to households where the mother is economically active as well as households where she is not. Most of these studies suggest that, in dual-earner families, what occurs is not an equal division of labour but rather a reallocation of tasks (Hoffman and Nye, 1974). Until 1977 no study found that husbands of employed wives spent more "absolute" time on child and household care than husbands of non-employed wives. This is not to say that differences were not discernible but these time-budget studies typically revealed proportional rather than absolute differences. Thus, a review of research in 1978 (Pleck and Lang, 1978) indicated that employed women did between twice and four times as much "family work" as their partners, whereas for women not working outside the home this rose to six times as much.

These findings are very similar to those obtained from a more recent English study (Brannen and Moss, 1988). This carefully controlled investigation involved interviewing women before the arrival of the first child, through the months afterwards, and when the women had eventually returned to work. It was found that not only did most men generally do less childcare but that they rarely assumed primary responsibility for it. The male role was that of helper or assistant rather than of equal partner. These mothers reported that they did well over half the childcare, with fathers undertaking routine tasks, such as feeding, less frequently than "most days". Nor did partners tend to take on more of the household chores to free their wives for the additional requirements of childcare. Household contributions were limited to clearing up after meals, some shopping and some cooking. Washing clothes, cleaning the house or ironing were seldom included and a number of the mothers said that they would rather do most jobs themselves because of their partners' perceived (or actual) incompetence. Similarly Hill (1987), based on his interviews with both parents in a number of Edinburgh households, reports on the evasive techniques employed by fathers. He identifies three mechanisms: voluntarism, which reflects the view that household duties are optional for men but obligatory for women; incompetence, which was sometimes demonstrated by poor performance but also sometimes a product of collusion by partners to preserve the mothers' sense of expertise; and distaste as, for example, when fathers excused themselves from changing nappies.

Fathers are viewed as equal contributors only in disciplining the children and in play activities. Although there is some evidence that men are gradually increasing their contribution to child and household care (Pleck and Lang, 1978), a recent report (Morris, 1990) concluded that the change is not yet sufficient to compensate for women's increased employment outside the home. Morris compared findings in the United States and the United Kingdom and suggests that women in part-time work who have young children, may have the worst of both worlds. Unfortunately, we do not know if women select part-time work because they, or their partners, are not prepared to share childcare equally or if these couples do not contribute equally because the women have chosen to work "only part-time".

A limitation of many studies is that fathers' views have not been obtained directly. As there is a tendency for more men than women to report childcare and household chores as being shared equally (see, for example, Jowell et al., 1989), this is an important omission.

There is relatively little research into how domestic duties are shared within families in Northern Ireland. However, a thoughtful review of the available literature (Montgomery and Davies, 1991) indicates that there are many similarities between the results obtained in Northern Ireland and elsewhere, and particularly as regards the weight attached to women's domestic responsibilities. In the present study, all mothers were asked about how childcare was or had been shared with their partners. Of the 593 respondents, over half considered "I do/did most of it", while 39% shared childcare on a 50/50 basis. Across the entire sample there was only one family in which all the childcare was done by the husband/partner. The fact that this unique father of three worked in catering may have been significant in equipping him with the combination of necessary skills and flexible working hours but he remains very much a man alone.

Table 1 relates specifically to those 387 mothers who, at the time of the survey, were not divorced, separated, widowed or single and had children under 16 years living at home. Regardless of employment status, over half (56%) of these mothers in the WWLS sample did most of the childcare, with the remainder considering that it was shared 50/50. If the mothers who work full-time, part-time or not at all outside the home are compared, it is apparent that those women who work part-time may indeed fare worst, just as Morris (1990) suggests.

Additional factors which were explored included age of mothers, possession of higher educational qualifications, occupational class (as determined by mother's occupation), religious persuasion, number of children, ages of children and age of the youngest child. Apart from "age of mothers" (see Chapter 2), none of these factors had a statistically significant effect on the way in which childcare was shared, although a strong trend suggested that age of youngest child may have been influential with parents of younger children more likely to share childcare. The number of children in the family and the extent of sharing childcare are given in Table 2. No clear patterns emerge, apart from, ironically, a higher proportion of those with only one child sharing childcare, and a slight reduction in the percentage of mothers providing all or most of the childcare with the arrival of the fourth or subsequent children.

Table 1:   Employment status and current sharing of childcare*

Childcare	Full-time work	Part-time work	Available for work	Not available for work	All
	%	%	%	%	%
I do it all	3	4	28	8	7
I do most of it	38	52	52	54	49
It is shared 50-50	58	44	20	38	44
He does most of it	-	-	-	-	-
He does it all	1	-	-	-	-
Total %	100	100	100	100	100
N	99	124	25	139	387

*Breakdowns in this table do not include those who were divorced or separated. In addition, economic activity figures do not include those who were waiting to take up work, or who were temporarily/permanently sick, retired or on YTP schemes.

Table 2: Number of children in the family and % of sharing in childcare

Childcare	Children					
	1	2	3	4	5-10	All
	%	%	%	%	%	%
I do it all	5	3	10	6	14	7
I do most of it	34	54	57	50	41	50
It is shared 50-50	61	43	32	44	46	44
He does most of it	-	-	-	-	-	-
He does it all	-	-	1	-	-	-
Total %	100	100	100	100	100	100
N	62	137	94	64	44	401

As childcare is an all-inclusive term, women were also asked which parent undertook various day to day activities related to childcare. These are shown in Table 3. From a depressing set of statistics, perhaps the most dismaying of these findings is the first. 3% of fathers have never played with their children, and what is more distressing is that these fathers are found in families both large and small alike.

The information that 7% of fathers with children under 16 have never fed their children in the mothers' absence, that 21% have never got up to see to a child during the night and that 22% have never washed or bathed a child, provides useful insights into the difficulties which may be encountered by mothers if they wish to remain in full-time or part-time work outside the home.

Table 3: Sharing in daily childcare activities for children ≤ 16 at home.

	Never	Sometimes	Often	Total %	N
Has husband/partner:	%	%	%	%	
play(ed) with child(ren)?	3	25	72	100	401
put child(ren) to bed?	6	42	52	100	400
fed child(ren) alone?	7	45	48	100	400
read to child(ren)?	18	35	47	100	399
changed a nappy?	19	42	39	100	401
got up during night?	21	42	37	100	400
washed/bathed child(ren)?	22	41	37	100	400
taken child(ren) to doctor?	48	39	13	100	401

No significant social class differences (as defined by working mother's occupation) were found on any of these aspects of childcare, as typically demonstrated by the frequency with which partners of working mothers currently with children under 16 actually put children to bed (Table 4). It could be argued that the exigencies of the fathers' work might well mean that they were not available during the day to share in feeding, changing nappies and, perhaps, in washing or bathing the children. However, this argument is less sustainable in relation to putting the children to bed or to getting up during the night.

Table 4: Mother's occupational class and frequency with which fathers put children to bed

	Occupation		
	Professional/ Intermediate	Skilled Non-manual	Skilled Manual All Part/Unskilled
Child to bed?	%	%	%	%
Never	6	7	12	8
Sometimes	31	26	23	27
Often	63	68	65	65
Total %	100	100	100	100
N	35	31	26	92

As previous research has demonstrated that mothers are more likely than fathers to look after sick children or to take them to the doctor, employed mothers were asked about getting time off from work. 65% of those in full-time work and 79% of those in part-time work had no difficulty about taking time off (Table 5), but only 54% of those in full-time work and 28% of those in part-time work were paid for any time taken off for these childcare purposes (Table 6).

Table 5: Accessibility of time off for mother when children are ill

	Full-time work	Part-time work	All
Time off work?	%	%	%
Yes, easily	65	79	73
Yes, with difficulty	24	9	16
No	3	3	3
Don't know	7	9	8
Total %	100	100	100
N	*95*	*117*	*212*

Table 6: Payment of mothers for time off when children are ill

	Full-time work	Part-time work	All
Payment for time off?	%	%	%
Yes	54	28	40
No	30	49	40
Varies	5	6	5
Don't know	12	17	15
Total %	100	100	100
N	*84*	*103*	*187*

Here differences in terms of occupational status did emerge. Mothers employed in professional, intermediate or skilled non-manual work were much more likely to be paid for time off than those in skilled, partially skilled or unskilled manual work (51% compared with 13%; Table 7), and to have the time treated as holidays (20% compared with 10%; Table 8).

However, 41% of women working part-time and 31% of women working full-time reported that their employers were prepared to make informal arrangements rather than to treat this time as either sick leave or holidays (Table 9).

Table 7: Occupational status and payment for time off when children are ill

	Occupational status				
	Professional/ Intermediate	Skilled/ Non-manual	Skilled/ Manual	Part skilled/ Unskilled	All
Payment?	%	%	%	%	%
Yes	50	52	11	16	39
No	20	37	71	58	40
Varies	8	6	7	-	6
Don't know	22	5	11	26	15
Total %	100	100	100	100	100
N	60	63	28	31	182

Table 8: Occupational status and how employers regard mothers' time off when children are ill

	Occupation status				
	Professional/ Intermediate	Skilled/ Non-manual	Skilled/ Manual	Part skilled/ Unskilled	All
Time off	%	%	%	%	%
Holidays	20	21	4	16	17
Sick leave	5	11	-	6	7
Informal	35	39	50	19	36
Has not occurred	32	18	11	26	32
Varies	8	11	-	13	9
Total %	100	100	100	100	100
N	60	62	28	31	181

Table 9: Employment status and how employers regard mothers' time off when children are ill

	Full-time work	Part-time work	All
Time off	%	%	%
Part of holidays	21	13	17
Part of sick leave	11	3	6
Informal arrangement	31	41	37
Has not occurred	25	37	32
Varies	12	6	9
Total %	100	100	100
N	84	102	186

Responsibility for Childcare

The first part of this chapter has concerned the extent to which childcare in Northern Ireland is shared between "partners". Complementing studies carried out in both the United States and in other parts of the United Kingdom, an interesting uniformity of practice is once again apparent. The impression which comes through, and which confirms the work of Rapoport and Moss (1990) in England, is that little has changed in the last twenty years in terms of responsibility for childcare. This accords with a recent small scale study (Tierney, 1989) of rural, working class parents in Northern Ireland in which both parents were interviewed. Tierney concluded that the only differences which were apparent between dual-earner families and those where the mother did not work outside the home lay in the way in which caring for sick children and taking children to the dentist or doctor was arranged. These differences were, in any case, slight. The Tierney study did not explore social class differences. However, these were apparent in very few of the aspects of childcare which were examined in the WWLS. In the light of the finding that some fathers do not play with their children, it is perhaps fortunate that there is no single linear association between the amount of time either parent spends with the child and the strength of attachment between them (Lamb, 1981). Although fathers spend less time with their children than mothers, they may still be the preferred parent and play a key role in the children's development. There is evidence that fathers are particularly important in helping to develop gender roles, as they differentiate their interactions between sons and daughters more than do mothers (Lamb, Frodi, Hevang, Frodi and Steinberg, 1982), and intellectual effects have also been documented (Ostermeyer, Trew and Turner, 1988). The importance of the father's psychological and social contribution to childrearing has been increasingly recognised over the last decade, especially as this effects school based learning (Radin, 1981; Wolfendale, 1983). As Richards (1982) suggests, it may well be that boys and girls differ in having more or less to gain from care by one or other parent. He argues that children should experience both male and female care.

The most serious financial implications of women's primary responsibility for childcare affects highly qualified women whose careers are jeopardised by any employment breaks. Joshi (1985) has calculated that this responsibility "costs" a representative mother six to seven years of exclusion from employment and, probably, twice as many years loss of average earnings. This is based not only on earnings lost through taking time off work to raise children but also involves work experience, increments and promotions. These effects make their mark for the rest of the mothers' working lives, and not just the time when the children are young. This is not to suggest that gender inequalities in income and employment opportunities occur exclusively or even mainly as a result of women's responsibility for childrearing but clearly childcare is a major piece in this complex mosaic. Simultaneously, there is no compelling reason why mothers need to automatically shoulder this responsibility unless they wish to do so (Moss, 1986), and there is considerable research which demonstrates that "mothering" may be learned through experience, observation and training (Bee, 1974; Tizard, 1986) and that such learning may be undertaken equally by men and women. This could lead to more working mothers sharing childcare with their partners on a 50/50 basis. Studies of families where this is the norm indicate that traditional views of sex roles are not immutable (Vogel et al., 1970) but vary as a result of individual experience, thus revealing more optimistically that societal stereotypes may also eventually change. There is some evidence that already such a change may be taking place, albeit very slowly. Studies in the United States suggest this (Pleck and Lang, 1978), and more recently an investigation in Sweden (Hwang, 1987) has found that "well-educated" fathers in the 25 to 35 age range participated far more in the care of their young children than was found in earlier studies. Evidence from the WWLS also suggests that younger men may be participating more in childcare than had previously been the case (see Chapter 2).

Meanwhile, any analysis of the labour market which ignores the domestic responsibilities of both men and women may also need re-examining. The majority of employed mothers in our study (73%) indicated that they could easily get time off work when their children were ill. This invites the speculation that flexibility on the part of employers may already play an important part in the continuing employment of working mothers, or conversely, mothers may be constrained to work for those employers who will facilitate time off for medical, educational and other child-related requirements. This is undoubtedly an issue worthy of further investigation.

Childcare and Working Mothers

Our society remains ambivalent about mothers who work and about children whose care is shared (see Chapter 10). Although the number of mothers in the workforce continues to rise, many experience a conflict between their views on the responsibilities of motherhood and their need or desire to work. This is especially apparent when mothers of young children in the labour market are studied. Those who decide to work, either full-time or part-time, are often guilt-ridden about leaving their children and frequently unaware of the growing body of research which indicates that alternative forms of childcare in themselves do not constitute a risk factor in children's lives (Scarr, Phillips and McCartney, 1990). Instead, it is the quality of the relationship between mother and child and the quality of the alternative care which is of most importance (Hoffman, 1984). The child looked after exclusively by an unhappy mother who feels imprisoned in the house is not in a fortunate position. Such a child may actually benefit directly from experiencing alternative care and indirectly from the release this affords the mother whether or not she uses this time to rest, to shop, to visit friends or to take up employment.

From the moment of birth, babies differ in temperament, showing wide variations in their reactions to people, places and objects, and hence to care experiences. In turn, those experiences also vary greatly. A child may be taken to a carer or the carer may come to the house; some children are cared for by relatives whom they already know and whose ways are likely to be very similar to those of their mothers. Other children are cared for by neighbours or by strangers, trained or untrained, whose relevant knowledge and experience may be considerable or slight, and whose behaviours may be quite different to those which they have previously encountered. They may be looked after alone or with other children by a childminder, or be placed in a creche or a nursery. It is not surprising that research demonstrates consistently that it is not the form but the quality of the alternative care which is most important. An extreme example is provided by the children who live with a full-time carer in a kibbutz and whom studies have found to develop normally and become securely attached to their parents (Fox, 1977).

What is quality in relation to childcare? Some aspects are obvious, including the training and experience of carers, the total number of children accepted, the adult-child ratio, the type and variety of toys and equipment and the size and composition of available play areas. The most vital of these dimensions of quality is the first (Clarke-Stewart and Gruber, 1984) and the others tend to follow from the presence of properly trained carers. Interestingly, it seems that experience with children does not replace child-related training. Arnett (1989) reports that training leads to improved caring. Therefore, ideally, carers should have both experience and training. A recent report from the Department of Education and Science (1990) on the quality of educational experience offered to three and four year-olds in Britain, makes specific recommendations concerning the nature of the training and experience which is desirable.

A less obvious aspect of quality is the stability of arrangements. Children who experience stable childcare develop normally, both emotionally, socially and linguistically, but those who experience multiple changes in carers and care settings seem to be at risk of less optimal development and these effects can last for some years (Howes, 1988). It seems probable that children who have to adapt to changes of carer every few weeks may feel less secure and that this in turn may influence adjustment and development. This has led some researchers to advocate properly staffed day centres in preference to childminders for young children. The centre provides a stable setting and several adults with whom the child develops multiple attachment relationships

(Ainslie and Anderson, 1984) so that the loss of one from time to time can be encompassed. The child with an individual childminder who is replaced by another minder may simultaneously experience a change from a familiar adult to a stranger, a change of location and a change of regime so that several adjustments are required of the child in addition to those arising from the loss of the previous carer.

Research needs to examine not only these issues but also the effects of the unavailability of childcare, particularly the unavailability of good quality, consistent care (Scarr, Phillips and McCartney, 1990). In the absence of affordable, quality childcare, most mothers in the UK have no real choice about returning to work or remaining at home. We do not know the effects of this lack of genuine choice on mothers and their children because no controlled studies can be carried out in the absence of opportunities for mothers to choose from a range of available, quality care to suit not only babies and young children but also older children who may require care after school and out of term time. What is clear, however, is that in the absence of suitable childcare, equal opportunities in employment remain for many women a mirage. Cohen (1990) identifies this as the key barrier to equal opportunities.

Since 1978, when the Equal Opportunities Commission for Northern Ireland first examined the issue of daycare (Evason, 1980), this link between available provision for the care of children of working parents and equality of opportunity has been well established. Moss (1988) has pointed out that the traditional "twin peaks" for women in employment in the UK: 20 to 24 and 45 to 49, is unique in the EC, and arises because so many women used to leave the workforce on the arrival of their first child. It stands in marked contrast to Belgium and France, for example, where a large percentage of women remain in employment after the birth of their first child, and to Denmark and Portugal where employment rates are fairly constant and very high for women between the ages of 20 and 49. Although evidence suggests that the "M" profile of female employment rates is now less discernible (see Chapter 3), the structural and financial difficulties faced by working mothers across the UK remain a real concern.

Family Size, Age and Mother's Employment Status

These statistics, taken in conjunction with the evidence which identifies the lack of adequate childcare as a key factor in mothers' decisions not to continue working (see Chapter 10), suggest the need to focus particularly on the nature of the childcare used by working mothers while their children are young. In contrast to most previous research, when working mothers were asked about their childcare arrangements, the WWLS disaggregated replies for pre-school children. Instead of using the inclusive category of "under five", the survey examined the forms of childcare used when children were less than three years old, when they were three to four years old as well as when they were five or older. In this way, it is possible to see the extent to which the nature of childcare varies with the age of the child. To set the scene, Tables 10 and 11 indicate how married and cohabiting women's employment status is influenced by both the number of children and the age of the youngest child in the family. Although over half were in work (57%), only 44% of these women were in full-time employment. A smaller proportion of women were working when children were under three although a higher proportion of these mothers with young children were working full-time.

Table 10: Mothers' employment status by age of youngest child

	Age of youngest child				
	Under 3	3 - 4	5 - 11	12 - 16	All
Employment status	%	%	%	%	%
Full-time work	29	19	20	31	25
Part-time work	19	36	42	36	32
Not in paid employment*	53	44	38	33	43
Total %	100	100	100	100	100
N	144	47	132	80	403

* Does not include those either sick (temporary or permanent), waiting to take up work or retired.

As well as their age, the number of children was also related to current employment status, with the arrival of the second child seemingly associated with a movement to part-time employment (Table 11), with this shift continuing as family size increases.

Table 11: Number of children and percentage of full-time to part-time workers amongst working mothers

	Number of children					
	1	2	3	4	5 to 10	All mothers
Employment status	%	%	%	%	%	%
Full-time	63	43	38	32	33	44
Part-time	37	57	62	68	67	56
Total	100	100	100	100	100	100
N	48	88	48	28	12	224

Forms of Care

A small minority of the mothers of children under three years of age (10%) have addressed the childcare problem by working at home and looking after their children at the same time, or by taking their children to work with them, or by exchange minding with a friend or neighbour. This latter form of care, which incurs no direct costs, relies upon the mothers making informal arrangements and is categorised in Table 12 under "complementary care". The availability of such care is naturally variable and it is clearly less dependable on a day-to-day basis than, for example, placement in a nursery where staff and facilities are provided during working hours for five days per week. Not surprisingly, given the shortfall in this type of provision in Northern Ireland, only 8% of mothers report using nurseries for children under three (categorised under "group care" in Table 12). The majority of children, 67%, were looked after by a relative (categorised under "family care" in Table 12), with 30% using childminders. Overall, 19% of respondents mentioned that they used a combination of arrangements, often including both family care and childminders.

Table 12: Forms of childcare used*

	Age of child			
	Under 3	3 - 4	5 and over	All
Childcare	%	%	%	%
Family care	67	53	59	60
Childminder	30	37	11	20
Complementary care**	10	21	44	32
Group care	8	44	1	11
N	*63*	*43*	*147*	*253*

* Respondents may have replied to more than one item so %s do not sum to 100.
** Working at home and minding at the same time, taking the child to work, exchange minding with a friend or neighbour.

For the three to four year olds, the percentage for whom care is provided by the family drops to 53% while 37% spend at least some time with childminders. It is noteworthy that as many as 47% of children in this age range are receiving a combination of care arrangements, including family and group care together with nursery and primary schooling on occasion. These complicated arrangements may reflect the difficulties working mothers encounter in finding, and possibly funding, childcare and the determination and organization which is required if they are to continue in employment. Take, for example, the situation of one mother whose pre-school child is reported as attending a private day nursery as well as being looked after by the father, an older sibling, another relative and a childminder who comes to her home! Another child accompanied mother to work, was cared for by father and by grandmothers but was also taken to a childminder and to two nurseries. The predicaments faced by these mothers and their children are by no means atypical and throw revealing light on the reasons why so many women have traditionally withdrawn from full-time work after the arrival of their first child (see Chapter 3).

Just over half (59%) of the older children (over five years old) of working mothers were looked after within the family, this form of care being mentioned either by itself (39%) or in combination with other arrangements (20%). Indeed, more than one arrangement was mentioned by 16% of women, with 11% mentioning childminders and 44% experiencing "complementary care". It is to be expected that the incidence of this form of care will rise with the age of the child as, once children are at school, complementary care becomes easier for mothers to arrange, particularly if they opt to work part-time and only during school hours. Thus the two most common options, family care and complementary care, reveal the efforts made by the working mother to use her personal circle of family and friends and to minimise the need to find professional childcare.

Costs of Childcare

The costs of childcare, as shown in Table 13, reflect the heavy dependence upon goodwill by employed mothers in Northern Ireland, and existing networks of mutual support, as nearly three quarters of the mothers who use childcare pay less than £20 per week. These findings are especially interesting because quality group care in a properly equipped daycare centre, with appropriate indoor and outdoor play areas and fully trained staff, currently costs not less (and frequently more) than £80 per child per week. The shortage of such facilities in Northern Ireland may be reflected in these figures but equally it could be argued that the cost of quality group care would put this beyond the reach of many families in any case. In practice, this means that professional care is not available to many mothers, as the cost of care is most usually met by the mother from her earnings (Brannen and Moss, 1988). It is likely that the relatively high cost of professional childcare, when viewed in the context of the women's low earnings, acts as a disincentive for mothers to remain in the workforce or to return to it. Childcare which is subsidised by pressing the family into service or by using childminders, who constitute the least expensive alternative, must be distorting the labour market and causing a systematic undervaluation of all those involved, not least the childminders themselves.

Table 13: Childcare costs per child per week

	Age of child		
	Under 5	5 and over	All
Cost	%	%	%
Free	20	82	62
< £20	20	6	11
£20 -£29	17	7	9
£30 - £39	17	3	7
> £40	26	3	11
Total %	100	100	100
N	60	125	185

Satisfaction with Childcare

Not unnaturally in view of their dependence upon relatives and friends for childcare, less than 1% of mothers openly expressed dissatisfaction with the care the child was receiving. 81% of those with children under three years of age and 78% of those with children of three and four years of age indicated that they were very satisfied, with only 6% in each group endorsing "not satisfied". At the same time, a significant number of mothers mentioned a complexity of arrangements, a complexity which these statistics cannot hope to untangle. Many older children experienced a combination of carers which involved being with a friend or neighbour after school or with grandmothers, father and other relatives during school holidays. However, 20% of childcare arrangements involved the mother in working only school hours or in term time or in some similar way minimising the need to find childcare. Overall a high level of satisfaction with childcare arrangements is not surprising since, if this were not the case, presumably mothers would make alternative arrangements or even leave their current employment to look after the children meanwhile or permanently. Also, it is difficult to know to what extent these responses reflect an assessment of the quality of childcare rather than availability.

Childcare Preferences

Elsewere in the UK, there appears to be a preference by parents of the under fives for group rather than individual childcare and for educational provision, with only a minority of mothers who are using childminders doing so from preference (Moss, 1988). This situation contrasts with WWLS findings insofar as nurseries were preferred by only 15% of mothers for their under threes, but this figure rose to 40% of mothers with reference to their three to four-year-olds. Table 14 may therefore reflect in part the low level of publicly funded daycare and nursery places in Northern Ireland, together with the existence of strong family networks. Between a quarter and a third of mothers preferred childminders for these age groups. This preference may be influenced by the fact that, in Northern Ireland, there are more registered childminders per 100,000 of the population aged 0-4 years than any other part of the UK (Report of Social Services Inspectorate for Northern Ireland, 1990). Thus, when mothers were asked about their preferences among the various types of childcare, these preferences seemed to relate more closely to their immediate experiences than to what they might choose if quality care of various individual and group kinds were available at affordable prices. This was equally true of mothers of older children, where 58% of choices involved family care and 46% complementary care.

Table 14: Childcare preferences*

	Age of child			
	Under 3	3 - 4	5 and over	All
Childcare preference	%	%	%	%
Family care	61	50	58	58
Childminder	24	31	14	19
Complementary care**	18	24	46	35
Group care	15	40	1	11
N	*62*	*42*	*146*	*250*

* Respondents may have replied to more than one item so %s do not sum to 100.
** Working at home and minding at the same time, taking the child to work, exchange minding with a friend or neighbour.

Childcare Arrangements

The second part of this chapter has concerned the childcare arrangements of women who continue working or resume employment while bringing up their children. The types of childcare which were used serve to illustrate the accuracy of a recent major report which demonstrated that, within the EC, the UK is one of the three countries with the lowest levels of publicly funded childcare services for children of all ages (Moss, 1988), the other two being Ireland and the Netherlands. Within the UK, Northern Ireland has the poorest provision. As Hinds (1989) has pointed out, there is considerable support for the view that

Northern Ireland is the most disadvantaged area in the EC with regard to childcare provision. It is hardly surprising, therefore, that here as elsewhere in the UK, many women have discontinuous employment careers after the birth of their first child, often involving part-time work and "downward mobility". In the absence of publically funded daycare, most working mothers, as we have found, must rely upon arrangements involving family care, complementary care and childminders.

How do these arrangements influence the children's development? Most psychological research on children's intellectual and social development has concentrated upon the mother-child dyad or upon peer and adult relationships in daycare and school settings. Comparatively little is known about the influence of father-child interactions and hardly anything at all about the contribution of other members of children's social networks. Grandparents, uncles, aunts and neighbours, not to mention older and younger children, have not been the focus of research. One result of this paucity of research is that we do not know how relationships within a child's social network influence one another. It is very difficult to judge, therefore, the effects of family or complementary care on children's development. A study in Sweden which examined father-child behaviours in families where the father looked after the child while the mother was at work, discovered that fathers interacted with their children in characteristically different ways to mothers (Lamb, Frodi, Hevang, Frodi and Steinberg, 1982). For example, fathers tended to be more involved in play while mothers displayed more affection. Other studies (Belsky, Gilstrap and Rovine, 1984) have also found consistent differences between the patterns of mothers' and fathers' interactions with children. Children's behaviour towards parents is similarly differentiated. These different patterns may have cognitive as well as social effects. A number of studies have found that mathematical and logical abilities may be encouraged in girls (but not in boys) by supportive father-child relationships (Ostermeyer, Trew and Turner, 1988).

Children who are cared for by grandmothers normally find themselves not only in the hands of experienced caregivers but also, at least in the case of the maternal grandmother, encountering many similarities to their mothers' behaviours. In evaluating the quality of care, experience has been linked to consistency and, hence, to the child's feelings of security, so it could be argued that these children are enjoying the "best" option within the possibilities subsumed as family care. When considering such care it is also worth noting that a familiar and interested adult contributes most to children's language development (Tizard, 1986).

The situation of the child looked after by an older sibling will be different but is it inferior? As Dunn and Kendrick (1982) point out, older siblings offer a unique contribution to socialisation. Tizard (1986) sees the older brother or sister as tending to be the more aggressive in the relationship but also being supportive and affectionate, while the younger child takes on an imitative and submissive role. However, much of this interaction is non-verbal so the older child contributes much less than a parent or grandparent to developing the younger child's language. The value of the older child as "minder" may well lie in raising the level of play of the younger child and in providing a role model. Dunn (1983) describes the special feature of sibling relationships as their variety and, as yet, there is little clear cut evidence about how these factors operate.

When we turn to the effects on children's development of being placed with childminders, there are few relevant studies. Moss (1987), who provides an excellent and insightful review of childminding research in Britain since 1965, found only two studies which attempted to compare the development of "minded" and "non-minded" children. Both of these deal with very young children and one concentrates solely upon language and social adjustment (Raven, 1972 [cited in Moss, 1987]). The other is more wide ranging and considers the development of children in different types of daycare (Moss, 1986). Raven found no effects attributable to childminding while the other study found no signs of language retardation in the minded group. Similarly, there were few differences in social development by 18 months of age. However, a number of studies have expressed reservations about the emotional and social development of "minded" children who are seen as detached, passive and inactive (Mayall and Petrie, 1983). Jackson and Jackson (1979) attribute this to the quality of care which some children receive while others point to the effects on the children of experiencing daily a situation in which everything belongs to someone else and the rules are different from those of home (Moss, 1987). Other findings are more positive, showing that minders meet the emotional and physical needs of the children although there is often an absence of intellectually stimulating play (Davie, 1986; Shinman, 1981). As Moss points out, there is no reason to assume that children's experience with childminders "must be or will be uniform and constant" (1987, p.29) so it is hardly surprising that the results of studies should vary according to location, age of the children, number of children minded and, most vitally, the central focus of each study. However, those who take a positive view of childminding (for example, Davie, 1986) and those who have a more negative opinion (for example, Bryant, Harris and Newton, 1980) agree on one finding; the childminder is not a substitute mother. In any case, replications of the mother-child relationship occurring between minder and child could produce emotional conflict for all three (Mayall and Petrie, 1983).

To the extent that minders combine looking after children with their normal domestic routine, the variety in the children's days is much as it might be at home. It follows that the range of toys and educational activities is more limited than in a good day nursery, where quality of care is more closely monitored and trained staff are employed. Perhaps this is why Bryant, Harris and Newton (1980) and Moss (1986) both found that only a minority of mothers who use minders initially wanted this form of care. Many children in these English studies ended up with minders because other forms of care were not available. This may be equally true of Northern Ireland as the mothers in our sample who intended to return to work but had not yet done so showed a higher preference for nursery day care than for childminders. However, those working mothers who used childminders, whether as first choice or from necessity, usually seemed reasonably satisfied with the level of care provided. A recent study of children in the first year of primary school in Northern Ireland (O'Hanlon, 1989), found that minded children and a "home" group were similar on various language tests and on popularity with peers, while a comparative nursery day care group did rather better than either on socialising skills, adjustment to school and spontaneous learning. This study involved mostly unregistered minders and expressed reservations about the stability of minder care. All the mothers were interviewed and those of minded children indicated more causes for concern than those of children in the other two groups.

Perhaps the best explanation for differences found in the outcomes of the various forms of care is provided by Tizard (1986). She identifies familiarity as of central importance. Familiarity facilitates attachment and responsiveness in the child which in turn encourages social skills and intellectual development. Children benefit especially from the reassurance which stems from the continuing presence of familiar adults and children. This also enables children to establish friendships which serve both a developmental and protective role. The children in our study who were experiencing family care and/or complementary care and/or whose childminders were known to their families and seldom changed were likely to have in common this factor of familiarity. It seems probable that any form of childcare which influences the child's social world so as to enhance his or her present levels of play and enjoyment may produce similar positive developmental outcomes. Tizard describes these as "modest, but from the point of view of the child, sufficiently important" (1986, p.36).

It is clear that the role of the husband/partner in childcare touches on a great many fundamental issues and concerns, not least the welfare of all family members and including children, fathers as well as mothers. The problem lies in trying to reconcile the best interests of all, in a society in which some mothers must work, many mothers wish to work, and all would wish to be entitled to freedom to consult their preferences in the absence of externally imposed constraints. Demographic changes across many parts of Europe are making employers rethink working practices, while environmental concerns are drawing attention to the quality of life in general. Concurrently, psychological research is demonstrating that the traditional parental roles can and sometimes (if rarely) do change in dual-earner families. This is apparent not just in relation to the allocation of duties but also to the quality of the mother-child relationship. It has been shown, for example, that working mothers play with their babies more than mothers at home (Pedersen, Cairn and Zaslow, 1982) and that supportive fathers increase mothers' responsiveness to their children (Crockenburg, 1981). Fathers have been shown to have the capacity to be very efficient caregivers to their children (Lamb, Frodi, Hevang, Frodi and Steinberg, 1982); fathers provide characteristically different patterns of adult-child interaction but are equally proficient in giving children care, love and security. At present, few fathers appear to be fulfilling their potential in this regard.

As regards childcare arrangements for working parents, the survey has served to demonstrate just how *ad hoc*, informal and often complicated childcare arrangements continue to be for many working mothers in Northern Ireland, and particularly for children in the pre-school years. The availability of extended family networks may bring many benefits but stability and simplicity of childcare arrangements does not always appear to be prominent amongst these. In the light of the previous discussion, the effects of these arrangements not only on women's employment opportunities but also on the development of the children themselves must lead to genuine cause for concern. This said, children differ in the ways in which they react both to their mothers and to other carers when they are looked after by relatives or childminders or placed in some form of group care. What suits one child and keeps him or her happy and contented may have quite opposite effects on another. It follows that there are no best forms of care but only those which are most appropriate for a particular child and family. Also, children's and families' needs are subject to change for a wide variety of reasons. As such, nothing in the findings should be taken as endorsing current practice or as advocating a particular form of change. Rather the survey has sought to discover childcare facts and opinions from a representative sample of women in Northern Ireland today. And this brings us to an important methodological issue. This arises because firstly, childcare is a significant and emotive concern for women; secondly, society expects mothers to foster children's physical, emotional and intellectual development; and thirdly, there is a clear and generally accepted view of what constitutes "good mothering". Good mothering includes maximizing the quality and quantity of mother-child interaction in the early years and ensuring the mother's availability "on demand" at least during the childhood years. It follows that there are pressures on women, as mothers, to order their lives in certain ways and to answer questions about childcare in conformity with society's expectations. Perhaps it is not surprising that studies which have questioned both men and women tend to find discrepancies between these separately obtained reports. The present investigation of childcare is based solely upon interviews with women and in that lies both its strength, in obtaining information from those most involved in childcare, and its weakness, in not being able to incorporate the directly obtained views of husbands/partners and fathers. Research which gives both partners the opportunity to express their opinions on current practice and desirable future developments is likely to be even more informative, as are studies which focus on the children's experiences and their development, including an examination of the effects on children of different arrangements and allocations of childcare.

References

Ainslie, R.C., and Anderson, C.W. (1984). 'Day care children's relationships to their mothers and caregivers: An inquiry into the conditions for the development of attachment.' In R.C. Ainslie (ed.), *The Child and the Day Care Setting.* New York: Praeger.

Anderson-Kulman, R.E., and Paludi,M.A. (1986). 'Working mothers and the family context: Predicting positive coping.' *Journal of Vocational Behaviour, 28,* 241-253.

Arnett, J. (1989). 'Issues and obstacles in the training of caregivers.' In J. Lande, S. Scarr and N. Gunzenhauser (eds.), *Caring for Children: Challenge to America.* Hillsdale, New Jersey: Erlbaum, pp. 241-256.

Bee, H. (1974). *Social Issues in Developmental Psychology.* New York: Harper and Row.

Belsky, J., Gilstrap, B. and Rovine, M. (1984). 'The Pennsylvanian Infant and Family Development Project.' *Child Development, 65,* 692-705.

Brannen, J. (1987). *Taking Maternity Leave.* T.C.R.U. Working and Occasional Papers, 7. London: University of London Institute of Education.

Brannen, J. and Moss, P. (1988). *New Mothers at Work: Employment and Childcare.* London: Unwin.

Bryant, B., Harris, M. and Newton, D. (1980). *Children and Minders.* Oxford: Grant McIntyre.

Clarke-Stewart, A. (1980). 'The father's contribution to children's cognitive and social development in early childhood.' In F.A. Pedersen (ed.), *The Father-Infant Relationship.* New York: Praeger.

Clarke-Stewart, A. and Gruber, C. (1984). 'Day care forms and features.' In R.C. Ainslie (ed.), *The Child and the Day Care Setting.* New York: Praeger, pp. 35-62.

Cohen, B. (1990). *Caring for Children: The 1990 Report.* Edinburgh: The Scottish Child and Family Alliance.

Crockenburg, S.B. (1981). 'Infant irritability, mother responsiveness, and social support influences on the security of infant-mother attachment.' *Child Development, 52,* 857-865.

Davie, C. (1986). *An Investigation into Childminding Practice in North Staffordshire.* London: Department of Health andSocial Services.

Department of Education and Science (1990). *Starting with Quality.* The report of the committee of inquiry into the quality of the educational experience offered to 3- and 4-year-olds, chaired by Angela Rumbold. London: HMSO.

Dunn, J. (1983). 'Sibling relationships in early childhood.' *Child Development, 54,* 787-811.

Dunn, J. and Kendrick, C. (1982). *Siblings.* London: Grant-McIntyre.

Evason, E. (1980). *Just Me and the Kids: A Study of Single Parent Families in Northern Ireland.* Belfast: Equal Opportunities Commission for Northern Ireland.

Fox, N. (1977). ' Attachment of Kibbutz infants to mothers and metapelet.' *Child Development, 48,* 1228-1239.

Gilbert, L.A. (1988). *Sharing It All: the Rewards and Struggles of Two Career Families.* New York: Plenum Press.

Herbst, P.G. (1960). 'Task differentiation of husband and wife in family activities.' In N.W. Bell and E.F. Vogel (eds.), *A Modern Introduction to the Family.*   New York: The Free Press of Glencoe.

Hill, M. (1987). *Sharing Child Care in Early Parenthood.* London: Routledge and Kegan Paul.

Hinds, B. (1989). *Women and Social Policy in Northern Ireland: Childcare Provision and Employment.*   Belfast: Gingerbread (NI) (Mimeographed).

Hoffman, L.W. (1984). 'Maternal employment and the child.' In M. Perlmuttor (ed.), *The Minnesota Symposia on Child Psychology: Vol. 17.   Parent-child Interaction and Parent-child Relations in Development.*   Hillsdale, New Jersey: Erlbaum, pp. 101-127.

Hoffman, L. W. and Nye, F.I. (1974). *Working Mothers.*   San Francisco: Jossey-Bass.

Howes, C. (1985). 'Relations between early child care and schooling.' *Developmental Psychology, 24,* 53-57.

Hwang, P. (1987). 'The changing role of Swedish fathers.' In M.E. Lamb (ed.), *The Fathers' Role: Cross-cultural Perspectives.* Hillsdale, New Jersey: Lawrence Erlbaum Associates.

Jackson, B. and Jackson, S. (1979). *Childminders: a Study in Action Research.*   London: Routledge and Kegan Paul.

Joshi, H. (1985). 'Gender inequality in the Labour Market and the domestic division of labour.' Paper given to the Cambridge Journal of Economics Conference, *'Towards New Foundations for Socialist Policies in Britain'.* Cambridge, 26-29 June 1985.

Jowell, R., Witherspoon, S. and Brook, L. (eds.) (1989). *British Social Attitudes: The Fifth Report.* Aldershot: Gower.

Lamb, M.E. (ed.) (1976). *The Role of the Father in Child Development.* New York: Wiley.

Lamb, M.E. (ed.) (1981). *The Role of the Father in Child Development.* New York: Wiley.

Lamb, M.E., Frodi, A.M., Hevang, C.P., Frodi, M., and Steinberg, J. (1982). 'Mother- and father-infant interaction involving play and holding in traditional and non-traditional Swedish families.' *Developmental Psychology, 18,* 215-221.

Mayall, B. and Petrie, P. (1983). *Childminding and Day Nurseries: What Kind of Care?* London: Heinemann.

Montgomery, P. and Davies, C. (1991). 'A woman's place in Northern Ireland.' In P. Stringer and G. Robinson (eds.), *Social Attitudes in Northern Ireland.* Belfast: Blackstaff Press.

Morris, L. (1990). *The Workings of the Household: a US-UK Comparison.*   Cambridge: Polity Press.

Moss, P. (1986). *Childcare in the Early Months.* TCRU Working and Occasional Papers, 3. London: University of London Institute of Education.

Moss, P. (1987). *A Review of Childminding Research.*   TCRU Working and Occasional Papers, 6. London: University of London Institute of Education.

Moss, P. (1988). *Childcare and Equality of Opportunity.*   Brussels: CEC.

Newson, J. and Newson, E. (1970). 'Concepts of parenthood.' In K. Elliott (ed.), *The Family and its Future*. London: CIBA Foundation Symposium, University of London.

O'Hanlon, K. (1989). *The Effects of Early Childcare Provision on the Language Skills, Popularity and Social Adjustment of Children in Primary 1*. Unpublished MSc Thesis, Queen's University, Belfast.

Ostermeyer, M.C., Trew, K. and Turner, I.F. (1988). 'Father-daughter emotional relationships and mathematical attainment in primary schools.' *Research in Education, 40*, 1-9.

Pedersen, F.A., Cairn, R. and Zaslow, M. (1982). 'Variation in infant experience associated with alternative family roles.' In L. Laosa and I. Sigel (eds.), *The Family as a Learning Environment*. New York: Plenum Press.

Pleck, J.H. (1985). *Working Wives/Working Husbands*. Beverly Hills, CA: Sage.

Pleck, J. and Lang, L. (1978). *Men's Family Role: its Nature and Consequences*. Wellesley, Mass: Wellesley College Centre for Research on Women.

Radin, N. (1981). 'The role of the father in cognitive, academic and intellectual development.' In M.E. Lamb (ed.), *The Role of the Father in Child Development*. New York: Wiley.

Rapoport, R. and Moss, P. (1990). *Men and Women as Equals at Work*. TCRU Working and Occasional papers, 11. London: University of London Institute of Education.

Raven, M. (1972). 'A Comparison of the Language Competency and Social Behaviour of Childminded and Non-childminded 3- and 4-year-old children.' Unpublished MSc dissertation described in P. Moss (1987), *A Review of Childminding Research*. TCRU Working and Occasional Papers, 6. London: University of London Institute of Education.

Richards, M.P.M. (1982). 'How should we approach the study of fathers?' In L. McKee, and M. O'Brien (eds.), *The Father Figure*. London: Tavistock.

Scarr, S., Phillips, D., and McCartney, K. (1990). 'Facts, fantasies and the future of child care in the United States.' *Psychological Science, 1*, 26-35.

Shinman, S. (1981). *A Choice for Every Child? Access and Response to Pre-School Provision*. London: Tavistock.

Social Services Inspectorate for Northern Ireland (1990). *Review of Social Services Departments, Policies and Provision in Relation to Preventative Child Care: With Particular Reference to Under Fives*. Belfast: HMSO.

Tierney, C.E. (1989). *Child-rearing Practices: Parental Roles and Influences in Single and Dual Wage-earner Families*. Unpublished dissertation. The Queen's University, Belfast.

Tizard, B. (1986). *The Care of Young Children: Implications of Recent Research*. TCRU Working and Occasional Papers, 1. London: University of London Institute of Education.

Vogel, S.R., Brovermann, I.K., Brovermann, D.M., Clarkson, F.E., and Rosenkrantz, P.S.(1970). 'Maternal employment and perception of sex roles among college students.' *Developmental Psychology, 3*, 384-391.

Wolfendale, S. (1983). *Parental Participation in Children's Development and Education*. London: Gordon and Breach.

Chapter 9

INFORMAL CARE

Eithne McLaughlin

Introduction

The concept of community care for people who are highly dependent on others is not new. The seeds of this approach can be detected in policy documents relating to those with a mental handicap or disability in the first decade of this century (see Jones, 1960). By the late 1950s, the Royal Commission on the Law relating to Mental Illness and Mental Deficiency (Cmnd. 169, 1957) had recommended a clear shift in emphasis from hospital to "community"-based care (Jones, Brown and Bradshaw, 1978). Since the 1950s, this policy has grown and developed. In particular, the importance of people who need care staying with their family and in their own home has begun to overshadow the earlier objective of integrating people who need care into the community through the establishment of small-scale units in residential areas (for example, Cmnd. 4683, 1071). Even more recently, the policy thrust has been towards families having the financial responsibility to provide care, rather than the health or social services. While policy documents in the 1960s and 1970s (for example, Cmnd. 4683, 1971) called for more domiciliary services to be provided by local authorities to highly dependent people, those in the 1980s have increasingly seen family members as substitutes for such services (for example, Cmnd. 8173, 1981). In other words, in both Northern Ireland and Great Britain, the 1980s has seen a change of emphasis in community care policy away from the statutory provision of services for highly dependent people living in private households, and towards the roles, responsibilities and, critically, labour of family members as the primary providers of "community" care.

This change of emphasis has occurred at the same time as an increasing proportion of the population have found themselves related to a very elderly and/or disabled person who has care needs. Better standards of nutrition, health, health care, housing and working conditions have each contributed to large and continuing increases in the numbers of very elderly and disabled people (see Craig, 1983). By 1985, between 3 and 3.5 million people in Great Britain needed help from others to go about their daily activities (see Martin, White and Meltzer, 1989; Smyth and Robus, 1989).

In terms of equality of opportunity between men and women, it is significant that the shift in community care policy towards the labour of family members and continuing increases in the numbers and proportions of people needing care, have coincided with an increase in the numbers and proportions of women in employment and seeking employment. It is not necessarily that women who are employed are generally less likely to take on, or continue, caring responsiblities for family members (see Parker 1990:27-28). Rather, when they do so, caring commitments for disabled and elderly relatives may, like caring for children, impact on the nature of the employment held. To date, government policy has not addressed this issue. Instead debate and activity has centered around the needs of women with dependent children. In many Western countries, caring responsibilities for disabled people are now more pervasive, or invasive, than caring responsibilities for very young children. In Europe, Britain and Northern Ireland, the time has come to widen the debate to include the impact of all kinds of caring activity on women's, and less often men's, employment (McLaughlin, 1989).

Women and Informal Care

Until comprehensive national data became available in the late 1980s, it was generally accepted that women were those who provided most of the unpaid care received by elderly and severely disabled people in private households. Data from the 1985 General Household Survey in Britain, however, showed that many more men are involved in providing care than had previously been suspected (12% of men compared with 15% of women, Table 1). Meanwhile in Northern Ireland, the disparity between the proportions of men and women involved in caring is larger than in Great Britain (9% of men compared with 14% of women, Table 1).

The WWLS contained 166 women who had caring responsiblities for disabled or elderly relatives or friends, giving a slightly higher estimate of the incidence of women's caring responsiblities than the 1985 Continuous Household Survey (17% compared with 14%).

Table 1: % of adults (16+) who were carers by whether dependant lived in same or different household, N.I. and G.B. 1985

	Male		Female	
	NI	GB	NI	GB
% of Adults caring for someone	%	%	%	%
In same household	4	4	6	4
In different household	5	8	8	11
Total %	9	12	14	15

Sources: N.I. - PPRU CHS Monitor 1/86, Table 17 ; G.B. - Green 1988, Table 2.2.

Although the similarity in the proportions of men and women providing care in Britain in 1985 suggests some movement towards equality between the sexes, behind this lies significant differences in the patterns of caring by men and women. In both Britain and Northern Ireland women are much more likely than men to be providing care when they are of working age (Tables 2 and 3). The peak age for female carers is very clearly the middle ages of 40 to 60 years (Tables 2, 3 and 4).

Table 2: % of adults who were carers by sex and age, 1985 (Great Britain)

	Age in years				
	16-29	30-44	45-64	65+	All
Sex	%	%	%	%	%
Male	6	11	16	14	12
Female	7	16	24	12	15
All	7	14	20	13	14
N					2,470

Source: Green, 1988, Table 2.4.

Table 3: % of adults who were carers by sex and age, 1985 (Northern Ireland)

	Age in years				
	16-24	25-44	45-59	60+	All
Sex	%	%	%	%	%
Male	4	10	12	8	9
Female	6	18	22	11	14
N					752

Source: PPRU Monitor 1/86, 1986, Table 16.

Table 4: % of women who were carers by age (WWLS)

	Age in years					
	< 20	21-30	31-40	41-50	51-60	61+	All
%	10	3	16	27	25	15	17
N	3	7	35	63	45	13	166

In Britain, for example, 24% of women aged 45-64 are carers compared with 16% of men. In Northern Ireland in 1985, 22% of women compared with 12% of men aged 45-59 were carers, whilst the WWLS showed 27% of 41-50 year old and 25% of 51-60 year old women caring. There are significant sex differences here, bearing as they do on women's and men's employment prospects for those under pension age. Where male carers provide a great deal of care, they are typically husbands over pension age caring for their spouses (Parker 1990). In addition, women are more likely than men to provide very high levels of care (see Parker, 1990) and it is very high levels of informal care which have the most direct adverse effect on employment prospects.

The amount and nature of informal caring varies greatly from keeping an eye on an elderly neighbour to providing total care and supervision, usually to a close relative on a co-resident basis. As Table 5 shows, in the WWLS over half (56%) of the co-resident carers provided total care for their dependants, while carers who did not live with the dependant were likely to do household chores (34%) or generally keep an eye on the person (32%). Among carers who were not living with the dependant person, such responsibilities usually involved daily (36%) or nearly daily visiting (33%) (Table 6).

Table 5:   Nature of care provided by residence of carer

Nature of care	Carer lives with dependant	Carer does not live with dependant	All carers
	%	%	%
Keep eye on	27	32	31
Care for completely	56	4	19
Household chores	13	34	28
Shopping/transport	4	14	11
Company/visiting	-	15	11
Total %	100	100	100
N	48	118	166

Table 6: Frequency of visits by non-resident carers

Frequency	%
Daily	36
Several times a week	33
Once/twice a week	21
Less than once a week	3
Varies	7
Total %	100
N	118

In the WWLS, most carers were caring for their own or their husband's parents (Table 7). Only about one in five were caring for more distant relatives and one in ten for non-relatives. 16% of carers were caring for two dependants, most usually both their elderly parents.

Table 7: Relationship of dependant to carer

Relationship	One dependant %	Two dependants %*
Husband	3	-
Child	6	-
Mother	36	69
Father	16	42
Mother-in-law	10	31
Father-in-law	3	19
Other relative	17	27
Friend/neighbour	9	11
N	*140*	*26*

* Respondents replied to more than one item so %s do not sum to 100 in this column.

Informal Care and Employment

Informal care can have substantial material opportunity costs including loss and restriction of employment (for example, reduction of hours at work, fewer opportunities for overtime, restricted career development and promotion, loss of pension rights), reduced income and increased expenditure. Such costs will vary depending on how old the carer is when they begin caring, the intensity, nature and level of the care provided, and the extent to which care is shared with other informal carers and the welfare state (through domiciliary services or day care for the disabled person needing care). As Parker (1990) has commented, "It is still the case that the full economic costs (and indeed value) of informal care remain to be calculated".

The largest cost to individual carers will occur if they lose all, or do not return to, paid employment because of their caring responsibilities for a disabled or elderly person. As Table 8 shows, carers in the 1985 General Household Survey (GHS) who were providing high (20 to 49 hours of care a week) or very high (50 or more hours of care a week) levels of care were less likely than other carers, or the general population, to be in employment, particularly full-time employment.

Thus in the 1985 GHS, 33% of the total population under pension age were not employed, compared with 67% of those providing 50 or more hours of

Table 8: **Employment status by amount of care provided, population under pension age, 1985 Great Britain GHS.**

		Extent of care			
	All	All carers	< 20 hrs	20 to 49 hrs	50+ hrs
Employment status	%	%	%	%	%
Full-time employed	52	44	48	36	21
Part-time employed	15	20	20	22	12
Not employed	33	36	32	42	67
N		*1827*	*1467*	*180*	*180*

Sources: Green, 1988, Table 2.9; and McLaughlin, 1991, Table 3.2.

care a week. Neither data on hours of care provided nor employment status of carers from the 1985 Continuous Household Survey (CHS) for Northern Ireland have been published. Table 9 shows data from the WWLS on the hours of care provided by carers. Although the bands used to collect information on hours of care provided per week differed between the WWLS and the 1985 GHS, Table 9 suggests that a roughly similar proportion of female carers in Northern Ireland and all carers in Great Britain are providing 20 or more hours of care a week; that is, the level of care associated with lowered full-time employment rates.

Table 9: **Weekly hours of care given, WWLS and 1985 GHS**

WWLS		1985 GHS	
Hrs per wk	%	**Hrs per wk**	%
Varies a lot	21		
0 - 4 hrs	9	0 - 4 hrs	37
4 - 8 hrs	18	5 - 9 hrs	20
8 - 16 hrs	22	10 - 19 hrs	19
16+ hrs	30	20+ hrs	24
Total %	100		100
N	*166*		*2460*

Source: 1985 GHS; and Green 1988, Figure 4A.

Women, Informal Care and Employment

Tables 10 and 11 from the WWLS show that, as in Britain, caring in Northern Ireland among women is associated with both higher rates of part-time work and lower employment rates. Because of the sample size of the WWLS, and because only a minority of carers are engaged in high levels of caring, a breakdown by hours of care was not feasible. Having said that, it may be worth noting in relation to Table 10 that 32 of the 50 carers (64%) who were providing more than 16 hours of care a week were not employed. Table 11 shows that non-employed women who identified themselves as informal carers were also less likely to be seeking paid work than their non-carer counterparts.

Table 10: Whether caring by employment status

	Carers	Non-carers	All
Employment status	%	%	%
Full-time employed*	28	39	37
Part-time employed	27	19	21
Non-employed	45	42	42
Total %	100	100	100
N	166	834	1000

* For the purposes of this analysis, those waiting to take up a job, those temporarily sick, those in full-time education and those on YTP (n=41) were included in the full-time employed category.

Table 11: Whether non-employed women were seeking work by whether care provided

	Carers	Non-carers	All
Seeking work	%	%	%
Seeking	6	14	13
Not seeking	94	86	87
Total %	100	100	100
N	80	375	455

Although these associations between caring and increases in part-time employment rates and lowered employment rates are reasonably clear from the data, direct causality cannot be inferred. It may be that it is women whose labour market attachment is already weak who find themselves "selected", or are self-selected, from within the family circle to fulfill the role of carer. Qureshi and Simons (1987) have demonstrated the existence of "a systematic set of rules for deciding [who should care for elderly people] between available network members" (see also Qureshi and Walker, 1989). The closeness of kinship ties, gender, marital status, proximity (in same house, in close-by or distant separate house), strength of labour market attachment and extent of other caring commitments, for example, for young children, all interact to produce a hierarchy of expectation and obligation within family circles.

In relation to labour market attachment, an unmarried son or daughter who is, and has been, in stable employment will not be likely to provide care for a dependant parent. In contrast, a married daughter, or even daughter-in-law, whose children are no longer highly dependent, and who has either not yet returned to the labour market or who has returned in a part-time capacity to a relatively low-status, low-paid job, is a likely candidate. On the other hand, an unmarried son or daughter who is unemployed is more likely to provide care than a married daughter who is in a full-time "good" job or who has substantial childcare commitments. As regards gender specifically, an unemployed son is less likely to provide care than his sister if she is also unemployed.

Although these interactions are complex, it remains married women in their middle years who form the majority of carers of working age, as Tables 12 and 13 show. This is because the proportion of unmarried people in the population is small, and because married women typically have "unstable" employment histories, and often experience downward occupational mobility after a period out of work to care for children.

Table 12: Informal care by marital status

Marital status	Carers %	Non-carers %	All %
Single	16	24	22
Married/cohabiting	76	65	67
Divorced/separated	4	7	6
Widowed	4	5	5
Total %	100	100	100
N	166	834	1000

The interaction of gender and labour market attachment in selecting carers within family circles is particularly significant in Northern Ireland. The relatively weak employment position of women in Northern Ireland in comparision with Great Britain may go some way to explaining the greater preponderance of women providing informal care in Northern Ireland.

Carers themselves may not be aware of the full effects of care provision on

Table 13: Informal care by age

Age in years	Carers %	Non-carers %	All %
20 or under years	2	3	3
21 - 30 years	5	29	25
31 - 40 years	21	22	22
41 - 50 years	38	21	23
51 - 60 years	26	16	18
61 plus years	8	9	9
Total %	100	100	100
N	166	834	1000

their employment status and employment history for two reasons. Firstly, because it is often those family members whose labour market attachment is weakest (most often because of past caring commitments for children and less often because of unemployment) and secondly, because it is only at the very highest levels of care provision that a direct, immediate and highly visible effect of care on employment occurs. Where a woman's responsibilities for children have overlapped with gradually increasing care responsibilites for disabled and elderly adults, it may be difficult for her to distinguish in an abstract way between these phenomena in her own (very non-abstract) life.

In the WWLS, although higher levels of part-time work were evident among all carers, and although very few carers providing high levels of care to dependant adults were in any paid work, only 33 of the 166 carers (20%) said that caring had affected their employment, as Table 14 shows. This did, however, rise to 56% among those providing 30 or more hours of care a week (Table 15), most of whom regarded care as having completely prevented any paid work on their part.

Table 14: Whether and how providing care has affected paid work.

Effect	%
Prevented paid work	13
Restricted hours	5
Take days off	1
Other	1
Did not affect paid work	77
Don't know	3
Total %	100
N	166

Table 15: Weekly hours of care given by whether employment affected

	Varies	0-16	16-30*	30+	All
Employment:	%	%	[N]	%	%
Affected	9	9	[5]	56	20
Not affected	89	90	[12]	37	77
Don't know	3	1	[1]	6	3
Total %	100	100		100	100
N	35	81	[18]	32	166

* Presented as raw data given N < 20

Neither the effect of caring on paid work, nor the definition of oneself as an informal carer, is necessarily clear-cut from the point of view of women carers themselves. Among the 80 non-employed women providing informal care, 27% gave care as their reason for not working, and this rose to 52% among those providing 30 or more hours of care a week (Table 16). However, informal carers in this sample often had other caring responsibilities, for children and husbands, which they felt had more impact on their employment status than informal care for a disabled or elderly adult.

Table 16: Reasons for non-employment, giving priority to (a) labour market conditions and (b) informal care, by whether informal care provided*

Reasons	All Carers	Carers 30+ hrs pw	Non - carers
Redundant/unemployed	13	13	12
Ill health	15	9	17
Education/training	3	-	6
Caring for children/home	37	26	50
Informal care	27	52	7
Other	6	-	8
N	80	23	375

*Respondents may have replied to more than one item so %s do not sum to 100.

Table 16 also shows that some women who did not describe themselves as having informal care responsibilites in response to the direct question about this in the survey interview, nevertheless seemed to have such responsibilities and indeed gave them as a reason for their non-employment (26 out of 375). This raises important methodological and theoretical questions about the extent to which, and under what conditions, informal care constitutes a visible and definable "role" with which women can identify. The role of "married woman" in itself is, by definition, a caring role, and certainly married women carers were less likely than single women carers to say that their employment had been affected by informal care responsibilities (20% compared with 31%, Table 17).

Table 17: Whether employment was affected by marital status of carer (% of carers)

| | Marital status of carer | | | |
Employment:	Married /cohabiting	Ex-married*	Single	All
	%	[N]	%	%
Affected	20	-	31	20
Not Affected	77	[12]	69	77
Don't Know	3	[1]	-	3
Total %	100		100	100
N	127	[13]	26	166

* Presented as raw data given N < 20

Informal Care and Women's Incomes and Earnings

Where informal carers attempt to combine caring responsibilities with paid employment, research in Britain (see Parker, 1990, for a review) has found that the nature of their employment is likely to be restricted. This may mean, for example, working in part-time jobs, jobs where the hours fit around the availablity of others to provide substitute care (for example, evening jobs), being unable to change jobs or relocate, and hence having to accept restrictions on career advancement. So, for example, in the WWLS, women informal carers were somewhat less likely to welcome the idea of promotion than non-carers, less likely to be in jobs where promotion was a possibility, and less likely to have a job (Table 18).

The results of this process of segregation can also be seen in the earnings and incomes of women carers compared with women non-carers and men. Table 19 shows the gross weekly pay of both all carers and high level carers compared with non-carers in the WWLS. Although the number of employed carers providing 16 or more hours of care a week is small, it is noticeable that

Table 18: Attitude of women to promotion by whether care provided

	Carers	Non-carers	All
Promotion	%	%	%
Definitely welcome	7	11	10
Probably welcome	2	3	3
Possibly welcome	1	2	2
Not welcome	10	8	8
Don't know	1	1	1
Not possible in present job/no job	80	76	77
Total %	100	100	100
N	*166*	*834*	*1000*

a third of these employed women, compared with 21% of all employed carers and 16% of employed non-carers, earned less than £50 gross a week (Table 19). Table 19, however, also suggests that employed carers are more likely than other employed women to be in high-earning jobs. Thus, over a quarter of employed carers providing 16 or more hours of care a week earned in excess of £300 a week, compared with 14% of all employed carers and just 6% of employed non-carers. This is likely to be a reflection of the capacity of carers to buy in substitute care which would allow them to continue employment alongside caring, as only women in well paid jobs would benefit financially from such a strategy and such women are clearly in a minority in the population as a whole.

Table 19: Gross weekly pay by whether, and how much, care provided, % of employed women

£ gross per week	Carers 16+ hrs per wk*	All carers	Non-carers	All
	[N]	%	%	%
up to 50	[6]	21	16	16
51-100	[3]	29	25	26
101-150	[1]	20	26	25
151-200	[1]	6	16	14
201-300	[2]	10	11	11
301-400	[4]	8	5	5
401-900	[1]	6	1	2
Total %		100	100	100
N	*[18]*	*80*	*432*	*512*

* Presented as raw data given N < 20

Whether informal carers lose all employment, or can retain only low-paid, part-time employment, or can maintain a high-paying job by buying in large amounts of substitute care, there will often be negative personal income consequences, and indeed negative household income consequences. The majority of two (or more) adult households in both Britain and Northern Ireland today contain two earners (see Chapter 2). The loss of women's earnings within these households is highly significant because of the impact on both household and personal standards of living (see McLaughlin, 1991). Analysis of household income, weighting for differences in the numbers of adults and number and ages of children in each household, in the WWLS, showed that among households with between 1.5 and 2.5 equivalent single adults, only one out of 14 informal carers providing 30 or more hours of care a week had above average joint household incomes, compared with 45% of all informal carers and 40% of non-informal-care-giving households.

It should be a matter of public and policy concern that households providing high levels of care to severely disabled people are likely to have reduced standards of living because of providing care. The impact of this on the quality of life attained by highly dependant people living in the same household as their carer, and the impact on carers' own quality of life, are issues which community care policies have so far treated as peripheral to the thrust of community care in the UK (see McLaughlin, 1991). If, however, community care is to be a better alternative to residential care for very disabled people, these are not issues which we can afford to treat as marginal.

Informal Care and Equal Opportunities

In the last twenty years, feminist scholarship has been instrumental in drawing attention to the effects of women's childrearing responsibilities on their employment histories. It has also demonstrated the many ways in which the welfare state fails to challenge, and even perpetuates, inequalities between men and women in society and within couples and families (see, for example, Pascall, 1986; Brannen and Wilson, 1987). Feminist activism has also succeeded in putting equality of opportunity on to the political and policy agenda, although this remains very much unfinished business. Research on informal care in turn brings to light new complexities which need to be addressed both in the academic study of women's employment, gendered labour markets, and social policy, and in activism around equality of opportunity issues.

As this chapter has shown, women in Northern Ireland are disproportionately likely to provide informal care compared with their male counterparts, especially in their later middle-age. For a significant minority of these women, caring will be time consuming. Half the women in the WWLS who lived with a dependent person cared for them completely and a third of those who did not live with their dependant nevertheless visited them every day. Where caring is time-consuming, it is associated with lowered rates of employment. Half of those providing 30 or more hours of care a week in the WWLS attributed their non-employment directly to the provision of care. Employed carers were less likely than other women to welcome promotion, and the data suggest that employed carers are particularly likely to be engaged in low-paid (less than £50 gross a week) and part-time work. The data also suggest that only a few women at the top of the earnings range keep on a full-time job and pay for substitute care when they are providing high levels of care (16 or more hours a week).

To date, debate on the kinds of measures necessary to bring about improvements in equality of opportunity have focused on a range of issues such as maternity rights, childcare provision and equal pay for work of equal value. To this must now be added measures which address the employment problems and needs of women and, to a lesser extent, men, who are responsible for the care of severely disabled people. Such measures include levels of, and access to, day-care provision and publicly provided domiciliary services for severely disabled people, care leave entitlements for employed women or men caring for disabled people, appropriate safeguarding of informal carers' pension entitlements (occupational and statutory), and adequate social security protection for informal carers if they do have to give up paid work for substantial periods of time. This is by no means an exhaustive list and yet such a list shows how much broader a discussion of equality of opportunity policies needs to be if all the varied caring responsibilities which women are likely to face in their lives are to be addressed.

References

Brannen, J. and Wilson, G. (eds.) (1987). *Give and Take in Families: Studies in Resource Distribution.*   London: Allen and Unwin.

Cmnd. 169 (1957). *Report of the Royal Commission on Mental Illness and Mental Deficiency, 1957.* London: HMSO.

Cmnd. 4683 (1971). *Better Services for the Mentally Handicapped, 1971.*   London: HMSO.

Cmnd. 8173 (1981). *Growing Older, 1981.*   London: HMSO.

Craig, J. (1983). *The Growth of the Elderly Population.*   Population Trends, No. 32. London: OPCS.

Davies, C. and McLaughlin, E. (eds.) (1991). *Women, Employment and Social Policy in Northern Ireland: A Problem Postponed?*   Belfast: Policy Research Institute.

Green, H. (1988). *1985 General Household Survey Informal Care Report.* London: HMSO.

Jones, K. (1960).   *Mental Health and Social Policy, 1845-1959.* London: Routledge and Kegan Paul.

Jones, K., Brown, J. and Bradshaw, J. (1978).   *Issues in Social Policy.* London: Routledge and Kegan Paul.

Martin, J., White, A., and Meltzer, H. (1989).   *Disabled Adults: Services, Transport and Employment.*   London: HMSO.

McLaughlin, E. (1991). *Social Security and Community Care: The Case of the Invalid Care Allowance.* London: HMSO.

McLaughlin, E. (1989). *Community' Care and Solo Women in Europe.* Expert Report for the Cross-national Study of the Socio-economic Circumstances of Solo Women in the EC. Brussels: CEC.

Parker, G. (1990). *With Due Care and Attention: A Review of Research on Informal Care, 2nd Edition.* London: FPSC.

Pascall, G. (1986). *Social Policy: A Feminist Analysis.* London: Tavistock.

PPRU (1986). *Continuous Household Survey Monitor, 1/86.* Department of Finance and Personnel: Belfast.

Smyth, M. and Robus, N. (1989). *The Financial Circumstances of Families with Disabled Children Living in Private Households.* London: HMSO.

Qureshi, H. and Simons, K. (1987). 'Resources within families: Caring for elderly people.' In J. Brannen and G. Wilson (eds.), *Give and Take in Families: Studies in Resource Distribution.* London: Allen and Unwin.

Qureshi, H. and Walker, A. (1989). *The Caring Relationship: Elderly People and their Families.* London: Macmillan.

Chapter 10

ATTITUDES AND MOTIVATIONS

John Kremer

Introduction

Questions relating to women's attitudes, orientations and motivations are to be found throughout the length and breadth of the WWLS. In order to impose some structure on this diverse material, the present chapter has been organized around four headings. The first of these addresses the stereotype of the woman worker, including its derivation and the extent to which the facts and the fiction of women at work coincide. The next section focuses attention on women's responses to their own life experiences, including their attitudes towards their own work and their reasons for working. Part three considers the vexed question of job satisfaction, how satisfied women are with their work and opportunities for advancement. The final section moves beyond women's responses to their own lives and deals with attitudes towards female employment in a more general sense, including the circumstances under which it is felt that women should or should not work, and attitudes towards women's rights and roles at work.

The chapter obviously covers a great deal of information, and before embarking on this coverage, a few words of caution and orientation may be appropriate. In the first instance, important as our attitudes and motivations may be, it should not be assumed that our thoughts and feelings will always have a direct bearing on behaviour. Indeed, if the history of attitude research has taught us anything it is just how complex the relationship between thought and action is in reality (Ajzen, 1988). Two examples which are pertinent to the WWLS may serve to illustrate some of these complexities. Take the case of a working mother with pre-school children. For various reasons, she may have to work but despite her own circumstances she may still be in general agreement with a statement that for women as a whole it is wrong for mothers with young children to go out to work. Taking a further example, irrespective of similarity in personal circumstances, when asked to list the reasons why they work, women in the 1990s may spontaneously mention factors different from those cited in the 1980s or earlier. Personal, economic or domestic circumstances may or may not have changed substantially over time but such factors alone will not always provide sufficient explanation for shifts in attitudes. Instead, in response to the social climate, women may have different perceptions of themselves, their roles, and thus their reasons or explanations for acting in certain ways. Therefore women in the 1930s who stayed at home to raise children may have been content to say that this was because it was woman's natural state, or because their husband wanted them to. In contrast, women in similar circumstances in the 1990s may be more likely to mention individual choice.

Turning to work motivation, orientation and job satisfaction, close scrutiny reveals that the concepts themselves and the relationships between these concepts are not straightforward. One illustration is how women's domestic commitments impact on their perception of paid employment. Description of the conflict between home and work often begins by looking at the historical process of industrialization. Industrialization removed much of paid employment from the home and simultaneously placed the burden of homecare, childcare and domestic organization squarely on the shoulders of women. In the words of Blau and Winkler (1989, p.266), "The broad thrust of industrialization diminished the relative status of women by creating a gender division of labour in which, after marriage, women were responsible for home work and men were responsible for market work.". During the industrial and post-industrial eras, employment opportunities for women have been predominantly in lower paid, unskilled jobs, with an implicit expectation that they should move in and out of paid work as family circumstances dictate, and with a further assumption that the home should come first. Translating this into employment, the popular model of the dual labour market (Barron and Norris, 1991) characterises women as predominating in the secondary employment sector, which is marked by greater instability, fewer prospects and poorer working conditions. Given this model, it could be assumed that measures of job satisfaction will show women in general as being less content with their work than men, and yet paradoxically research surveys have consistently found higher levels of job satisfaction amongst women, and even greater satisfaction amongst part-time workers and those working from home (see Hakim, 1991 for discussion).

To understand why this is the case requires close examination of what these measures of job satisfaction are actually tapping, and the relationship between job satisfaction and work commitment, either in relation to general employment or a particular job. In terms of traditional research dealing with attitudes to women and work, it is fair to say that, with notable exceptions (for example, Feldberg and Glenn, 1979; Dex, 1988; Hakim, 1991), there have been few attempts to grapple with such issues. Instead the priority has usually been to measure attitudes, to relate these to biographic and demographic variables, and to describe evidence of change over time and place. Over the last sixty years such research has been useful in giving some indication of attitudes to, and of, women at work, and along the way has provided ammunition for challenging certain widely held beliefs as to why women choose to work in the first place, what they get out of their work, and even more significantly, the accuracy and usefulness of the stereotype of the woman worker, and it is towards this issue that we first turn.

The Stereotype of the Woman Worker: Myths and Realities

Given the dual labour market model and what are seen as traditional attitudes towards women's roles in society, it is generally accepted that a lacklustre stereotype of the woman worker has prevailed, at least during the first half of this century (Dex, 1988). The belief has been engendered that a woman's commitment to work must be more tenuous, and consequently her attitudes to her own work will be less positive. Therefore it is assumed that the typical woman worker will show less resistance to movement out of work in order to accommodate changing domestic circumstances and particularly to facilitate childcare. As we are all aware, stereotypes provide rough and ready cognitive pigeonholes for dealing with large amounts of information quickly but rarely do they help us to genuinely understand individual experience or behaviour. It is therefore imperative that we look behind and beyond the stereotype to see the true picture of women's responses to work and thus test the foundations on which the stereotype is constructed. For example, are women more or less willing or committed to work than men?

Being a single-sex survey, the WWLS does not allow us to deal with this comparative question directly but previous research can be used to set the scene. Table 1, derived from European Women and Men in 1983 (Commission of the European Communities, 1983), demonstrates that although women are less likely to be in paid work than men in the first place, the overwhelming majority of those who do work prefer to be in paid employment, and the majority of those not in work, and particularly those aged under 50, would prefer to be in employment. In addition, the percentage of women preferring to be in work does not appear to correlate with the actual percentage of women working in any particular country.

Looking further at the construction of the sex role stereotype, a fascinating picture is revealed when the preferences (and presumed preferences) of husbands and wives to the wife working are compared (Table 2). A telling statistic is that husbands assumed that wives were less willing to work, and they were also convinced that their wives were of the same opinion. The majority of men (39%) preferred that their wives did not work, yet 63% of wives preferred to work. It is also significant that European wives were more accurate in guessing their husband's preference for wife working than was true of husbands guessing wives' preference. It is certainly the case that many men remain to be convinced that women wish to work and they are also

Table 1: Men and women's work experience and women's preference, across the EC

| | % in Work | | % of women preferring to be in employment | | |
	Men	Women	Working	Not working 15-49 yrs	50+ yrs	All
Country						
Belgium	62	26	79	61	31	54
Denmark	62	49	82	72	18	61
West Germany	62	25	86	55	27	52
France	50	37	73	64	48	63
Ireland	56	24	93	54	31	57
Italy	59	32	87	80	64	78
Luxembourg	67	30	ns	ns	37	51
Holland	55	32	90	58	31	62
United Kingdom	57	40	84	62	37	63
Greece	62	23	76	83	61	74
All	58	33	82	65	41	63

Source: Derived from data included in CEC, 1983

Table 2: Husbands' and wives' preferences for wife working across the EC

	Preference for wife working			
	Wife's preference:		Husband's preference:	
	According to herself	As according to husband	As according to wife	According to himself
Country	%	%	%	%
Belgium	52	41	36	30
Denmark	62	59	54	53
West Germany	50	58	46	44
France	64	52	44	34
Ireland	51	39	33	32
Italy	76	61	47	43
Luxembourg	42	39	26	16
Holland	59	49	47	43
United Kingdom	65	54	51	37
Greece	75	58	48	43
All	63	55	46	39

Source: CEC 1983, p.93

unaware or deliberately blinkered to women's aspirations. The erosion of traditional stereotypes is clearly made more difficult given such attitudes and beliefs amongst many men. It is also made more difficult if organizations make decisions based upon such stereotypes. Those women surveyed in the WWLS who had applied for work in the previous five years were asked if they felt they had ever failed to get a job because of their sex (Table 3). In total, 17% of the sample felt that they had been discriminated against, and the reasons given are all too familiar in terms of traditional stereotypes.

Table 3: Reasons for not getting a job*

Reasons	%	N
May leave to start a family	53	34
Would take too much time off work	33	21
Could not cope with the job and look after the home	25	16
Were not strong enough	16	10
Were not commited/serious about the job	16	10
Others	27	17
N		*384*

* Respondents may have replied to more than one item so %s do not sum to 100.

That traditional stereotypes persist and present hurdles to many women's career aspirations is beyond dispute, but how do women's attitudes and orientations tally with this stereotype? For example, do men and women differ with regard to their feelings about work? To answer this question, findings from a number of previous surveys are relevant (for example, Agassi, 1982; Martin and Roberts, 1984; Witherspoon, 1985; 1988; Kremer and Curry, 1985; Commission of the European Communities, 1987; Dex, 1988). One particularly salient example is the Social Attitudes in Northern Ireland survey (Montgomery and Davies, 1991), in which working men and women were asked to rate the importance which they attached to various factors at work (Table 4). Sex differences, where they appear, are far from impressive. Indeed the similarities in replies are more remarkable than the differences, with the exception of "flexible working hours" and those items dealing with helping and caring. In line with these findings, and allowing for key variables (most significantly, domestic responsibilities and occupational status), research has generally failed to reveal major sex differences in terms of attitudes to work, and especially amongst the young (Agassi, 1982; Witherspoon, 1985; Dex, 1988). This conclusion has been challenged more recently by Hakim (1991), who has aimed to reconcile the discrepancy between, on the one hand, women's high job satisfaction and, on the other hand, their relatively poor working conditions.

Table 4: Important factors in work: Northern Ireland Social Attitudes Survey

	% rating as very important or important	
	Men	Women
Factors	%	%
Job security	98	96
Interesting job	94	93
Good opportunities for advancement	90	90
High income	85	83
Job that is useful to society	72	80
Job that allows someone to help others	69	77
Job that allows someone to work independently	66	63
Job with flexible working hours	40	53
Job that leaves a lot of leisure time	42	38

Source: Montgomery and Davies, 1991, p.78

Hakim argues that the similarities in work orientation scores between women and men do not reflect upon underlying similarity between the sexes but instead upon women and men's different life goals. This, she argues, comes through most strongly when comparing men's and women's commitment to work as measured by questions asking if the person would wish to continue working irrespective of financial necessity. For a substantial proportion of women, their main concern is identified as a "marriage career", with their career at work assuming secondary importance. Thus for many women, expectations are lower and satisfaction rates are subsequently higher as these expectations are more easily met. A part-time worker who registers a high score on an index of job satisfaction could be assumed to be highly motivated in her work and to be oriented towards doing well in her job but according to Hakim, the reality may be somewhat different. This person may be satisfied with her work not because of intrinsic interest in the job itself but because the work is convenient and does not interfere with other parts of her life which she sees as more important. In addition, if her expectations about what she will get out of her work are already low, or if her work offers her escape from an even less attractive lifestyle, then she is also more likely to be satisfied than is the person who has greater choice, or high hopes and expectations which are not realised.

Whilst this point may have some validity, it is premised upon a notion of "commitment" which may not take due regard of our capacities as information processors, nor our ability to have a strong "commitment" to more than one life domain simultaneously. The problem of pinpointing fundamental sex differences in terms of work commitment also remains a difficult task. For example, although more men would continue working irrespective of financial needs than women (Hakim, 1991), how far this reflects on women's actual experience of poorer working conditions and less rewarding jobs, and how far upon different life priorities in the first place is still open to debate. What Hakim does demonstrate is the shortcomings of existing survey data and their inability to provide comprehensive answers to questions such as why individuals, both women and men, choose to work and what they derive from their work. To develop our comprehension of these issues social researchers must draw on expertise from a range of disciplines. One example is occupational psychology where research on work motivation and job satisfaction is underpinned by increasingly sophisticated process models of motivation at work. These models describe a wide range of personal and situational variables which mediate the relationship between effort, performance, reward and job satisfaction (e.g. Porter and Lawler, 1968), and where the relationship between motivation, work performed, perceptions and valuation of rewards received, and ultimately job satisfaction, is seen as a unique and idiosyncratic cognitive blend.

Women's Attitudes and Orientations Towards Their Work

A systematic evaluation of the substance behind the stereotype of the woman worker reveals the foundations of the stereotype to be far from secure. Beyond this discussion, it then becomes appropriate to move away from generalities and instead consider how women themselves view their own work in the 1990s. As part of the WWLS, those women currently in paid work were asked to list all the reasons why they were working (Table 5). As would be expected, financial considerations were mentioned most often, a finding which is common to employment surveys of both women and men. By way of comparison, a 1986 Northern Ireland survey of attitudes to work (Kremer and Curry, 1986) found that both men and women were likely to record the need for money as the single most important reason for working at that time. Alongside pay, it is significant that so many of the WWLS sample also cited the intrinsic rewards which they derived from work. These included the stimulation of work and feeling useful, and, significantly, at the same time only 8% referred to partner's wishes. In the light of the earlier discussion it is also interesting to note that replies from part-time and full-time workers were so similar, apart from fewer part-time workers (71%) indicating that pay was important to them.

Table 5: Reasons for working by employment status*

	Employment status		
	Full-time	Part-time	All
Reasons	%	%	%
I need the money	87	71	81
I like the stimulation of going out to work	63	65	64
Work makes me feel I'm doing something useful	47	47	47
I often get bored and fed up without work	40	44	42
I have too much time on my hands without work	25	26	25
My husband/partner likes me to work	8	9	8
I spend too much time with family/friends	2	4	3
N	*327*	*207*	*534*

* Respondents may have replied to more than one item so %s do not sum to 100.

Working women were next asked how true each of the following statements about work were for them at present (Table 6). In this case, the results can be compared directly with those derived from the earlier work of Martin and Roberts (1984) in Great Britain, with figures from the WES included in italics in the right hand set of columns. Comparing these data, it would appear that the intrinsic rewards (or attractions) associated with work are relatively more important for women in the WWLS. In 1991, 80% believed it to be definitely true that "Working makes me feel I'm doing something useful", and 79% "Enjoy the stimulation of going out to work", in comparison with 61% and 60% respectively in 1980. By comparison, financial dependence on work was not perceived to be as crucial in 1990. 36% stated it was definitely true that their family could not manage without their wage; in 1980 this figure was 43%. In the light of other analyses (see Chapters 5 and 7) it is unlikely that the female wage is materially less significant to families in 1990. Instead, as a consequence of placing greater emphasis on intrinsic rewards, extrinsic factors may have become relatively less important in terms of thinking about their work. However, this is an issue which may be worthy of further investigation.

Comparing full-time and part-time responses, on certain items large differences are apparent. For example, 83% of those in full-time work would look for work immediately if they lost their job, in comparison with 60% of part-time workers. 50% of full-time workers stated that they often become tired because of their work, but only 25% of part-time workers replied that this was definitely true. Likewise, full-time workers were more likely to agree that they did not have sufficient time to do everything, nor to see family and

Table 6: Perceptions of current work by employment status*

How true is it that:	Full-time work				Part-time work				All			
	Def true	Part true	Not true	Total %	Def true	Part true	Not true	Total %	Def true	Part true	Not true	Total %
	%	%	%	%	%	%	%	%	%	%	%	%
I/my family could not manage unless I was earning	45	23	32	100	21	27	52	100	36	24	40	100
									43	*27*	*30*	*100*
I don't need to work for the money	10	15	75	100	21	22	57	100	14	18	68	100
									11	*25*	*64*	*100*
If I lost my job I would look for another straight away	83	8	9	100	60	20	20	100	74	13	13	100
									66	*18*	*16*	*100*
It wouldn't bother me if I lost my job and couldn't find another one	14	11	75	100	23	18	59	100	17	14	69	100
									12	*19*	*69*	*100*
I like the stimulation of going out to work	81	14	5	100	77	19	4	100	79	16	5	100
									60	*32*	*8*	*100*
I wish I didn't go out to work	5	16	79	100	4	13	82	100	5	15	80	100
									6	*18*	*76*	*100*
Working makes me feel I'm doing something useful	83	14	3	100	77	18	5	100	80	16	4	100
									61	*34*	*5*	*100*
I have less time than I would like to spend with my family and friends	26	25	49	100	12	21	67	100	20	24	56	100
									18	*36*	*46*	*100*
I often get very tired because of my work	50	30	20	100	25	23	52	100	40	27	32	100
									29	*44*	*27*	*100*
I never have enough time for everything	43	32	25	100	31	23	46	100	39	28	33	100
									31	*43*	*26*	*100*
I would not continue to work if my partner disapproved	15	15	70	100	19	20	61	100	17	17	66	100
									[not included in WES]			
N			327				207					534

* %s sum to 100 by row

friends. These results confirm the common finding of higher scores for part-time workers on job satisfaction measures but should not detract from other evidence (see Chapter 2) that simultaneously part-time workers are less likely to receive help from their partners in the home, for example with childcare or housework. Domestic circumstances also played a very significant part in determining attitudes towards work. For example, 30% of those working with at least one child under three said it was definitely true that they had less time than they would like with family and friends, in comparison with 14% of those with no children. Similarly, 55% of those with children under five said that it was definitely true that they "never have enough time for everything", compared with 28% of those without children.

Moving beyond the sample as a whole, those women who had applied for work in the last five years were asked to list any factors which were important to them when deciding to apply for jobs (Table 7).

Table 7: Important factors in deciding to apply for jobs*

Factors	%
Work you like doing	74
Good rate of pay	71
Convenient hours of work	52
Secure job	42
Convenient to home	42
Friendly people to work with	40
Good prospects	36
Pleasant work environment	31
Opportunity to use your ability	31
Support from husband/partner	14
Familiar work	13
Job gives you status in the community	6
Good child care facilities	
N	*379*

* Respondents may have replied to more than one item so %s do not sum to 100.

Interestingly, 81% of those aged under 30 mentioned "Work I like doing", in comparison with 63% of those aged over 40. This age difference possibly serves to highlight the increasing importance attached to the intrinsic value of work for women in the 1990s; younger women were more willing to state that choice and personal interest were as important, if not more important, than financial or domestic concerns. Given that younger women have significantly more qualifications and greater experience of education (see Chapter 4), these differences may well reflect on a realistic appraisal of greater opportunity and choice for the younger age cohort. Pay was regarded as significant irrespective of personal circumstances, and indeed it is noteworthy how variables such as occupational status did not appear to influence replies to this question. Given the considerable domestic burden which women still shoulder (see Chapters 2 and 8), it is not surprising that domestic circumstances were significant in key respects. For example, those with children were less likely to mention good prospects (26%) than those without children (52%). In a similar vein, 83% of single women, or those who were married but had no children, mentioned intrinsic interest in their work, in comparison with 70% of those with children. By way of comparison with previous research, Table 8 is presented from the WES report (Martin and Roberts, 1984). Martin and Roberts asked their female respondents to rate the importance of various considerations when looking for a job.

Table 8: Important factors when looking for work by employment status: WES

	% rating as essential/very important		
	Full-time	Part-time	All
Factors	%	%	%
Work you like doing	93	88	91
Friendly people to work with	85	88	86
Job security	83	68	76
Convenient hours of work	65	88	75
Good rate of pay	79	68	74
Opportunity to use ability	78	62	71
Easy journey to work	53	66	59
Prospects	58	37	49
N	*1877*	*1477*	*3354*

Source: Martin and Roberts, 1984, p.72

Rather than listing those items which the individual identified as important, Martin and Roberts asked that each item in turn should be rated in terms of importance, hence the differences in percentage rating scores between the surveys. Direct comparison is not possible but as regards the rank ordering of items, intrinsic interest is evidently to the fore in both surveys, but with socio-emotional concerns at work being mentioned relatively more frequently in 1980. It may or may not be significant that good rate of pay is ranked higher in the present survey.

Taking into account both Tables 6 and 7, it is clear that intrinsic reasons and motivators are extremely important, and have become even more significant over the years for women. The perception, if not the reality, of choice and personal freedom is salient when charting equality of opportunity and women's rights. It should not be forgotten that Martin and Robert's work was carried out over a decade ago, and during the 1980s women's perception of greater freedom may have afforded a higher priority to items associated with personal choice and to intrinsic motivators, rather than seeking external justification with reference to factors such as working conditions, flexibility and security.

When taken as a whole, these results challenge the view that women themselves conform to the traditional stereotype of marginal workers. Intrinsic interest in their work is given a high priority by women, and their commitment to work appears to be far from short term or transient. This point is further underlined by the finding that 68% of women who were either in paid employment or looking for work, expected that they would continue to work until retirement. The equivalent figure for men may well be higher but this should not detract from the fact that over two thirds of women wish to continue working and only 17% stated they would not, with the remaining 15% undecided. Variables such as age, marital status, children and social class did not appear to significantly affect replies to this question.

Job Satisfaction

Having considered factors which are important in determining perceptions of work, attention now turns to the satisfaction which women feel they derive from their work. Previous employment surveys have tended to rely upon relatively simple measures of job satisfaction. Unfortunately, these may not always have been able to identify which aspects of their work individuals find more or less satisfying. At the same time, researchers have been disenchanted with outcomes from these questionnaire items, given that they consistently reveal high levels of satisfaction which stand regardless of a range of factors (for example, Brown, Curran and Cousins, 1983). Whether this uniformity of response reflects upon questionnaire design or upon genuinely high rates of job satisfaction across the workforce is a question which remains unresolved, but undoubtedly any questionnaire response is likely to mask a considerable number of individual reasons and personal interpretations of job satisfaction.

The primary job satisfaction measure used in this survey was based upon the Worker Opinion Survey (WOS). The WOS was originally developed by Cross (1973) to consider various aspects of job satisfaction, and in its original form included six subscales relating to different facets of the job, namely Pay, Promotion, Immediate Superior, Co-workers, the Job Itself and the Organization. Five of the scales were subsequently included in the WWLS (the Co-workers subscale was omitted as not all respondents would currently work alongside others, and item 8 from the Job Itself scale, "The job is better than other jobs I have had", was also excluded, given that some respondents may have no experience of other work). Each item was scored as either 1 (Yes); 2 (Unsure) to 3 (No). Summative scores for the Pay, Promotion, Immediate Superior and Organization subscales fell within the range 24 (very satisfied) to 8 (very dissatisfied). The Job Itself scale was scored between 21 (very satisfied) and 7 (very dissatisfied). Mean scores on each scale are presented in Table 9.

Table 9: Worker Opinion Survey mean scores by employment status

WOS Scale	Full-time		Part-time		All	
	mean	N	mean	N	mean	N
Pay	16.9	327	17.5	204	17.1	531
Job Itself	16.2	327	16.4	204	16.3	531
Superior	20.6	295	21.1	184	20.8	479
Organization	19.3	295	19.5	185	19.4	480
Promotion	16.5	292	15.6	175	16.2	467

In line with earlier research (for example, Beechey and Perkins, 1987), job satisfaction scores for part-time and full-time women workers were similar. With regard to Pay, the Job Itself, Superior and the Organization, part-time workers were marginally more satisfied with their work, although these differences were small. As previously mentioned, Hakim (1991) argues not only that there is a need for more refined indices of job satisfaction in employment research but also that any measure of job satisfaction will tell us less about the quality of the work experience itself and more about the life goals, expectations and orientations of different groups of workers. Even using more refined measures of job satisfaction, the WWLS results do not refute this contention for despite palpably poorer working conditions, part-time workers only demonstrate significantly lower levels of satisfaction with regard to prospects for promotion. Clearly there is the need for further research and informed discussion, and particularly as regards the concept of job satisfaction and how it relates to work motivation, work orientation, expectations and life experiences.

Looking at other variables which have a significant effect on job satisfaction, as regards the Pay subscale, marital status and religion were both influential. Single women (mean score = 16.2) were less satisfied with their rate of pay than were married women (17.6), perhaps reflecting on fewer opportunities for married women, or the difficulties which they encounter as working mothers. For reasons which were not immediately obvious but which may warrant further investigation, Catholics (17.6) were also more contented than Protestants (16.3). As regards the Job Itself, perhaps predictably, occupational status played a significant role. Professional women (17.9) exhibited greater satisfaction with their work than skilled/non-manual (16.3), skilled/manual (14.7) or partly skilled/unskilled workers (15.4). In addition, younger women were somewhat less content with their jobs than older women; those aged under 25 obtained a mean score of 15.5 in comparison with 16.5 for those aged 45 years or older. Once more an awareness of greater opportunities and unfulfilled expectations amongst the young may reflect in lower job satisfaction, although clearly this would also require further investigation. Few variables appeared to influence attitudes towards Immediate Superior, or the Organization as a whole. However, once more occupational status influenced satisfaction with Promotion prospects. Women in professional/intermediate jobs (17.6) showed themselves to be happier with promotion prospects than skilled/non-manual (16.3), skilled/manual (14.8), or partly skilled/unskilled workers (15.1).

As part of the 1980 WES, Martin and Roberts simply asked women how satisfied they were with various aspects of their current jobs. They too found that the majority of women were satisfied with many aspects of their working lives (Table 10).

Table 10: Levels of job satisfaction by employment status: WES

	% rating as very/fairly satisfied with their own job		
	Full-time	Part-time	All
Factor	%	%	%
Work you like doing	88	89	88
Opportunity to use ability	76	72	75
Prospects	73	65	69
Good rate of pay	75	83	79
Job security	86	84	85
People you work with	92	90	91
Convenient hours of work	89	94	91
Easy journey to work	85	87	86

Source: Derived from Martin and Roberts, 1984

At face value, the picture presented in both surveys is of a contented workforce but such generalizations are likely to be misleading when set in the context of the previous discussion. The traditional stereotype of the women worker may be a distortion of reality but at the same time it may be dangerous to construct a new stereotype which ignores individual differences, expectations and experiences. This is revealed, for example, through a consideration of promotion at work, and women's responses to the prospects of promotion. As well as completing the WOS Promotion subscale, all women who had ever been in paid employment were asked if they had ever been promoted at some stage during their working lives, or if they had ever deliberately refused the chance of promotion (Table 11). Approximately one third of all the women interviewed had been promoted at work. Looking at that subset of the sample who were currently in paid work, of those in full-time work 46% had received promotion, in comparison with 33% of those in part-time work. Fewer than 10% of women had ever refused promotion (N = 85). These women tended to be somewhat older, with 50 (59%) aged over 40 years but otherwise they were not distinguishable from the sample as a whole. Table 12 lists the reasons why these women had refused promotion.

Table 11: Acceptance and refusal of promotion

	Accepted promotion	Refused promotion
Frequency	%	%
Yes, once	19	2
Yes, more than once	14	7
No	68	91
Total %	100	100
N	*955*	*955*

Table 12: Reasons for refusing promotion*

Reason	%
Did not want more responsibility/don't like giving orders	40
Happy in post/like the job I'm doing	38
Interfered with family commitments	16
Did not want to be 'above' fellow workers	14
Don't like new work	12
Expected to leave job soon	11
Was not sufficiently qualified	5
Other	17
N	*85*

* Respondents may have replied to more than one item so %s do not sum to 100.

Perhaps significantly, the most common reasons were not related to outside interests or commitments but were associated with satisfaction with their current post. Again, this may be used to reinforce the picture of a reasonably contented workforce but conversely may once more raise unanswered questions about the source of this satisfaction, and the reasons why women did not want more responsibility at work. Those currently in jobs where there was the possibility of promotion (N = 230) were then asked if they would welcome the opportunity of being promoted (Table 13).

Nearly two thirds would welcome promotion, although domestic circumstances and the nature of their work do play significant roles. For example, 56% of those without children stated that they would definitely welcome promotion, in comparison with one third of those with two or more children. Similarly, 52% of those in professional/intermediate jobs would definitely welcome promotion but only 28% of those in partly skilled/unskilled employment. Women who replied no or don't know to this question (N = 87) were asked which factors were important in helping them decide not to seek promotion (see Table 14, where % figures refer to % who listed that factor).

Table 13: Welcome opportunity for promotion

Welcome:	%
Yes, definitely	43
Yes, probably	11
Yes, possibly	8
No	35
Don't know	3
Total %	100
N	*230*

Table 14: Reasons for not seeking promotion*

Reasons	%
Did not want more responsibility/don't like giving orders	64
Happy in post/like the job I'm doing	63
Interfered with family commitments	22
Don't like new work	8
Expected to leave job soon	7
Was not sufficiently qualified	7
Too old	6
Other	7
N	*87*

* Respondents may have replied to more than one item so %s do not sum to 100.

Tables 12 and 14 are remarkably similar, with an almost identical rank ordering of items in each. Lack of self-confidence, low self-esteem, avoidance of success and fear of failure have all been identified as factors which contribute to women's under achievement at work, and these psychological constraints do come through, albeit implicitly, in both these tables. At the same time it should not be forgotten that the percentage of working women who have either refused promotion or would not welcome promotion is still relatively small, and these may or may not also be the women who Hakim (1991) identifies as having " marriage careers" or interests away from work. With this in mind it is relevant to consider the reasons why those women in the WWLS who were not in paid employment stated they were not working at present (Table 15).

Table 15 : Reasons for not working at present*

Reasons	Sole response	%	All responses	%
To look after children	154	33	191	42
Illness/injury	67	15	75	16
To look after other dependent	32	7	51	11
Marriage	13	3	34	7
Retired	31	7	31	7
To continue education	21	5	23	5
Contract ended	9	2	20	4
To start a family	5	1	16	3
Made redundant	10	2	15	3
Unable to find work	2	0	10	4
Unhappy with work	5	1	7	2
Don't want to work	9	2	7	2
N			*460*	

* Respondents may have replied to more than one item so %s do not sum to 100.

Childcare and domestic considerations are clearly dominant here but it is also noteworthy that so few women stated that the reason why they no longer worked was either because they were unhappy at work (2%) or because generally they did not want to work (2%). Of the women not in paid work, 58 (13%) were currently looking for work. However, when the remainder were asked to indicate when they might start applying for jobs again, 21% were uncertain, 4% said within one year; 15% between one and five years, 7% over five years, and 54% said never. It is perhaps significant that 68% of those replying never were aged 51 or older, and only three women aged under 30 thought that they would never work in the future. In addition those who were currently working but contemplated having children/more children (N = 108) were asked how soon they would expect to return to work. 65% maintained that they would continue working and only 5% felt it likely that they would give up work completely. Even in the case of those not working at present and who were expecting to have children/more children (N = 36), 58% hoped to start work at some time before their youngest child started school.

Standing back from these figures, the picture which is painted is certainly not one of a homogenous group of women, and certainly not a marginalised or peripheral labour force which is biding its time between bouts of domestic duty. Instead the portrait represents a conglomeration of individual values and priorities. Above all else the analysis warns us of the perils of constructing stereotypes or images of the "typical woman" when experiences and orientations differ so markedly between individuals. It is true that there are a minority of women who, at the present time, would not welcome promotion, or who do not have long-term aspirations to return to full-time employment. Simultaneously, there are many women who have strong commitments to their careers and yet again there are those who show interest divided equally between home and work. To simply categorize women as falling into one camp or the other, as either career or marriage oriented, may be a false dichotomy. Instead, people are each capable of dealing with a number of priorities, and these priorities will undoubtedly change over time and place. At any one time, women will prioritise certain parts of their lives and will make choices but these choices and these priorities will inevitably change in response to changing circumstances.

Attitudes to Women at Work

Women's personal experiences and their attitudes towards these experiences tell one half of the story, of equal importance are women's attitudes towards working women as a whole. As previously mentioned, these do not always tally, and it would not be unusual to find some mismatch between a woman's personal circumstances and what she believes is right for women in general. Looking back over this century, societal attitudes to the idea of women working have been less than positive and particularly as regards the employment of married women (see Dex, 1988). For example, in a national opinion survey carried out in the United States in the 1930s, fewer than 20% of women agreed that married women should be in full-time work. The 1943 Women at Work Survey revealed that 30% of women did not believe in a woman working after marriage, and in total, 58% considered that a woman's place was at home unless financial necessity compelled otherwise. By 1965, the position had changed somewhat (Hunt, 1968), with 89% of women approving of a married woman working if she had no children, but only 20% giving their endorsement if children were of pre-school age. In the Irish Republic, Fine-Davis (1983) found that in 1975, 48% of employed married women maintained that it was bad for young children if their mothers went out to work but by 1981 only 35% agreed with the statement. Such dramatic shifts have been noted across the

United Kingdom and Europe as a whole during the 1980s (Commission of the European Communities, 1987; Dex, 1988; Witherspoon, 1988).

One factor which has influenced attitude change has been the gradual rise in women's involvement in the labour market over time. Looked at in gross terms, as women's participation has increased, simultaneously more favourable attitudes to working women have been noted. However, it would be fallacious to assume that the relationship between economic activity and attitudes is linear or causal. For example, Dex (1988) argues that at least before the 1960s, attitude change may well have proceeded independently from changes in female economic activity rates. Overall, however, evidence would point to change, albeit gradual, and the development of more liberal attitudes towards women at work. Despite this general trend, predictive models should not automatically assume a natural and inexorable movement towards more liberal attitudes and greater freedom but must allow for economic and political fluctuations which may halt or even reverse the tide. For example, during periods of recession, female employment may rise but this will reflect in increasing numbers in part-time, seasonal or contractual work (Beechey, 1986). Simultaneously as male unemployment rates increase, men may feel that their "right to work" is threatened by women working and attitudes towards women working may become less positive as a consequence. Men's attitudes were not the direct concern of the WWLS but the survey does provide an opportunity to look at evidence of change in women's attitudes in response to the economic and political changes which took place during the 1980s. To begin, all respondents were asked their views as to whether or not a woman should work given various home circumstances, together with the response which they thought their husband/partner would make. The results are summarised in Table 16.

Looking at the figures overall, two features are striking. Firstly, a woman's right to choose features prominently and particularly when young children are not a consideration. Secondly, partner's/husband's wishes do not appear to be regarded as very important. In each of the first three sets of figures (single, married with no children, married and children left home), upwards of 90% of the sample maintained that the woman herself should make the decision about whether or not to work. In contrast, a far higher proportion of women believe that a mother with young children should stay at home. When children are at school this still only represents 10% of the sample (and only 4% of women aged under 40 years) but for pre-school children this figure rises to 41%. Looking at other significant variables, as would be expected older women tended to hold more traditional attitudes, or at least their existing attitudes may have been more resistant to change. For example, 55% of those aged over 50 years believed that a married woman with pre-school children should remain at home, but only 36% of those aged under 20 years endorsed this sentiment.

Table 16: Attitudes towards women working by employment status

Single, no family

	All	Work full-time	Work part-time	Unemp (avail.)	Unemp (unavail.)	Partner's attitude
Her decision	91	93	90	86	91	91
Work if she needs money	9	7	9	13	9	8
Stay at home	0	0	1	0	0	0

Married, no children

	All	Work full-time	Work part-time	Unemp (avail.)	Unemp (unavail.)	Partner's attitude
Her decision	92	94	92	90	90	92
Work if she needs money	7	6	8	8	8	7
Stay at home	1	0	0	0	1	1
Do what partner decides	0	0	0	2	1	0

Married, children left home

	All	Work full-time	Work part-time	Unemp (avail.)	Unemp (unavail.)	Partner's attitude
Her decision	91	94	94	86	88	90
Work if she needs money	8	6	6	13	11	7
Stay at home	0	1	0	1	0	2
Do what partner decides	0	0	0	0	0	1

Married, children all at school

	All	Work full-time	Work part-time	Unemp (avail.)	Unemp (unavail.)	Partner's attitude
Her decision	68	75	70	63	62	67
Work if she needs money	22	19	23	24	23	16
Stay at home	10	5	7	14	14	17
Do what partner decides	0	0	0	0	1	1

Married, children under school age

	All	Work full-time	Work part-time	Unemp (avail.)	Unemp (unavail.)	Partner's attitude
Her decision	40	50	43	31	29	38
Work if she needs money	19	18	20	27	18	12
Stay at home	41	32	37	42	53	50
Do what partner decides	0	0	0	0	0	0
N	1000	327	207	86	279	667

Interestingly, this figure fell to 29% amongst those aged between 21 and 40 years and accordingly those most likely to have pre-school children. Amongst those women who were not available for work (that is, looking after the home full-time), 52% agreed that a woman in these circumstances should stay at home but the number of children which a woman has herself did not appear to significantly influence replies.

It is significant that when describing their partner's likely response, women believed their partners would be less likely to give the woman freedom to choose. Older women in particular believed that their partner's replies would be more dogmatic. For example, 60% of those aged between 41 and 60 thought that their partner would maintain that a woman with young children should stay at home. Also, 54% of Catholic women thought this the case but only 45% of Protestants, and yet religion was not a significant variable in terms of the women's own responses to these situations.

Apart from looking at variations within the sample, comparisons can also be made with earlier surveys carried out in Great Britain in 1965 and 1980 (Hunt, 1968; Martin and Roberts, 1984), and also the 1987 British Social Attitudes Survey (Witherspoon, 1988), as presented in Table 1.

Table 17: Attitudes towards women working - comparative results

% agreeing that the woman ought to remain at home

	1965 %	1980 %	1987 %	WWLS (1990) %
Married, no children	1	1	1	1
Married, children all at school	20	11	7	10
Married, children under school age	78	60	45	41

% agreeing that it is up to the woman to decide

	1965 %	1980 %	1987 %	WWLS (1990) %
Married, no children	75	62	69	92
Married, children all at school	35	50	61	67
Married, children under school age	5	15	26	40

Source: Derived from Hunt, 1968; Martin and Roberts, 1984; Witherspoon, 1988

Taking into account important differences in the question format ("Ought to work if she is fit" was not included in the WWLS, hence percentage scores on other items will have increased, albeit slightly given low response to this item in previous surveys), it would seem that the liberalisation of attitudes towards working women has continued. Witherspoon (1988) has described the shift in attitudes to working mothers during the 1980s as tantamount to a sea-change, and it would appear that the tide is continuing to run strongly. It is also true that, contrary to popular belief, Northern Ireland has not been immune to this shift in attitudes across the United Kingdom. This is evident despite the relatively poor childcare provision for the under fives in Northern Ireland (see Chapter 8). The right of the woman to choose for herself came through more strongly in the WWLS than in earlier work, although there were still reservations as regards those with pre-school children.

Received opinion tells us that Northern Ireland is more traditional than the rest of the United Kingdom along a number of dimensions, yet when it comes to specific issues, hard evidence to support this general claim is not easy to come by. One prime and very salient example concerns attitudes towards women, where "accepted wisdom" has it that attitudes are more traditional than in Great Britain (see Chapter 2). In a postal survey of 1000 men and women across Northern Ireland, Kremer and Curry (1986) found that attitudes to women were not markedly dissimilar from those obtained from British samples, but, as expected, there were within-sample differences. For example, women's attitudes correlated negatively with age, such that older women held more traditional attitudes. Montgomery and Davies (1991), working with data derived from the British Social Attitudes survey in Northern Ireland, also failed to be impressed by differences between Northern Ireland and Britain as regards general attitudes to women and employment issues but were more struck by contrasts in terms of a range of social issues. Once more, the present survey may be able to shed further light on the existence of cross cultural differences, as well as significant demographic factors at work within Northern Ireland itself.

The shortened version of the Attitudes to Women Scale (Spence, Helmreich and Stapp, 1973) is one of the most popular devices for considering attitudes to the rights and roles of women in society (Beere, 1979). The anglicised twenty-two item version or AWS-B (Parry, 1983) includes questions dealing with both work and non-work issues, and has been shown to be influenced by a number of variables including sex, age, social class, education and employment status. Kremer and Curry (1987) divided the scale into those items dealing with work and non-work/social domains, and discovered that it was the work items which accounted for almost all differences in scores between women and men. These eleven items dealing specifically with work related issues were included in the WWLS. Each item is scored on a five-point scale, with total scores ranging from 0 (traditional) to 44 (liberal).

The mean score obtained for the WWLS sample (N = 998) was 33.9. This compares with a mean score for women of 32.5 obtained in the 1986 Northern Ireland Attitudes towards Women Survey (Kremer and Curry, 1986). A breakdown of responses for each item is shown in Table 18, together with the mean score by item, which may fall between the range of 0 (traditional) and 4 (liberal). The mean scores obtained from the Kremer and Curry (1986) survey for each item are also shown in italics.

Age comes through as the most significant variable, along with domestic circumstances and economic activity. Those aged under 40 years who are single,

Table 18: AWS-B (Work) items

Item	Strongly Agree %	Agree %	Neutral %	Disagree %	Strongly Disagree %
There should be more women leaders in important jobs in public life, such as politics	38	39	16	6	2
		Mean = 3.1 (1986 mean = 2.8)			
If a woman goes out to work, her husbandshould share the housework, such as washing dishes and cleaning	62	32	3	2	2
		Mean = 3.5 (1986 mean = 3.5)			
Women should have completely equal opportunities in getting jobs and promotion as men	64	30	3	2	2
		Mean = 3.5 (1986 mean = 3.4)			
Women should worry less about being equal with men and more about becoming good wives and mothers	9	22	21	31	17
		Mean = 2.3 (1986 mean = 1.9)			
Women should not be bosses in important jobs in business and industry	4	5	6	43	41
		Mean = 3.1 (1986 mean = 2.8)			
Daughters in a family should be encouraged to stay on at school and go to college as much as sons in the family	63	29	2	4	2
		Mean = 3.1 (1986 mean = 3.0)			
It would be ridiculous for a woman to drive a train or for a man to sew on shirt buttons	4	11	8	42	35
		Mean = 2.9 (1986 mean = 3.0)			
A woman's place is in the home looking after her family, rather than following a career of her own	6	13	17	37	28
		Mean = 2.7 (1986 mean = 2.5)			
Women have less to offer than men in the world of business and industry	2	7	7	43	41
		Mean = 3.1 (1986 mean = 3.0)			
There are many jobs that men can do better than women	8	46	13	22	12
		Mean = 2.2 (1986 mean = 1.6)			
Girls should have as much opportunity to do apprenticeships and learn a trade as boys	52	40	3	3	2
		Mean = 3.4 (1986 mean =3.2)			

Mean scores for the AWS-B, by key variables, are presented below.

Age	20- yrs = 35.7; 21 - 30 yrs = 35.5; 31 - 40 yrs = 35.1; 41 - 50 yrs = 33.7; 51 - 60 yrs = 31.1; 60+ yrs = 30.8,
Religion	Catholic = 34.3; Non-catholic = 33.6
Marital Status	Single = 35.2; Married = 33.6; Div. = 34.6; Widowed = 29.6
School Type	Mixed-sex = 33.9; Single-sex = 35.0
Number of Children	0 = 35.2; 1 = 33.5; 2 = 34.4; 3 = 33.2; 4 = 33.3; 5 = 31.8; 6 = 31.7; 7+ = 33.9
Economic Activity	Full-time = 35.6; Part-time = 34.4; Unemployed (available) = 32.8; Unemployed (unavailable) = 32.3
Occupational Status	Professional/intermediate = 36.0; Skilled/non-manual = 35.3; Skilled/manual = 35.3; Partly skilled/unskilled = 32.4
Educational Quals.	None = 33.3; Vocat./ other = 34.8; Academic/prof. = 35.8

working full-time and have no children are likely to hold the most liberal attitudes of all. On almost all items, more liberal attiudes have been recorded in the WWLS in comparison with the 1985 survey (Kremer and Curry, 1986), although the magnitude of change is often small and direct comparison is problematic given the different sampling procedures employed in the two surveys. A scan across each item in turn reveals that liberal attitudes are very much the norm, for example with women over the age of 60 still recording a mean score of over 30. Indeed, given that the distribution of replies is so skewed towards the liberal pole, doubts must be raised as to the long term viability of the AWS-B as a measure of attitudes towards women and as a discriminator of individual differences.

The extent of liberal attitudes is to be welcomed but at the same time it is undoubtedly significant that two items which elicited amongst the least liberal attitudes were both dealing with the relationship between paid work and perceived domestic responsibilities ("Women should worry less about being equal with men and more about becoming good wives and mothers" and "A woman's place is in the home looking after her family rather than following a career of her own"). The conflict between home and work continues to dominate discussion of gender role attitudes and to impose considerable psychological strain on working women and particularly mothers. According to Scott and Duncombe (1991),

> *It is unlikely that women will reap the benefits of employment unless there are substantial changes in female labour market conditions and substantial shifts in normative beliefs about gender roles. In particular, unless high quality childcare and flexible work hours become widespread, working mothers will continue to experience role conflict in terms of guilt and anxiety about not being a full-time parent, especially when their children are young. Moreover, unless beliefs about gender roles change, and women stop being defined as primarily responsible for family care, women who are in paid work will ahve to struggle to do a double shift of employment and family care whilst still fearing that their families may suffer (Scott and Duncombe, 1991, p.20).*

Conclusion

What general conclusions can be drawn from this chapter? In the first place, it is worth reiterating the point that despite the persistence of the traditional stereotype of the woman worker in popular consciousness, this stereotype tells us little about the reality of individual experience. A further stereotype which enjoys widespread support concerns the general conservatism and traditionalism of the people of Northern Ireland. Although there is evidence to suggest that Northern Ireland is special in terms of moral and religious concerns (Sneddon and Kremer, 1991), it may be unwise to generalize to other spheres, including the world of work. Despite historical differences in female economic activity rates across the United Kingdom, and less marked but still noticable present day differences (McWilliams, 1991), there is little evidence that women in Northern Ireland hold substantially different attitudes to work in comparison with women in Great Britain, and there is evidence to suggest that attitudes in this 1991 survey are more liberal than those found in earlier work, either here or in Great Britain.

This is encouraging. It is also encouraging that in the face of inequality of opportunity which women still face at work and the smokescreen of traditional stereotypes, there is little evidence to suggest that women regard themselves as representing a marginalised or peripheral workforce. This is revealed in a number of ways, for example by the significance which many working women attach to intrinsic rewards derived from their work (Table 5), and also by the commitment shown to their work, irrespective of high rates of job satisfaction per se (Table 8). According to Hakim (1991), these high levels of job satisfaction must not be taken at face value, because for many women their primary life goals and interests may be away from work and a simple index of job satisfaction is not able to take these different orientations and expectations into account. Individuals, of either sex, may record satisfaction with their jobs not if they achieve, succeed or "grow" at work but merely if their work is convenient for them, leaves them free time for other activities and if it meets their basic needs. It is argued that for many women, these other activities often centre around the home but in pursuit of this argument we should not lose sight of the fact that work also fulfills a purely instrumental function for many men. Using a gender model to describe women's work commitment but a job model to interpret men's commitment is a temptation which must be avoided (Feldberg and Glenn, 1979); the alternative is to simply add support to traditional stereotypes. Possibly a stronger argument can be made that each individual's life experiences, priorities and circumstances (which obviously in turn are influenced by that person's sex) are likely to have a much larger impact on their attitudes to their work. Despite the considerable number of employment surveys which have been undertaken over recent years, it is true to say that our understanding of concepts such as work motivation, orientation and job satisfaction remains poor. Alongside the complexities of the relationship between attitudes and behaviour, as described earlier, there is a need for social researchers to address these issues in a more sophisticated fashion, and to remind themselves continually that behind each table and set of statistics there exist women and men who are unique human beings with a unique set of experiences.

When endeavouring to compare results from the WWLS with previous research, it became very apparent that even subtle differences in the form of questions made a considerable impact upon the nature of the replies. Such issues cannot and should not be ignored in social research; what questions are asked and how they are asked are the two most important factors determining outcome. It is often said, quite rightly, that the same statistics can be used to tell a thousand different tales but the story actually begins earlier with the formulation and design of questions. Often these influences are subtle. For example, in the present survey when quizzed as to their attitudes and opinions, women were normally asked to select from lists of items those ones which they felt were important or relevant to them. Previous research has been more inclined to ask respondents to rate items in terms of importance but often those surveyed have been required to respond to each item, irrespective of its true salience to them as an individual. Current attitude research would suggest that social scientists may have been misguided to work from the assumption that individuals necessarily and automatically hold attitudes on all issues and at all times. Increasingly research is now looking at the relative time taken to reach attitudes, or answer attitudinal questions, this serving as an index to the accessibility of that opinion to us as an individual (Fazio, 1990). It may be that the earlier research has unwittingly failed to discriminate between those items and values which are spontaneously recognised as significant by the respondent, and those items to which a forced response ascribes significance. The WWLS has certainly not avoided cuing entirely, as ready-made lists of alternatives were provided, but whereas previous work would suggest that a considerable number of factors are all identified as important by a majority of women (for example, Table 7), the WWLS results at least suggest less unanimity of response, and an even more open-ended set of questions would undoubtedly reveal even less consensus.

Dex (1988) and Witherspoon (1988) have both described large shifts in attitudes towards women working during the 1980s, and there is little to suggest that this change is not continuing apace, in Northern Ireland as elsewhere. The relationship between this attitudinal shift and changes in female employment patterns is, however, extremely complex, and certainly warrants further investigation. Here longitudinal research would be invaluable. Echoing the words of Dex (1988), attitudes may have some impact upon hours worked and a woman's decision to work but yet again behaviour may subsequently reflect in attitudes, or the two may co-exist independently. In the light of this complexity, generalizing from one woman's experience to the next is not only dangerous it is a corruption of the data. Again, surveys may reveal general trends but rarely are they able to tell us much about how individuals view their world or impute meaning to their world, and a recognition of this limitation is vital.

Within the WWLS, the two most significant factors which influenced attitudes towards women working were the respondent's age and domestic circumstances. For example, older women tended to be less tolerant of mothers going out to work, but against this, the overwhelming majority of the sample were prepared to say that it is up to the woman herself to determine when and if she should work (Tables 17 and 18). There was more ambivalence towards accepting that women with pre-school children should work but how far this finding reflects upon a principled stand concerning the responsibilities of motherhood and how far it reflects upon a practical evaluation of existing childcare services, or how these two interact, must remain a matter for conjecture. Nevertheless, it was also true that the two items on the attitudes towards women scale which elicited the most traditional replies were related to the conflict between the worlds of work and home, and dealing with this conflict psychologically remains an issue for many women.

Across the WWLS, it is noticeable that the vast majority of women were explaining their current circumstances with reference to intrinsic factors (for example, see Table 5), or were increasingly willing to give other women scope to choose their own lifestyles (Table 18). Irrespective of whether or not they were working, or their domestic circumstances, women were more likely to maintain that the decision was a personal one. Undoubtedly, in turn these choices may have been shaped by outside forces, including the influence of significant others and current circumstances but women were willing to affirm their agency. Research dealing with causal attribution (for example, Deaux, 1976) has traditionally described sex differences such that men are more likely to assume personal agency than are women; men say they choose but women say they have choices imposed upon them. Could it be that women's external attribution bias is becoming less powerful, and consequently women may now be more willing to describe themselves as controllers of their destiny; as agents rather than puppets? This is not to deny that considerations such as pay are still very important in terms of day-to-day existence, nor that the inequitable division of labour within the home continues to exert a massive impact on women's employment opportunities; rather it is to recognise that women's own perception of their capacity for influence and change may be shifting. In terms of long term goals of equality of opportunity at work as we rapidly approach the millenium, such evidence is certainly cause for optimism and is likely to be a powerful force for social change.

References

Agassi, J.B. (1982). *Comparing the Work Attitudes of Women and Men.*   Lexington, Massachusetts: Lexington Books, D.C. Heath.

Ajzen, I. (1988). *Attitudes, Personality and Behaviour.*   Milton Keynes: Open University Press.

Barron, R.D. and Norris, G.M. (1991). 'Sexual divisions in the dual labour market.' In D. Leonard and S. Allen (eds.), *Sexual Divisions Revisited.*   Basingstoke: Macmillan Press.

Beechey, V. (1986). 'Women's employment in contemporary Britain.' In V. Beechey and E. Whitelegg (eds.), *Women in Britain Today.*   Milton Keynes: Open University Press.

Beechey, V. and Perkins, T. (1987). *A Matter of Hours: Women, Part-time Work and the Labour Market.* Cambridge: Polity Press.

Beere, C.A. (1979). *Women and Women's Issues: A Handbook of Tests and Measures.* California: Jossey-Bass.

Blau, F.D. and Winkler, A.E. (1989). 'Women in the labour force: An overview.' In J. Freeman (ed.), *Women: A Feminist Perspective.* Mountain View, California: Mayfield Publishing Co.

Brown, R., Curran, M. and Cousins, J. (1983). *Changing Attitudes to Employment?* Department of Employment Research Paper No. 40. London: HMSO.

Brown, R. (1991). 'Postscript to women as employees: Some comments on research in industrial sociology.' In D. Leonard and S. Allen (eds.), *Sexual Divisions Revisited.* Basingstoke: Macmillan Press.

Commission of the European Communities (1983). *European Women and Men in 1983.* Brussels: CEC.

Commission of the European Communities (1987). *Men and Women of Europe in 1987. Supplement No. 26. Women of Europe.* Brussels: CEC (Women's Information Service).

Cross, D. (1973). 'The Worker Opinion Survey: A measure of shop-floor satisfaction.' *Occupational Psychology, 47,* 193 - 208.

Deaux, K. (1976). 'Sex: A perspective on the attribution process.' In J.J. Harvey, W.J. Ickes and R.F. Kidd (eds.), *New Directions in Attribution Research (Volume 1).* Hillsdale, New Jersey: Erlbaum.

Dex, S. (1988). *Women's Attitudes Towards Work.* Basingstoke: Macmillan Press.

Fazio, R.H. (1990). 'Multiple processes by which attitudes guide behaviour: The mode model as an integrative framework.' *Advances in Experimental Social Psychology, 23,* 75 - 109.

Feldberg, R. and Glenn, E. (1979). 'Male and female: Job versus gender models in the sociology of work.' *Social Problems, 26, 5,* 524 - 538.

Fine-Davis, M. (1983). *Women and Work in Ireland: A Social Psychological Perspective.* Dublin: Council for the Status of Women.

Hakim, C. (1991). 'Grateful slaves and self-made women: Fact and fantasy in women's work orientations.' *European Sociological Review, 7, 2,* 101 - 121.

Hunt, A. (1968). *A Survey of Women's Employment (Vols I and II).* London: HMSO.

Jowell, R. and Witherspoon, S. (1985). *British Social Attitudes: The 1985 Report.* Aldershot: Gower.

Kremer, J. and Curry, C. (1986). *Attitudes towards Women in Northern Ireland.* Belfast: Equal Opportunities Commission for Northern Ireland.

Kremer, J. and Curry, C. (1986). 'Attitudes towards women in Northern Ireland.' *Journal of Social Psychology, 127, 5,* 531 - 534.

McLaughlin, E. (1991). 'Introduction: A problem postponed.' In C. Davies and E. Mclaughlin (eds.), *Women, Employment and Social Policy in Northern Ireland: A Problem Postponed.* Belfast: Policy Research Institute.

McWilliams, M. (1991). 'Women's paid work and the sexual division of labour.' In C. Davies and E. Mclaughlin (eds.), *Women, Employment and Social Policy in Northern Ireland: A Problem Postponed.* Belfast: Policy Research Institute.

Martin, J. and Roberts, C. (1984). *Women and Employment: A Lifetime Perspective.* London: HMSO.

Montgomery, P. and Davies, C. (1991). 'A woman's place in Northern Ireland.' In P. Stringer and G. Robinson (eds.), *Social Attitudes in Northern Ireland: 1990/91 Edition.* Belfast: Blackstaff Press.

Parry, G. (1983). 'A British version of the Attitudes towards Women Scale (AWS-B).' *British Journal of Social Psychology, 22, 3,* 261 - 263.

Porter, L. W. and Lawler, E.E. (1968). *Mangerial Attitudes and Performance.* Homewood, Illinois: Dorsey Press.

Scott, J. and Duncombe, J. (1991). 'A cross-national comarison of gender-role attitudes: Is the working mother selfish?' *Working Papers of the ESRC Research Centre on Micro-social Change.* Paper 9. Colchester: University of Essex.

Spence, J.T. and Helmreich, R. (1972). 'The Attitudes towards Women Scale: An objective instrument to measure attitudes towards the rights and roles of women in contemporary society.' *JSAS Catalogue of Selected Documents in Psychology, 2, 66.*

Spence, J. T., Helmreich, R. and Stapp, J. (1973). 'A short version of the attitudes towards women scale (AWS)'. *Buttetin of the Psychonomic Society, 2,* 219-220.

Webb, M. (1989). 'Sex and gender in the labour market.' In I. Reid and E. Stratta (eds.), *Sex Differences in Britain: 2nd Edition.* London: Gower.

Witherspoon, S. (1985). 'Sex roles and gender issues.' In R. Jowell and S. Witherspoon (eds.). *British Social Attitudes: The 1985 Report.* Aldershot: Gower.

Witherspoon, S. (1988). 'Interim report: A woman's work.' In R. Jowell, S. Witherspoon and L. Brook (eds.). *British Social Attitudes: The 5th Report.* Aldershot: Gower.

Chapter 11

EQUAL OPPORTUNITIES

Sheila Rogers

The Way to Equality

Equality of opportunity is a term which immediately brings to mind concepts such as fair play and justice, with equal chances for all, unfettered by discriminatory criteria or prejudiced attitudes which limit rather than enhance, or which build barriers to progress instead of opening doors to opportunity. The primary aim of this chapter is to place a discussion of equality in the context of the WWLS findings. This will highlight some of the realities of women's working lives before going on to look at ways in which the cause of equality may be advanced through the implementation of equal opportunities programmes and the utilisation of positive action initiatives. As such the orientation of the chapter is very much towards the future; looking not only at what is true but what could and should be true of women's experience in the workplace.

Equality of Opportunity : The Legislative Framework

For working women in Northern Ireland the idea of equality was first translated into legislation with the passing of the Equal Pay Act (Northern Ireland) 1970. In Great Britain, the elimination of discrimination and the promotion of equality began to take on a formal meaning in 1974 with the publication of the Government's White Paper "Equality for Women" (Home Office, 1974). This policy document pointed out how wasteful a failure to provide equality of opportunity could be both for the individual, who does not develop her talents, and for the economy generally, when the abilities of the majority of the population are undervalued and under-utilised. The White Paper set the scene for the introduction, in 1975, of the Sex Discrimination Act in Great Britain, and in 1976 the Sex Discrimination (Northern Ireland) Order extended the legislation to Northern Ireland.

The Equal Opportunities Commission for Northern Ireland was established under the 1976 Order with a remit to eliminate discrimination, to generally promote equality of opportunity between the sexes and to keep under review the provisions of the Sex Discrimination (Northern Ireland) Order 1976 and the Equal Pay Act (Northern Ireland) 1970. The Commission, which is an independent statutory body, utilises a number of mechanisms and strategies to carry out these duties. Through enforcement of the legislation, the

Commission may assist individual women and men whose legal rights have been infringed. It undertakes research to inform its work and may conduct formal investigations into sectors or industries where discriminatory practices may be in operation. The Commission also has an important role to play in promoting equality of opportunity, by educating the public about their rights and obligations and encouraging employers and trade unions to implement equal opportunities programmes.

In the field of employment both the Equal Pay Act (Northern Ireland) 1970 and the Sex Discrimination (Northern Ireland) Order 1976 impose legal obligations on employers and provide protection for individuals - minimum standards which offer a safety net below which they should not fall. The Equal Pay Act (Northern Ireland) 1970 stated that women and men were to be paid the same when they did the same or broadly similar work. In 1984 the Act was amended to incorporate the concept of equal pay for work of equal value which meant that women and men should be paid the same if their work, even though completely different, was equal in value in terms of the demands upon them in areas such as decision making, skill or environmental conditions. In practice, however, the equal value amendment has had only a limited impact upon the differential rates of pay of women and men; the operation of the legislation is cumbersome, complicated and costly and six years after the 1984 amendment only two cases in Northern Ireland had been concluded (Maxwell, 1989; EOC(NI), 1991). It has been argued that radical changes, both administrative and legislative, are needed if the concept of equal pay for work of equal value is to become a reality (Equal Opportunities Commission for Northern Ireland, 1990).

The second piece of legislation, the Sex Discrimination (Northern Ireland) Order 1976, as amended by the 1988 Order, has resulted in somewhat more progress being made toward the elimination of discrimination between men and women. In the field of employment, the Order renders it unlawful to discriminate on grounds of sex or marital status directly or indirectly in the following ways :

- *in the arrangements made for determining job offers (selection and recruitment practices);*
- *in the terms on which a job is offered;*
- *by refusing (or deliberately omitting) to offer a person a job;*
- *in access to opportunities for promotion, transfer or training;*
- *in any other benefits, facilities or services provided to employees;*
- *in dismissals and any other unfavourable treatment to which employees may be subjected.*

The central theme of the Order - that there should not be less favourable treatment on grounds of sex or married status - has been utilised through litigation to extend the level of protection for working women. For example, in M -v- Crescent Garage (Case No 24/83SD) the Tribunal held that sexual harassment amounted to less favourable treatment on grounds of sex and was, therefore, unlawful (COIT, 1983). Likewise, in the more recent case of McQuade -v- Lobster Pot Restaurant (Case No 427/89SD), less favourable treatment on grounds of pregnancy was found to be direct discrimination (COIT, 1989).

Northern Ireland women may also claim rights under the Treaty of Rome and a number of European Community Directives on equal treatment. It is expected that the European arena will increasingly provide the forum for the extension of rights and protections in areas including maternity and pregnancy, rights for part-time workers and parental leave among others. It is now time for government to undertake a complete overhaul of domestic legislation with a view to producing a unified Code which would comply with both the spirit and the intent of European Community law.

Despite the existence of equality legislation, however, the Northern Ireland labour market remains deeply segregated, both horizontally and vertically, along gender lines (NIAAS, 1990). For example, even though women now represent 48% of the total number of employees in Northern Ireland the data on the sectoral and occupational employment patterns of women still presents a stark picture of gender segregation. Four out of every five women work in the services sector but only 18% in construction, manufacturing and agriculture/ energy (DED, 1988). The occupational data show just as clearly the segregated nature of women's work with two-thirds of all women employed in only three occupational areas, namely clerical and related, professionals in health and welfare and catering, cleaning, hairdressing and other personal services. Men, on the other hand, fill only eight percent of clerical and related jobs (DED, 1988).

Much of the work women do is characterised by low pay and low status. This is borne out by the fact that women's average gross hourly earnings remain at only 78.6% of men's (DED, 1989). It would indeed appear that little has changed since 1974 when the White Paper noted, "Most women do low grade jobs in a narrow range of industries and services for much lower rates of pay than unskilled men" (Home Office, 1974). It is somewhat disheartening to note that the pace of change since 1974 has been halting. The next sections look at some of the issues, at home and in the workplace, which may impact upon and influence the speed with which greater equality will be achieved. It will be argued that more than a legislative framework is required in order to hasten progress towards the goal of equality of opportunity. What is needed is a serious commitment on the part of employers and the implementation of policies and measures which take account of the reality of women's lives as unpaid carers at home and as paid members of the labour force.

Equality of Opportunity and the Reality of Women's Lives

The WWLS has once more shown how the tasks associated with running a house, and caring for children in a partnership household, continue to fall primarily to women (see Chapter 2 for further discussion). For example, despite the fact that the overwhelming majority of women (93%) felt that housework ought to be shared by partners, 71% of all women in the survey with a partner reported that they were responsible for all or most of the housework with partners sometimes or often helping with cooking, cleaning or shopping but seldom with the washing or ironing (Table 1).

Table 1: Frequency of partner carrying out selected household tasks

Frequency	Washing %	Ironing %	Cooking %	Cleaning %	Shopping %
Never	74	82	26	36	39
Sometimes	20	15	53	46	39
Often	6	3	21	18	22
Total %	100	100	100	100	100
N	668	668	668	668	668

Nor does the woman's responsibility diminish once there are children to care for. As Table 2 shows clearly, the arrival of children is not associated with a reduction in housework to free time for childcare activities. Indeed, the presence of children, who themselves will create additional housework, has very little influence on the division of labour within the home.

Table 2: Responsibility for housework by number of children

Housework	Children None %	1 %	2 %	3 %	All %
Woman does most/all	68	67	73	71	71
Shared equally	28	31	26	25	26
Man does most/all	4	2	1	4	3
Total %	100	100	100	100	100
N	53	94	204	317	668

A woman's traditional role as care-giver influences her ability to participate fully in the workforce. Thus, for example, of the 41 women who changed from full-time to part-time work, 78% did so wholly or partly because of childcare responsibilities, and 62% of all women with children felt that bringing up a family had influenced their availability for work. Much has been written about Northern Ireland's dismal record in the area of childcare provision where there are significantly fewer places in day nursery and nursery education than elsewhere in the United Kingdom (see Chapter 8 for further discussion). Figures for 1988 show that Northern Ireland had only 233 places in registered playgroups per 1,000 population for children aged three and four years compared to the United Kingdom average of 335 places (Cohen, 1990). It is clear that the issue of childcare is important in terms of equality of opportunity yet only 3% of the women stated that childcare was provided at their place of work and not one working woman's childcare needs were met through a nursery or créche run by her employer. In addition to childcare the ageing population may eventually have an effect on the participation rates in employment of care givers. This can already be seen from the survey in that, of 166 women who had caring responsibilities other than childcare, 20% felt that this has affected their working lives.

Equality of Opportunity: Women's Experiences in the Labour Market

The terms and conditions of employment under which a woman works can influence her ability to combine her domestic and work responsibilities. Provisions such as flexi-time or career breaks can offer alternatives to traditional working patterns. Paid maternity leave can facilitate a mother's return to work after her baby is born and the availability of a pension scheme offers some security for the future. The findings of the WWLS indicate, however, that many Northern Ireland women do not have access to these schemes or benefits (see Chapter 6).

Under a flexible hours scheme a woman can choose, within limits, her daily start and finish times, and she may be able to bank additional hours to take as paid leave. This can help when planning for childcare. However, only 20% of working women in the WWLS had the opportunity to work flexi-time, with the scheme being available to significantly more full-time than part-time workers. At the same time, of those working a fixed day, 42% indicated a preference for flexi-time arrangements.

The availability of a career break scheme may provide a welcome opportunity to those women who can afford time away from work for childcare or other purposes. According to a 1990 survey conducted by the Institute of Manpower Studies, of 2,259 employing organizations in Great Britain, only 4%

of respondents had a career break scheme in place (Institute of Manpower Studies, 1990). The situation in Northern Ireland would appear to be somewhat better as most major public sector and some private and voluntary sector employers have career break schemes. This is borne out by the WWLS which showed that 8% of women in work reported that they had access to such a scheme. However, while women in Northern Ireland seem to be better off in this regard, the percentage of working women with access to a career break scheme is still abysmally low.

In recent years the Equal Opportunities Commission for Northern Ireland has seen a significant increase in the number of complaints from individuals alleging discrimination on the grounds of pregnancy and maternity (Equal Opportunities Commission for Northern Ireland, 1991). Obviously the availability of paid maternity leave is an essential pre-requisite to enable women to co-ordinate the dual roles of mother and worker. In this regard the existing statutory scheme is inadequate as it provides for only nine-tenths pay for six weeks, followed by a flat rate of pay for twelve weeks and then only if a woman fulfills a number of criteria and has a specified period of continuous employment. Some larger employers have enhanced their maternity schemes beyond the statutory minimum but the survey evidence would seem to support the contention that more attention needs to be paid to this issue. Only 50% of women currently in employment received their full salary during maternity leave and 15% reported that they were not entitled to any leave at all (Table 3). The difference between full-time and part-time workers is particularly stark in this area with 29% of part-timers reporting that they do not get maternity leave. Also significant is the apparent lack of awareness among women about their entitlement, with 30% of part-timers and 21% of full-timers indicating that they did not know whether or not they would be eligible for maternity leave.

Table 3: Maternity leave by full-time and part-time employment status

	Employment status		
	Full-time	Part-time	All
Maternity leave	%	%	%
Unpaid	5	4	5
Part salary	34	22	30
Full salary	54	45	50
No leave	7	29	15
Total %	100	100	100
N	236	134	370

The retirement years can be greatly enhanced if worries about financial matters have been alleviated because a woman has been able to contribute to an occupational pension scheme during her working life (Groves, 1987). Occupational pension benefits can provide the additional funds which would help ensure a way out of the poverty trap which is a fact of life for so many older people. However, only 35% of working women in the WWLS stated that they belong to such a scheme.

In the context of an unequal division of labour on the home front and the impact of domestic responsibilities on women's working lives adequate, affordable childcare, maternity protections and flexible working arrangements, all influence the extent to which women will be able to participate fully in the labour market. Full participation also depends on women's access to training and promotion opportunities. Training is one way in which occupational or horizontal segregation can be broken down by encouraging women to consider non-traditional career options. Likewise, the opportunity to climb the promotion ladder offers the chance to tackle the effects of past practices which have resulted in vertical segregation.

The availability of appropriate and accessible training is an essential element in fitting individuals for promotion and, through assisting career development, training can contribute to the furtherance of equality of opportunity for women and men. To achieve this, however, employers need to take the issue of training seriously and make efforts to facilitate and encourage employees to progress within their organizations. Only by doing so can the barriers which have resulted in horizontal and vertical segregation within the labour market start to be removed.

With this in mind, it is somewhat discouraging to note that half of the working women in the WWLS reported that they received no formal job training whatsoever, with married women less likely to be trained than single women. Of the 246 women who had received training the most frequently mentioned was "On the job" training (40%) followed by training provided at work (26%). Part-time workers were less likely to receive training with 64% reporting they had no formal training as opposed to 40% of full-time workers. Of those who had received training 36% said the duration was less than one week. 89% of women who worked in a mixed gender environment and who had been given training stated that it was similar to the training received by their male colleagues. However, almost 8% felt that they had received either less or much less training than the men. Given that the Sex Discrimination (Northern Ireland) Order 1976 requires that there should be no discrimination in access to training opportunities it is encumbent upon employers to ensure that the principles of equality are being adhered to in practice.

Over a third of all working women (36%) felt that there were no further training opportunities for them at their place of work (Table 4) yet at the same time 60% of both married and single women stated that they would welcome further training.

Table 4: Would welcome further training by marital status

	Single	Married	All
Further training?	%	%	%
Yes	67	56	60
No	33	44	40
Total	100	100	100
N	*75*	*154*	*231*

Excluding those over fifty years of age who, not surprisingly, expressed less interest in further training, the desire for more training is consistent across all age bands. Interest in further training is most popular within the 31-40 age range and does not appear to dissipate once children are born, with 58% of women with between one and four children expressing an interest in more training.

Statistics show that even in areas of employment where women predominate they tend to be clustered in the lower graded posts and there is a significant under-representation of women in senior positions throughout industry, the public sector and professional organisations. Traditional attitudes and stereotyped views about the position of women at work, in particular that women do not want responsibility, can muddy the perceptions of senior managers whose responsibility it is to select candidates for promotion. Yet women themselves show a willingness to take on that added responsibility (Table 5). 91% of all women reported that they had never refused or deliberately avoided a promotion with only slightly fewer married than single women having done so.

Table 5: Refused/deliberately avoided promotion by marital status

	Single	Married	All
Refused promotion	%	%	%
Yes	8	9	9
No	92	91	91
Total	100	100	100
N	*193*	*659*	*852*

Of the 85 (9%) who reported having refused a promotion only 32 (38%) indicated "additional responsibility" as a reason. 29 (34%) liked their present job and 14 (16%) cited family commitments.

Only 32% of all women reported that they had ever been promoted at work and married women appear to be less likely than single women to receive promotion, with only 32% of married women stating that they had ever been promoted in their present job as opposed to 35% of single women.

The majority of women in work (64%) would welcome a promotion in their present job although married women were somewhat less keen to be promoted than their single colleagues (Table 6). However, amongst those with children, the evidence suggests that the number of children within the household is inversely related to enthusiasm for promotion (Table 7).

Table 6: Would welcome promotion in present job by marital status

Promotion?	Single %	Married %	All %
Yes	79	58	66
No	21	42	34
Total	100	100	100
N	72	134	206

Table 7: Would welcome promotion in present job by number of children

	Children					
Promotion?	None %	1 %	2 %	3 %	4+ %	All %
Yes	78	64	53	55	43	64
No	22	36	47	45	57	36
Total	100	100	100	100	100	100
N	87	39	45	29	23	223

There are many women who have never been promoted in their working lives yet at the same time the majority of women are willing to consider moving up the occupational ladder. This would seem to confirm the existence of the infamous "glass ceiling" for women, a ceiling which seemingly has less to do with a lack of personal ambition and more to do with stereotyping and structural constraints on women's careers. In addition, there is some evidence to suggest that a woman's marital status in itself may influence whether or not she is promoted, a matter which, of course, should not form part of any employer's promotion decisions.

Training, promotion, benefits and the role of women as care givers are all issues which need to be addressed positively by employers in order to lower barriers to women's progress. It is noteworthy that women themselves are quite clear in their belief that there should be equality of opportunity between the sexes (Table 8).

Table 8: Women should have equal opportunities in getting jobs and promotion

Agreement	%
Strongly agree	64
Agree	30
Neutral	2
Disagree	2
Strongly disagree	2
Total %	100
N	*998*

Progress towards the attainment of equality of opportunity requires a commitment not only towards the concept in theory but, most importantly, to the idea in practice. The means whereby this can be accomplished are discussed in the next section.

Equality of Opportunity : The Way Forward

At first blush the concept of equality seems straightforward. After all, are we not merely talking about everyone, men and women alike, having equal rights and being treated fairly? In reality, however, the road to equality is one which is made up of many intricate and complex routes, any one or all of which may impact upon an individual's ability to participate fully in economic life.

It is likely that the traditionally held belief that women workers are marginal and secondary to the labour market has influenced the progress made on equality issues. Indeed, the extent to which women's work is viewed as incidental to the labour market may be inversely proportional to the level of commitment to the achievement of equality of opportunity demonstrated by employers. Yet it is fair to say that unless all women and men have the opportunity to compete for the whole range of jobs and careers then the pool from which an employer can select will continue to be limited and the "best person for the job" or merit principle cannot operate. Equality is both an individual and a collective issue and employers must take care to ensure that, as far as possible, they remain sensitive to this when considering the approach to take to the provision of equality at work. For example, developing non-discriminatory recruitment practices will assist in ensuring a level of equal opportunity. However, even the most perfect system may not provide equity on an individual level because of personal circumstances, such as the lack of adequate childcare or the need for flexible working hours, which may impinge upon an individual's ability to take advantage of particular opportunities.

Employers need to develop a broadly-based approach which recognises both individual and collective concerns. It is not enough to take a minimalist view of equality for this will bring about little change. Simply complying with the law will not, in and of itself, bring about equality of opportunity. This can only be accomplished by creating an environment for change within an organization and developing and implementing a comprehensive programme of action.

The way in which jobs have been defined in the past may have led in some measure to the job segregation which exists today, in Northern Ireland as elsewhere. The idea of "men's work" and "women's work" has been based on beliefs about what is appropriate or acceptable for a man or woman to do, and indeed, what men and women are capable of doing. It is suggested that, because of past practice, such job segregation will continue unless steps are taken to counter traditional attitudes and stereotyping. These attitudes and assumptions have led to the erection of barriers to the full participation of men and women in all parts of the workforce and, as we have already seen, have reserved childcare, housework and associated duties for women.

The provision of equality of opportunity requires an employer to take a number of steps which, while important in and of themselves, together form an integrated equal opportunities programme.

Issuing a Policy Statement

The first step is the development of an equal opportunities policy statement which sets the scene within which the component parts of the provision of equality of opportunity will operate. It must take into account the particular circumstances of the employer and contain a firm commitment to the goal of equality for all. It must be supported from the top of the organization and communicated to all employees. It is a framework for the future and must be a dynamic and operational document if employees and potential employees are to take the commitment to equality seriously, and feel that, indeed, it is a goal toward which the employer is working and is one which has direct and very real meaning for them as individuals. Nothing will bring the concept of equality into disrepute quicker than a commitment in name only.

Analysis and Monitoring

The second step is monitoring and analysis. A monitoring system is an invaluable tool which an employer can use to plot the progress of equality within an organization. Initially it offers a snapshot view of where women and men are in terms of jobs, grades and various other criteria but, perhaps more importantly, it allows for a longitudinal view of change or the potential for change within an organization and presents the employer with the opportunity for, and the evidence on which to base, positive action initiatives which will help counter the effects of past discriminatory practices. Monitoring should not be seen as an intrusive exercise into personal details of individual employees and care must be taken to ensure that it is not perceived as such. Rather, it is an integral and essential component of any serious effort to bring about equality of opportunity.

Drawing up a Programme of Action

Armed with an analysis of the workforce an employer may then embark on the development of a programme of action which will start to redress identified imbalances and problem areas and challenge attitudes and stereotypes which may be contributing to the continuation of discriminatory practices and behaviour within the organization. This will require a review of practices and procedures and the implementation of a variety of positive action steps.

Positive/affirmative action can be defined as any lawful steps an employer may take to achieve greater equality of opportunity at work. The Sex Discrimination (Northern Ireland) Order 1976 contains a number of legislative permissions which allow for positive action initiatives in the field of training and the provision of special encouragement where there has been an under-representation of one or other sex in specific areas of employment. Thus, for example, an employer with no female managers could organise a single-sex training course for female employees to equip them with management skills; a local authority could sponsor a Public Service Vehicle (PSV) course for women which will give them the skills necessary to compete, on equal terms, with men for vacancies for which this qualification is required. Similarly, special encouragement by way of advertising can be used to attract applications from men or women for posts in which they have been under-represented in the past. Such initiatives, it should be pointed out, aim both to implement and complement the obligations placed upon employers by the sex discrimination and equal pay legislation. Positive action can encompass a myriad of measures which will help overcome the effects of discrimination past and present. It provides the employer with the opportunity to institute measures which will alter employment practices and patterns which may, in the past, have resulted in unequal treatment of men or women. Positive action is, therefore, a powerful tool with which to tackle structural barriers which impede the achievement of equality. It is not reverse discrimination. This implies the preferential treatment of men or women at one or more points of the employment relationship. Reverse discrimination can also embrace the situation where, for example, gender is viewed as a consideration when evaluating applicants for posts or indeed as the sole consideration through the establishment of quotas. All forms of reverse discrimination are unlawful in Northern Ireland.

The components of a positive action package taken together can constitute a programme of action which will enhance the opportunities open to employees or potential employees and offer to the employer the benefits which will derive from providing true equality of opportunity at work.

An equal opportunities perspective should lead employers to carefully examine the ways in which jobs are defined and characterised. What criteria are set? Are they relevant to the current duties of the post? Are traditional assumptions and attitudes creeping into the job descriptions or personal specifications? Are these likely to impact adversely on women or men? For example, whereas in the past, many jobs required a certain degree of physical strength is this still necessary and, if not, has the job description been rewritten to reflect the reality of the job today? Is the experience criteria, contained in many job descriptions, overstating what is actually required to do the job? If so, this may impact less favourably on female applicants many of whom may have taken time out of the labour market to raise a family. Similarly, the setting of age criterion may indirectly discriminate against women because of their absence from the paid workforce for periods of time. Are the qualifications stated those which are essential for the post in question? The tendency to define jobs on the basis of who has held the post in the past rather than what is essential to carry out the duties of the job today may result in the perpetuation of past practices which have led to gender segregation and have militated against the provision of equality of opportunity.

How an individual sets about finding work and how jobs are filled are areas which offer scope for positive action initiatives. The location of advertisements can influence the pool of applicants for a post and therefore any programme of action for equality must carefully assess advertising practices. Just as restricting press advertisements to one major Northern Ireland newspaper may result in a failure to reach either the Catholic or Protestant community, so too can the location and the content of advertisements effect whether or not men or women will respond in proportion to their numbers. Evidence shows that official unemployment figures tend to minimise the number of women who are out of work (Equal Opportunities Commission for Northern Ireland, 1990). This is particularly true of women, living with spouses, who are not entitled to receive Income Support once their Unemployment Benefit ends and who then disappear from the unemployment statistics unless they themselves register as unemployed (see Chapters 5 and 7 for further discussion). Employers and others striving to work toward equality of opportunity need to be aware of these realities and must be ready to take steps to counter them.

The Sex Discrimination (Northern Ireland) Order 1976 permits positive action advertising to encourage applications from the under-represented sex for a particular type of work. This offers employers the opportunity to raise awareness and challenge some of the underlying assumptions which may exist about the appropriateness of such work for the under-represented group. Traditional recruitment practices can serve only to perpetuate the existing profile of a workforce and employers who continue to use methods such as word-of-mouth recruitment and unsolicited applications may be operating not only contrary to the principles of equality of opportunity but may also be acting unlawfully.

The selection process is fraught with the potential for actions which are contrary to the interests of equality of opportunity (Kremer, 1991). From the design of the application form to the final interview this process must be carefully examined and regularly reviewed to erase any traces of discriminatory practices. Some employers now realise that it is inappropriate to include questions about children, marital status, spouse's occupation or the like on application forms; indeed such questions may constitute evidence of unlawful discrimination. Many employers, however, have not yet taken steps to rid their procedures of such questions. From the potential employee's perspective such enquiries into their private affairs can be seen as intrusive and irrelevant and they may question the intention of the inquirer to select in a non-discriminatory manner.

The shortlisting and interview stages can and do result in contraventions of the principles of equality of opportunity with women, in particular, being subjected to questioning about personal matters which are irrelevant to the duties of the post applied for. It is not only overt discriminatory behaviour which occurs but also less obvious and perhaps unintentional treatment which nevertheless results in unlawful actions and a failure to provide equality of opportunity to all.

A programme of action must also include a review of promotion practices to ensure that they are as free as possible of discriminatory elements. This must include training in non-discriminatory practices and procedures for managers and others charged with the responsibility for selection. Managers must also become sensitive to the ancillary issues which may influence whether or not women and men can take full advantage of opportunities for promotion, in particular domestic and other responsibilities. Likewise, in the area of training. As we have seen, women are demonstrating a willingness to receive further training, and in particular when training does not interfere with domestic commitments. Employers need to ensure that all employees have the opportunity to take advantage of the benefits which training can provide. The Sex Discrimination (Northern Ireland) Order 1976 permits employers to provide training for women and men where they have been under-represented in the workforce. Much more attention needs to be paid to these under-utilised opportunities to enhance and develop the skills of female workers.

In recent years the popularity of alternative working arrangements has grown. Initiatives such as job-sharing, career breaks, flexi-hours and part-time hours have each become more common and acceptable ways of working. Such schemes may help women workers to combine their domestic and work responsibilities, and as such have a place within a comprehensive equal opportunities programme. As with any initiative, however, care must be taken to ensure that the terms and conditions which attach to the scheme do not adversely impact upon either sex.

Job-share schemes may offer an attractive alternative to employees who do not want or are not able to work full-time (Walton, 1990). Such schemes, if properly designed, will protect employment rights and offer pro-rata holidays and other benefits. Times of work can usually be decided by the sharers themselves, thus providing even greater flexibility. Through job-sharing an employer can improve the quality and frequency of part-time work and facilitate progress towards the goal of equal opportunity. Career breaks can provide a welcome opportunity for employees to free time for the purposes of child-rearing, caring and the like. For the employer, too, a career break scheme can be beneficial since it can help to ensure that, rather than losing valued employees because of external commitments, those employees are likely to return to the workforce following their break. These schemes, however, constitute an extended unpaid leave period away from work and thus, in real terms, are not accessible to all women. In fact, as 79% of survey respondents who were in employment cited the need for money as a reason for working, for these women a career break may be impractical. Employers need also to look at their maternity provision, an integral part of any equal opportunities programme. They must ensure that their female employees are not treated less favourably on grounds of pregnancy - a major barrier to the achievement of equality of opportunity. The current statutory scheme is seriously flawed and employers are urged to review and enhance their maternity schemes.

The plight and the rights of part-time workers also require urgent attention. As has been mentioned previously these workers, who are primarily women, continue to receive significantly less favourable terms and conditions of employment than do their full-time colleagues. Quite apart from the potential for unlawful discrimination employers need to be encouraged to attach more value to the contribution made by their part-time employees.

Finally, employers must begin to set measurable targets and reasonable timetables for the achievement of equality. This is an essential element of a programme of action for it enables an employer to monitor the effectiveness of the measures which have been introduced to bring about change. Targets and timetables are not quotas and should not be seen as such. Rather they are akin to the types of mechanisms which many employers already have in operation in areas such as sales, or production levels. Targets and timetables facilitate long term planning and are integral to any serious attempt to achieve equality of opportunity for men and women in the workforce.

The working lives of women in Northern Ireland as elsewhere continue to be influenced and, indeed, to be hindered by the failure to provide equality of opportunity. It is now time for employers and employee representatives to take on board, in a serious way, the concept of equality and translate it into action. The result can surely only be an improvement in the day to day lives of employees, the facility to more easily combine work and family responsibilities and the development of individual potential - all of which will in the long run reap benefits for employee and employer alike.

References

Cohen, B. (1990). *Caring for Children: The 1990 Report.* Edinburgh: Family Policy Studies Centre.

COIT (Central Office of Industrial Tribunals and Fair Employment Tribunals) (1983). *M v Crescent Garage. Case No. 24/83SD.* Belfast: COIT.

COIT (Central Office of Industrial Tribunals and Fair Employment Tribunals) (1989). *McQuade v Lobster Pot. Case No. 427/89SD.* Belfast: COIT.

Commission of the European Communities (1988). *Equal Opportunities for Women and Men.* Brussels: CEC.

Department of Economic Development (1988). *Labour Force Survey.* Belfast: HMSO.

Department of Economic Development (1989). *New Earnings Survey.* Belfast: HMSO.

Equal Opportunities Commission for Northern Ireland (1990). *Comments on the Operation of the Equal Pay Act (NI) as Amended by the Equal Pay (Amendment) Regulations (NI) 1984 and Recommendations for Change.* Belfast: Equal Opportunities Commission for Northern Ireland.

Equal Opportunities Commission for Northern Ireland (1991). *Fifteenth Annual Report.* Belfast: Equal Opportunities Commission for Northern Ireland.

Groves, D. (1987). 'Occupational pension provision and women's poverty in old age.' In C. Glendinning and J. Millar (eds.), *Women and Poverty in Britain.* Brighton: Wheatsheaf Books.

Home Office (1974). *Equality for Women.* London: HMSO.

Kremer, J. (1991). *Recruiting and Selecting Fairly: A Summary Report.* Belfast: Fair Employment Agency.

Maxwell, P. (1991). 'Equal pay legislation: Problems and prospects.' In C. Davies and E. McLaughlin (eds.), *Women, Employment and Social Policy in Northern Ireland: A Problem Postponed.* Belfast: Policy Research Institute.

NIAAS (1990). *Northern Ireland Annual Abstract of Statistics.* Belfast: HMSO.

Walton, P. (1990). *Job Sharing. A Practical Guide.* London: Kogan Page.

Chapter 12

CONCLUSIONS

Pamela Montgomery and John Kremer

Introduction

The contributors to this volume have explored women's working lives, past and present, focusing on women's experience of both the labour market and the home. The chapters have highlighted the forces of change which have impacted on women's employment over recent decades and most especially the 1980s. In addition they have drawn attention to the complexity and diversity of women's working lives in the 1990s. Against this rapidly shifting scene, this concluding chapter aims to address some of the major policy issues which arise from the WWLS and to set out the measures which are necessary to ensure that women and men have the opportunity to be active and equal citizens in the 1990s and beyond.

The Fact and the Fiction of Women and Work

To focus exclusively on policy issues is to tell only part of the story. The climate against which policy may or may not be implemented and the belief systems which may influence behaviour and which serve to make traditional attitudes resistant to change are of equal concern. The first section of this chapter is therefore presented to consider, and to challenge, some of the common myths associated with women and work. To achieve this end it is sometimes necessary to move far beyond the data and into the realms of inference and speculation, an approach which stands in marked contrast to the following section or indeed the previous chapters This endeavour is nevertheless seen as useful and necessary in order to attempt to project into the coming decade and to begin to consider trends which may be in their infancy but which could have a considerable impact on women in years to come.

Bearing this in mind, it is still true that many of the most resistant and enduring beliefs about women are predicated upon the traditional stereotype of women as carers and homemakers. One of these beliefs is that women, and especially married women, are less committed to their paid employment and less concerned about their long term careers, promotion prospects, or training opportunities. The WWLS shows that in the 1990s there is little substance behind this supposition, either in terms of women's attitudes to work or in terms of women's actual behaviour. Rather, the survey has illustrated the dramatic changes in women's participation in employment over recent decades. For example (and notwithstanding earlier structural impediments to married women working, such as the marriage bar in certain professions), it is significant that before 1949, 26% of women left work on becoming married yet by the 1980s, this figure had fallen to 3% (Chapter 3). In addition, before 1949 fewer than a third of women (31%) changed jobs early in their careers to move to better positions yet by the 1980s the figure was closer to half (47%). These statistics are reinforced by those presented in Chapter 2 which demonstrate a sharp fall in the proportion of working women who have taken time away from work to raise a family.

Even in those instances where women's behaviour could be seen to conform more closely to traditional stereotypes, the precise reasons why they have made particular choices need to be examined closely. One example is women who decide to interrupt their careers to raise children. For some this decision may reflect upon personal beliefs about a woman's primary role as mother and childrearer, for others it may directly reflect their partner's wishes, and for others their choice may be a pragmatic response to a shortage or absence of publicly funded childcare services and, in turn, either therefore a general concern for their children's well-being or simply an inability to afford professional childcare (Chapter 8).

Above all else the survey also highlights the very real problems which working women must address in practically balancing the demands made by work and home (Chapter 2). Women have to deal with these conflicting demands continually but the routines and schedules which they employ should not be taken as support for an argument that women are therefore less committed to their work, or are somehow less ambitious than men (Chapter 10). To challenge this assumption necessitates a more accurate appraisal of the psychological processes of commitment and motivation. Whatever they may be, commitment and motivation are not finite substances which have to be apportioned competitively between conflicting demands. Instead, as complex information processors we have the ability to manage and accommodate a number of different priorities simultaneously, priorities which may or may not be of equal concern to us at a particular time.

Overall it would be fair to say that a lack of personal motivation or commitment to work does not constitute the major disincentive to women at work, instead structural impediments are of far greater significance. These structural obstacles must be removed before women are able to compete on equal terms in the labour market, and, for example, are able to take up training opportunities in sizable numbers. At the present time it is clear that, for very practical reasons, training holds far greater attraction for women when it takes place within normal working hours. At the same time, there is little evidence to suggest that current experience of education and training has done anything to break down traditional sex roles or the sexual division of labour (Chapter 4).

A perusal of popular magazines, both men's and women's, reveals the existence of a more modern myth which has grown over recent years, the idea of "new man", a man who rejects outmoded sexual divisions of labour both inside and outside the home and who thereby provides women with greater freedom of opportunity. The actual presence of new man in the lives of most women is not easy to discern. The message which comes through loud and clear from the WWLS is that in paid employment, many women continue to encounter sex discrimination (Chapter 11) and that within the home, the majority of married women remain largely responsible for unpaid caring and servicing work (Chapter 2). The number of households where chores were shared equally was depressingly small. Instead, the day-to-day work associated with household management and childcare remained predominantly women's work, and where men showed signs of making a greater contribution then it was chiefly in those areas which were less irksome, more sporadic and ultimately more enjoyable.

It would be misleading to disregard the limited evidence which suggests that some men are increasingly likely to make a greater contribution to unpaid work in the home but even this change may not be without its costs. On the one hand evidence of change is to be welcomed but simultaneously there then arises the possibility that by making inroads into women's areas of domestic responsibility and competence, men may come to believe that they have "mastered" (sic) these competencies and therefore they have an even greater right to dictate how the home is managed and how work is carried out in the home. There then arises the intriguing possibility that increasing men's perceived competency may in turn increase expectations and the pressure on women to be "good" wives and mothers. Therefore whilst traditional job segregation in the home placed an undue burden on women, it could be that change bears certain costs, either short-term or long-term.

Looking at women's involvement in the trade union movement (Chapter 6), it is a common misconception that women have been and therefore always will be less prominent in trade unions than men because of other commitments and demands on their time. This assertion was not borne out by the WWLS. Those women who chose to be involved as union officers were found to be not dissimilar from other women in terms of their family commitments but they were sufficiently motivated to shoulder the triple burden of work, domestic responsibilities and trade union activism. Trade unions are genuinely concerned about the underrepresentation of women in the trade union movement in general and considerable steps have been and are being taken to try to ameliorate the problem. To bolster this campaign, the WWLS demonstrates that there is no support for the traditional argument, perhaps stil advanced in certain quarters, that the current situation represents what must be and always will be; clearly efforts to facilitate women's activity in the trade union movement remain important and potentially rewarding.

It would be fair to say that the women's movement and equal opportunities campaigns have generally proceeded against a tide of male resistance. For example, an argument frequently heard from male employees in the course of equal opportunities training is that equal opportunities have already advanced too far and that, far from creating a level playing field, they have now placed men at a disadvantage at work. Chapter 11 on equal opportunities demonstrates that this argument is not tenable. Many employers have yet to abide by the letter of existing equal opportunities legislation, let alone the spirit of that legislation. Beyond this, the survey also shows that few organizations have adopted working practices and terms of employment which would increase women's opportunities and help them realise their true potential. For example, the number of employers which offer flexible working hours, full maternity rights, job sharing schemes or crèche/nursery facilities remains small (Chapter 5). If many men do feel threatened then, psychologically, this is understandable, if not acceptable, given the challenge to their long standing position of advantage which equal opportunities programmes present. However, for men to now argue that equality has been reached or that the playing field is even sloping in women's favour remains unsubstantiated.

An objective evaluation of current working practices reveals that far more remains to be done to ensure that women are able to realise their potential as paid workers, and this is especially true for women who are working part-time. Part-time or atypical work has a tendency to be seen as less significant and to be undervalued, and this process of undervaluation cuts in at least two directions. Men may see women's non-typical work as peripheral, and women may also come to underestimate their own contribution. For example, it may be significant that in terms of certain statutory entitlements, a part-time worker refers to someone employed for fewer than 16 hours per week. In reality only 13% of working women in the WWLS worked fewer than 16 hours and indeed many who were working more than 30 hours categorised themselves as working part-time when they should be classified as full-time workers, in terms of their statutory entitlements. Existing conditions of employment, and especially for those defining themselves as "part-timers", clearly do not meet statutory requirements (Chapter 5). Furthermore, women themselves appeared to be often unaware of their entitlement, many answering that they were not eligible for certain benefits because of their part-time status when in reality this was far from the truth (Chapter 5). To help dispel the myth of women's peripherality, and to help women enjoy the benefits and rights to which they are entitled by law, it is vital that this gap between perception and reality is closed.

A final point concerns the domestic political climate against which recent changes in the labour market have taken place. The 1980s represented the era of Thatcherism, a political ideology which history has shown to be bedevilled by many contradictions, not least between much-vaunted market forces and party dogma. Taking the case of working women, on the one hand Margaret Thatcher publicly continued to espouse traditional family values and women's domestic duties, yet her government was faced with the economic necessity of bringing women in increasing numbers into work. What happened to attitudes and stereotypes against this climate of contradiction? In truth there is no evidence of a turning back of the clock towards earlier values; indeed the liberalisation of attitudes towards women has continued apace throughout the decade (Chapter 10), perhaps demonstrating that in the battle of words between the party rhetoric of traditionalism and the reality of economic and market forces, the latter won the day.

The evidence and information is therefore readily available to challenge the fiction of women's working lives, and surveys such as the WWLS can play an important part in this process. Without access to comprehensive and dedicated surveys it is tempting to construct simple answers to complex questions and thereby paradoxically reinforce stereotypes and beliefs which have little bearing on reality. It is the responsibility of policy makers and researchers alike to certainly take cognisance of these stereotypes and belief systems, but then to use the facts and not the fiction of women's experience to formulate strategies which are able to address the concerns of these individuals. It is towards these strategies that we now turn.

Looking Forward: Women and Work in the 1990s

Numerically at least, women have come to occupy a far more prominent position in the labour market. Not only have more women joined the labour market in recent decades, the indications are that the pattern of women's employment is also undergoing change so that increasingly women are remaining in employment throughout the traditional childrearing years. Chapter 10 has also demonstrated the considerable shifts which have taken place in women's expectations and attitudes towards work. Where change is less in evidence is in relation to the relative position of men and women in employment. The WWLS shows clearly that 15 years on from the introduction of equality legislation, discrimination in employment is still evident and women continue to be disadvantaged in the labour market. Chapter 5 has shown that while the numbers of women in employment has increased, this increase can be attributed to the growth of part-time service sector jobs, jobs which are in the main characterised by poorer working conditions and contracts, low wages, low status and limited prospects. Overall, the labour market remains highly segregated by gender into "women's work" and "men's work". Women are concentrated in a highly limited range of jobs where they are found in the lower grades and in part-time work. For all of these reasons, women's earnings have remained substantially lower than those of men. Chapter 2 has shown that only 10% of women earn the same or more than their partner. Neither is dramatic change evident as regards the traditional division of labour in the home. Rather it is women who have overwhelming responsibility for the home and family regardless of their position in the labour market. Addressing women's continued disadvantage in the labour market and tackling the marginalisation of women's employment, will require a range of policy measures aimed at removing the structural barriers to women's participation in employment. These measures will need to tackle head on the implications of the continuing segregation in employment, and aim to integrate women more fully into the labour market.

In this regard, Chapter 11 has already noted that EC policy on equal opportunities has been a dynamic force for change in terms of women's rights across the EC. Article 119 of the Treaty of Rome requiring equal pay for women and men, and various equality directives, now numbering five, have created a platform of rights on equal treatment at Community level. Within the EC's Third Action Programme (OJC 142/1, 31.5.92), there is an explicit recognition that the success of any policy initiatives in the area of women's employment, is the enhancement of the rights and entitlements of women workers. However, the contributors to this book have highlighted the continuing inequalities and disadvantage which working women in the United Kingdom face in relation to, for example, maternity entitlements, pregnancy, as part-time workers and as workers in occupations and sectors which are low paid. To reiterate the conclusions in Chapter 11, what is now required is a complete overhaul of domestic legislation to produce a unified code which will comply with both the spirit and intent of EC law. This is clearly a matter for government and is a matter which must be addressed as an issue of immediate priority.

Also at the level of government, policy measures are required to facilitate the entry of women into employment and to remove barriers to participation. In this regard, Chapter 4 has highlighted the urgent need for a review of training policy and provision for women. While government has at last publicly recognised the under-utilisation of women's potential and their specific training needs, the shortfall between women's qualifications, their training needs and the needs of industry are still remarkable. Chapter 4 has highlighted that, at a time when women returners are being targeted by government as making up a shortfall in the labour market created by the falling numbers of young people available to enter employment in the 1990s, a high proportion of the pool of potential women returners are likely to have no formal qualifications. Further, women are under-represented in government training schemes. If women are to find their way into the labour market after a career break and once having done so are not to be confined to the low paid, low status jobs which have traditionally been the lot of women returners, then it is essential that education and training policy address this disadvantage positively. What are required are a range of education and training initiatives aimed specifically at women which are structured to meet women's training needs and which provide opportunities for non-traditional training.

As regards women in employment, there is also a clear role for employers to comply with the spirit and intent of equality legislation. In this regard employers have a key role in facilitating women's entry into employment, by breaking down the unhelpful occupational and horizontal segregation which characterises the labour market. Chapter 11 has highlighted the benefits for employers of tackling the issue of equality of opportunity comprehensively through, for example, implementing an equal opportunities programme. This will ensure that employers select the right person for the job and having done so, develop their talents and abilities to ensure that these are not undervalued or under-utilised.

Chapter 6 has shown that, in addition to a role for employers as regard women's employment, there is also a role for trade unions in integrating women more fully into the labour market, removing the structural barriers to women's employment, tackling the implications of the continuing segregation of the labour market and enhancing the rights and entitlements of women workers. Progress in all of these areas is ongoing and Chapter 6 highlights the range of material benefits currently associated with women's trade union membership. The chapter 6 illustrates, however, that as regards the integration of women into trade unions, much remains to be done. Further, the finding that over 40% of women in the WWLS worked in non-unionised enterprises and as such did not enjoy trade union protection points to the need for trade unions to step up work in this area.

A key aspect of any equal opportunities programme is the development of policies and practices which take account of women's and men's domestic responsibilities. In this regard, there is an urgent necessity for policy initiatives aimed at helping parents, both women and men, to combine the demands of home and work. Government has a central role to play in any policy initiative, in that progress will require the development of a coherent childcare policy and as Chapter 8 has highlighted, the provision of a range of childcare services sufficient to meet the needs of all parents, including working parents. While throughout the EC as a whole demands for childcare exceed existing supply, the UK has one of the lowest levels of publicly funded childcare services for children of all ages. Further, within the UK Northern Ireland is the most disadvantaged region in relation to childcare services. The impact of the scarcity of affordable childcare provision is illustrated in Chapter 8 by the complexity of the childcare arrangements many mothers are required to negotiate in order to ensure that they can remain in paid work. In addition to the stress this creates for mothers, this chapter also draws attention to the impact which such arrangements may have on children's development.

The need for measures to be developed to enable women and men to reconcile their occupational and family obligations is a central principle of the EC's third action programme on equal opportunities for men and women, exemplified in March 1992 when the European Council adopted a recommendation on childcare proposed by the Commission (OJ L 123/16, 8.5.92). The recommendation requires the provision of childcare services for parents who are either employed, in education or in training. In addition to the provision of childcare services, it also recommended that special leave should be provided for working parents with responsibility for the care and upbringing of children, that initiatives should be undertaken to create an environment, structure and organization of work which should take into account the needs of working parents, and that action should be taken by Member States to promote and encourage increased participation by men in childcare. Again, it is incumbent on the government to take forward Council commitments under this recommendation.

In addition to action by government, Chapters 5 and 11 indicate that action by employers is also required. Both chapters have drawn attention to the low incidence of measures which could facilitate men's and women's ability to combine domestic and work responsibilities and measures which, if available to men, could facilitate their greater involvement in childcare.

A number of contributors have drawn attention to the way in which the marginalisation of women's employment is reflected and is reinforced by the manner in which women's economic activity is recorded in official employment statistics (see Chapters 3, 5 and 7). These chapters have shown that classification systems developed to take account of the world of men's work, have at best marginalised female employment and at worst, as in the case of female unemployment, have excluded a large number of women entirely. Chapter 7 has highlighted how rather than improving over recent years, this problem has become worse due to increased stringency for the criteria for determining eligibility for unemployment benefit. As part of the process of making women's work visible and of integrating women into the labour market, there is an urgent need for a thorough review of how government statistical information is collected and compiled, a process which reflects women's as well as men's economic activity. The need to take action in this area is highlighted by Chapter 7 which shows that as they are currently collected, unemployment statistics are completely inadequate for assessing the full extent of women's unemployment. By severely underestimating the true extent of women's unemployment, concern about unemployment continues to be directed towards men. This chapter highlights the need for policy measures directed specifically at women's unemployment and non-employment.

Women's poverty and the need for policy measures and reforms targeted at alleviating poverty is touched on by a number of the contributors to this book. Chapters 2 and 7 have highlighted the interaction between male and female unemployment and the resulting division in society between those households in which both partners are working and those households in which neither partner is in employment. Chapter 7 has highlighted that in the latter type of family, women carry the burden of family poverty. Both chapters have drawn attention to the need for policy measures to address the causes of this interaction between male and female unemployment and point to the ways in which men, women and children are locked into poverty by a social security system which treats households rather than individuals as the relevant income units. This continues to be the case despite the fact that the norm of the male breadwinner which underpins this policy provision is no longer a reality for the majority of households.

What is now required is a broad review of the social security system to produce an individualisation of benefits which takes account of the reality of family life today. Without such changes, Chapter 7's bleak conclusion, that the management of men's, women's and children's poverty will be the fate of the majority of women for the foreseeable future, seems inevitable.

Women's management of poverty is also significant in relation to those providing informal care who are likely to have reduced standards of living because they provide this care. As Chapter 9 has noted, the impact of this responsibility on the quality of life of both those caring and those cared are issues which community care policies have not yet addressed. Policies which address the needs of carers, and in particular women with caring responsibilities whose employment prospects are more likely to be affected than those of men, are clearly now overdue.

Chapters 5 and 11 have drawn attention to the poverty trap which is the lot of older women whose interrupted career histories may leave many without adequate national insurance payments to ensure pension entitlement in their old age. Indeed, for the majority of working women in the WWLS, long term financial security may not be guaranteed given that two thirds did not have access to an occupational pension scheme. Recent policy developments in the area of pensions indicate that the government's general strategy is to limit state provision in order to provide room for company and personal pension schemes. The WWLS has indicated the way in which company and personal pension schemes may be of limited value to women, the majority of whom have poorer employment opportunities than men and by virtue of their interrupted career histories, are less likely to build up adequate entitlements for their old age. In this regard, the Equal Opportunities Commission in Great Britain have concluded that the basic state pension, with its built in provision for Home Responsibilities Protection, suits women's life patterns best (EOC, 1992). In this regard, the current debate concerning state pension ages needs to take account of these findings and equalise both sexes pension ages in a way that does not further disadvantage women.

Taken together these chapters have produced a wealth of information. These data seem all the more timely as we move through the 1990s, a decade which seems set, nationally at least, to be the decade of citizenship. If the concept of citizenship is to have meaning to women and is to make a genuine impact then it must be broad enough to encompass the day-to-day reality of women's lives. It will need to address the marginalisation of women's participation and involvement. It will also need to address inequality in the social, political and economic spheres.

That women's working lives have changed markedly over recent decades is not in question. What is now required is the development of a range of policies which take account of women's lives as they are lived in the 1990s. In this regard there is a clear role for government, working with and through employers and trade unions, in order to mould the 1990s into the decade of citizenship, for women and men alike.

Reference

Equal Opportunities Commission (1992). *A Question of Fairness: Response to the Department of Social Security's Discussion Paper, 'Options For Equality in State Pension Age'*. Manchester: Equal Opportunities Commission.

Appendix 1
TECHNICAL REPORT
Peter Ward and Donal McDade

Introduction

The WWLS was commissioned by the Equal Opportunities Commission for Northern Ireland in June 1990. The survey was designed and implemented jointly by John Kremer of the School of Psychology, the Queen's University of Belfast, and Research and Evaluation Services (RES), a specialist commercial research agency based in Belfast. John Kremer had primary responsibility for the conceptual design of the survey instrument and the layout/format of the interview schedule; RES for the implementation of the field work, technical/ statistical assistance with the design of the questionnaire, and all aspects of data preparation and processing. The validated data set was made available to the Equal Opportunities Commission for Northern Ireland in May 1991.

Questionnaire Design

The questionnaire (see Appendix 2) was developed with reference to a number of existing sources, the most significant being the Women and Employment Survey (WES) by Martin and Roberts (1984a). The technical report accompanying the WES (Martin and Roberts, 1984b) was also found to be useful in the earlier design stages, initially when beginning to think of how to draw together a framework for the questionnaire as a whole and later in the inclusion of specific questions which could form the basis for comparison.

The two primary constraints governing the design of the questionnaire were the time which would be necessary to complete the interview and the number of variables which would be eventually generated. With regard to the former, given that respondents received no concrete reward for their cooperation, it was felt that the interview should not normally extend far beyond an hour. Whilst the routing questions which were included throughout the interview schedule were able to take most respondents through the questionnaire more quickly, an absolute upper time limit of one and a half hours was established, based on the minority of women who were required to complete the schedule in its entirety.

In terms of the data set, to ensure that the findings would be readily available to interested parties in the future, the total number of variables was not permitted to exceed 500, this being the number which can be accommodated within the PC version of SPSSx. (Given the file space taken up by Section C it was decided to store these data in a separate file, together with a number of significant main variables from other sections to facilitate later analysis.)

In order to encompass all relevant information in a systematic way, and to facilitate routing during the interview, the questionnaire was divided into the following 10 sections.

Section A   General Information
Section B   Education
Section C   Previous Work History
Section D   Experiences of Work
Section E   Current Employment Status
Section F   Trade Union Involvement
Section G   Attitudes to Women and Work
Section H   Home
Section J   Childcare
Section K   Other Dependent Relatives

In terms of this book, sections and chapters generally correspond in the following way.

Chapter	Authors	Main Section(s)
1. Introduction	John Kremer and Pamela Montgomery	
2. Paid and Unpaid Work	Pamela Montgomery	H
3. Work Histories	Janet Trewsdale and Ann Toman	C
4. Education and Training	Carol Curry	B
5. Employment	Janet Trewsdale and Ann Toman	E
6. Trade Union Involvement	Robert Miller and Donal McDade	F
7. Unemployment	Eithne McLaughlin	E; H
8. Childcare	Irené Turner	J
9. Informal Care	Eithne McLaughlin	K
10. Attitudes and Motivations	John Kremer	D; E; G
11. Equal Opportunities	Sheila Rogers	D; E

Questions were included throughout the interview which were directed at gathering both biographical information on respondents' current and past circumstances, and also their attitudes, motivations and priorities. With regard to the latter questions, a number of possible formats were available but it was eventually decided that in the majority of cases, providing an extensive list of alternatives (usually on show cards) and asking women to indicate which items they felt were important, relevant or applicable to themselves would minimise response bias and cueing. In addition to a range of these "List all that apply" questions, and those derived directly or obliquely from previous surveys, items from both Cross's Worker Opinion Scale (Cross, 1973) and an anglicised version of Spence and Helmreich's (1973) Attitudes towards Women Scale were included to measure dimensions of job satisfaction and attitudes to women at work respectively.

The design of Section C, dealing with work histories, presented considerable logistical problems. On the one hand the section was important for yielding key information on women's working lives since leaving school; on the other hand the section could not be too cumbersome, time consuming or place too many demands on women's memories, stretching back perhaps fifty years. The section was eventually designed to capture all periods of employment and non-employment since leaving school, including movement from full-time to part-time employment, promotions/demotions, and reasons for changing employment status. During piloting, two versions of Section C were tested, one relying upon a detailed and highly structured format, the other comprising a series of open-ended questions. Following discussion with interviewers after the pilot survey, a final format was developed which incorporated the most useful dimensions of both approaches, namely a semi-structured approach but including prompt items (see Appendix 2).

Pilot Survey

A pilot survey was conducted during July and August 1990. The pilot had two principal objectives. Firstly to test the questionnaire in relation to timing, content, layout and interviewee acceptability and secondly, to test the validity of the chosen sampling framework. Interviews were carried out by four experienced female interviewers. After conducting the pilot interviews, the four interviewers met with the research team for a debriefing session during which the questionnaire was reviewed item by item. Interviews in the pilot study were carried out in nine wards covering four Local Government Districts (LGDs), namely Down, Derry, Larne and Belfast. These were chosen from amongst the 110 wards arising from the sample selection process to provide a mixture of urban and rural settings. A provisional target of 50 interviews was set for the pilot survey. 45 interviews were achieved by an agreed date and these were deemed to be sufficient for feedback purposes. Given that subsequent changes to the questionnaire were not substantive, the 45 interviews from the pilot survey were adapted to conform with the format of the final questionnaire and included as part of the main survey data.

The pilot indicated that firstly, only minor modifications to the structure and presentation of the questionnaire were necessary; secondly, that interviewee interest in the survey was generally high, that reaction was positive and that cooperation was good; thirdly, that the length of the interview was found to be acceptable; fourthly, that introductory letters sent to potential respondents were helpful in eliciting cooperation; and finally, that there were no problems as regards the sampling procedure.

Fieldwork

The overwhelming majority of interviews (over 90%) were carried out during October, November and December 1990, with the remainder taking place during January 1991. The interviewing was carried out by 46 experienced female interviewers employed by Research and Evaluation Services. Before interviewing, all fieldworkers were required to attend a half day briefing session. This dealt in detail with the content of the questionnaire and also included extensive coverage of its administration.

Individuals named in the sample were sought at their home address as listed and in all cases interviews were conducted in the respondent's home. Where individuals could not be contacted initially, three follow up calls were made (one of which had to be at a weekend), before the person was deemed unobtainable. If the first call at an address generated information that the named respondent was not likely to be contactable during the period of the fieldwork then no further calls were made. The average length of time taken for the interview was found to be approximately 75 minutes.

An individually signed letter was sent to each woman in the sample shortly before the interviewers intended to call. The letter explained why the survey was being carried out, the topics which would be covered in the interview and the importance of the survey yielding a valid cross-section of women respondents across Northern Ireland. Interviewers also presented a copy of the letter to those respondents who did not recall having received one originally. The letter was felt by interviewers to have been useful in securing co-operation with the survey.

Sampling Frame

The survey was designed to yield a representative sample of women aged between 18 and 65, living in private households in Northern Ireland. (The ˀsent retirement age for women of 60 years in the United Kingdom was ˥ed to 65 years in the WWLS, in the light of the ongoing debate as to ˥t ages for men and women across the European Community.) ˅ling frame for the survey was the 1990 Register of Electors, ˀ most complete listing of the adult population available. The register, which was published in February 1990, is inclusive of all individuals nominated on Electoral Registration Forms returned in September 1989. The Electoral Register is held at the office of the Chief Electoral Officer for Northern Ireland and is available to the public for purchase in whole or in part. The register is compiled on a Local Government District (LGD) basis, of which there are 26 in Northern Ireland, with individual registers at ward level. Wards correspond to small localised areas within a district and both the number of wards per district and the number of electors within a ward are variable. There are a total of 526 electoral wards in Northern Ireland. Since registration as an elector is now compulsory, there is reason to believe that the listing is comprehensive, especially as the register is updated annually.

One drawback of using this electorally based sampling frame was the inability to identify and eliminate from the sampling process those women who were above the age limit for the study. Women of all ages were therefore included in the sample selection process and those over 65 years of age were eliminated at the point of interview by means of a screening question relating to date of birth.

Sampling Design

Technically, the best procedure for sample selection when using the Northern Ireland electoral register is to amalgamate the registers for all 26 LGDs and to draw the required number of names on the basis of a purely random sample. However, for practical and financial reasons, surveys usually proceed on the basis of an adaptation of the pure random sampling procedure. The sampling method adopted for this survey was a two stage proportionate random sample. The rationale governing this choice of design was to ensure coverage of all 26 districts with proportionate representation of all districts and of selected wards within districts. Whilst both the number of wards per district and the number of electors per ward varied widely, Belfast was unique with more than three times more electors than the next largest district (214,158 compared to 67,825). Belfast also contained 51 wards compared with the district with the next highest number of wards, 30. For these reasons it was decided to select 10 wards to represent Belfast LGD whilst for the other 25 LGDs only four wards were chosen to represent each.

In stage one of the sampling process the required number of wards was selected at random from each district using tables of random numbers. In stage two, listings for the 110 individual wards identified from the stage one process were acquired from the electoral office. From each ward, a number of electors was drawn, the number being determined by the population of the ward in relation to the total number of electors included on all Northern Ireland registers. As the registers contain both males and females, and, as there is no gender breakdown provided, the sample design was based on the assumption that there were no significant gender imbalances within individual ward registers.

In selecting the names and addresses of potential respondents from each ward, a table of random numbers was again used to ensure each name listed had an exactly equal chance of selection. All numbers occuring during this process which corresponded to male electors were ignored, with males and females being identified on the basis of forename(s).

The survey aimed to achieve 1000 effective interviews. Taking into consideration estimates of the percentage of the sample which would be ineligible due to their age and the percentage loss found generally in surveys due to a variety of reasons, a wastage rate of at least one third was considered likely. To account for this, 50% more names were drawn from each ward than was the required number of interviews. To minimise the scope for "sampling within the sample" by interviewers at ward level, additional names were only provided to interviewers in small lots when their original ward list had failed to produce the required number of interviews. In the final analysis, 1684 names were issued to achieve 1000 interviews. Table 1 shows the number of interviews required from each LGD, on the basis of proportion, and compares this figure with achieved results.

Table 1: Required and achieved sample by LGD

Local Government District	Required No. of Respondents per Thousand	No of Responses Achieved	% Achieved %
Derry	54	54	100
Limavady	16	17	106
Coleraine	32	33	103
Ballymoney	15	16	107
Moyle	9	10	111
Larne	20	19	95
Ballymena	37	38	102
Magherafelt	22	21	95
Cookstown	19	17	89
Strabane	22	23	105
Omagh	27	28	104
Fermanagh	34	35	103
Dungannon	28	29	104
Craigavon	47	46	98
Armagh	31	34	110
Newry and Mourne	51	52	102
Banbridge	22	22	100
Down	35	36	103
Lisburn	60	57	95
Antrim	26	27	104
Newtownabbey	48	45	94
Carrickfergus	21	21	100
North Down	47	48	102
Ards	42	43	102
Castlereagh	42	43	102
Belfast	189	186	98
N	996*	1000	100*

*Subject to rounding

Table 2 shows the reasons for non-achievement of interviews with named individuals drawn in the sample. Excluding those who were not potential interviewees (i.e. those over 65 years moved address or deceased), 1242 names and addresses were issued to obtain 1000 interviews, yielding an effective response rate of 80.5%.

Table 2:   Breakdown of unused cases

	N	%
Over 65 years	331	48
Refused	124	18
Deceased	16	2
Sick	20	3
Moved address	95	14
Non-contact	98	14
Total	684	100

Sampling Errors

As a sample uses only part of a population to estimate certain attributes of that population there arises the problems of sampling and non-sampling error. Using a probability based sample design allows the calculation of sampling errors i.e. the actual error between the values of the sample estimates and the true population values. For a pure simple random sample design the sampling error of any percentage can be calculated from the formula:

$$\text{s.e. (p)} = \sqrt{\frac{p\,(100 - q)}{n}}$$

As the sample design used in the WWLS uses a cluster of wards then it would require the calculation of complex standard errors taking into account the spread of percentage estimates between wards. If a design effect were to be calculated it would be greater than one indicating that the design used is less efficient than that of a simple random sample design. However, given the design used in the WWLS it is unlikely that the confidence intervals for levels of the key variables would differ significantly from those based on a simple random sample. As such standard errors and confidence intervals have been calculated assuming a simple random sample design.

The sampling error is used to calculate the confidence interval of any proportion in the survey by using the formula:

$$\text{95\% confidence interval} = p + 1.96 \times \text{s.e. (p)}$$

Thus if 20 random independent samples were drawn from the same population 19 of them would expect to yield an estimate for the proportion, p, within this confidence interval.   Thus using the simple random sample would indicate error of ± 3% for the survey.   Table 3 shows the standard errors and confidence intervals for different levels of the key variables in the WWLS.

Table 3: Calculation of standard errors and confidence intervals for key variables in the WWLS

Age	%(p)	Standard Error of p (%)	95% Confidence Interval
18-20	6	0.8	4.6 - 7.6
21-30	25	1.4	22.3 - 27.7
31-40	22	1.3	19.4 - 24.6
41-50	23	1.3	20.5 - 25.5
51-60	17	1.2	14.6 - 19.4
61-65	7	0.8	5.4 - 8.6
Marital status			
Married	7	1.5	64.1 - 69.9
Single	22	1.3	19.5 - 24.5
Widow/Div./Separated	11	1.0	10.0 - 12.0
Religion*			
Roman Catholic	39	1.5	36.1 - 41.9
Protestant	57	1.3	54.5 - 59.5
Other	4	1.0	3.0 - 5.0
Economic activity			
Working full-time	33	1.5	30.1 - 35.9
Working part-time	21	1.3	18.5 - 23.5
Unemployed	5	0.7	3.6 - 6.4
Inactive	42	1.6	38.9 - 45.1

*Base for religion variable is 996. Base for all other variables is 1000.

Representativeness of the WWLS

In undertaking any survey it is important to assess the level of non-response bias. Non-response bias arises if the characteristics of the non-responders differ significantly from the respondents in the sample. To facilitate an evaluation of the representativeness of the WWLS sample, five of the key variables have been compared against similar variables used in the Northern Ireland Continuous Household Survey (CHS). Although the 1990 WWLS used a sample size of 1000 and the 1990/91 CHS used a sample of approximately 5000, question structuring and question coding are broadly comparable. Table 4 shows the distributions across each of the variables of age, religion, economic activity, marital status and socio-economic status for the WWLS and the CHS.

Table 4: Comparison of the WWLS with the 1990/91 Continuous Household Survey

Age	WWLS	CHS	% difference
18-20	6	6	(0)
21-30	25	25	(0)
31-40	22	24	(2)
41-50	23	20	(3)
51-60	17	17	(0)
61-65	7	8	(1)
Marital status			
Married	67	67	(0)
Single	22	21	(1)
Widow/Div./Separated	11	11	(0)
Economic activity			
Working full-time	33	34	(1)
Working part-time	21	20	(1)
Unemployed	5	4	(1)
Inactive	42	42	(0)
Religion			
Roman Catholic	39	37	(2)
Protestant	57	59	(2)
Other	4	4	(0)

Total % = 100% for all variables.

The table above shows that the sample estimates for each of the five variables are similar across both surveys. All of the percentage differences between levels of the five variables are within the range of sampling error. Although the WWLS sample exhibits a slightly lower proportion of respondents in the 31-40 age group this percentage difference is still within the 95% confidence interval of $\pm$ 3%.

In terms of religious denomination 2% more respondents in the WWLS sample recorded their religious affliation as Roman Catholic and 2% fewer recorded their religion as Protestant. A comparison of the economic activity variable showed no significant differences across any of the levels although the table shows a 1% difference in the proportions working full-time, part-time and unemployed. Again these differences are well within the sampling error for the survey.

Coding and Data Preparation

Close collaboration at the design stage ensured that the questionnaire was structured so as to permit up to 80% direct coding by the interviewer, thus maximising accuracy by eliminating transcription errors. Codes derived from recognised sources (including occupational and industrial classification) and those derived from an amalgamation of multiple response items were coded in-house by experienced coding staff.

After keying data into the computer through the SPSS PC+ package, standard validation procedures were applied to the crude data file. During the validation process both intra and inter variable checks were applied to ensure a valid data file for subsequent analysis. It is estimated that between 300 and 400 hours were subsequently spent in validation.

Analysis Variables

Coded Variables

A number of variables were accessible directly from the questionnaire. These are indicated below, together with the normal disaggregation used for compiling tables (if these differ from the original categories as shown in the questionnaire).

Age (<20 -; 21 - 30; 31 - 40; 41 - 50; 51 - 60; 61+) (q. A3)

Religion (Catholic; non-Catholic) (q. A8)

Marital Status (single; married/co-habiting; divorced/separated; widowed) (q.A4)

Number of Children (q.A7)

Educational Qualifications (none; GCSE or equivalent; GCE 'A' level or equivalent; higher [including vocational, professional or academic]) (qs.B4; B12; B18)

Age of Youngest Child (0 - 2; 3 - 4; 5 - 10; 11 - 15; 16 - 18) (q.A7)

Employment Status (full-time work; part-time work; YTP; full-time education; unemployed [available for work]; unemployed [not available for work]; retired; others) (q.E1)

Gross Personal Income (q.E35)

Net Personal Income (q.E36)

Net Partner's Income (q.H14)

Net Household Income (q.H17)

Housing Tenure (q.A1)

School Type (q.B1)

Derived Variables

Economic Activity: For the purposes of the WWLS, economically active included women who were:

> *In full-time work*
> *In part-time work*
> *Waiting to take up work*
> *On YTP*
> *Registered as unemployed.*

Economically inactive women were classified as

> *Unregistered unemployed*
> *In full-time education*
> *Temporarily unavailable for work (e.g. sickness)*
> *Permanently unavailable for work (e.g. retirement, sickness)*
> *Looking after children*
> *Looking after other relatives*
>
> *Looking after the home.*

It must be noted that of those 14 women who indicated that they were temporarily unavailable for work (due to illness) none had either a current job title nor current job. As such it was safe to conclude that these women were economically inactive.

Weighted Household Size: In order to take into account the differential impact on income of members of the household, by age, a modified version of the McClements scale was used. Such scales have been employed to consider income in surveys including the Family Expenditure Survey, with the weightings as shown:

Married couple	1.64
Non-married respondent	1.00
Adult non-respondent	0.69
Child, 16 - 18	0.59
Child, 11 - 15	0.44
Child, 5 - 10	0.38
Child, 3 - 4	0.29
Child, 0 - 2	0.15

Occupational Class: All occupational information generated through this survey was coded on the basis of the Office of Population Censuses and Surveys (OPCS) Classification of Occupations, 1980.

Industry: Sectorial information relating to occupations was coded on the basis of Central Statistics Office (CSO) Standard Industrial Classification (SIC revised, 1980).

Tabulations

1. Figures included in the tables are derived from the WWLS unless otherwise indicated.

2. Figures are normally presented as percentages, with columns normally totalling 100%.

3. Percentages equal to or greater than 0.5 have been rounded up (e.g. 56.5% = 57%).

4. A dash (-) is used to signify zero.

5. In certain tables, N values do not correspond to 1000 as invalid responses and "Don't knows" have been excluded.

6. "All" columns refer to sum of rows included in that table and not the entire sample. By way of example, in relation to sharing of childcare Table 12 in Chapter 2 refers to all married and cohabiting women between the ages of 21 and 59 (N = 537), whereas Table 1 in Chapter 8 refers to particular categories of women by employment status (N = 387) and Table 17 in Chapter 7 refers to all women with children (N = 593).

6. Where column N < 20, raw data is presented rather than percentages for that column.

References

Cross, D. (1973). 'The Worker Opinion Survey: A measure of shop-floor satisfaction.' *Occupational Psychology, 47,* 193 - 208.

Martin, J. and Roberts, C. (1984a). *Women and Employment: A Lifetime Perspective.* London: HMSO.

Martin, J. and Roberts, C. (1984b). *Women and Employment: Technical Report.* London: HMSO.

Spence, J.T. and Helmreich, R. (1972). 'The Attitudes towards Women Scale: An objective instrument to measure attitudes towards the rights and roles of women in contemporary society.' *JSAS Catalogue of Selected Documents in Psychology, 2, 66.*

Appendix 2

THE INTERVIEW SCHEDULE

WOMEN AND EMPLOYMENT

in

NORTHERN IRELAND

1990

A Survey of Women's Experiences & Attitudes

prepared for the Equal Opportunities Commission for Northern Ireland

by

John Kremer

School of Psychology, The Queen's University of Belfast

&

Research & Evaluation Services
391 Lisburn Road, Belfast

WOMEN AND EMPLOYMENT

in

NORTHERN IRELAND

1990

SECTIONS

A – General Information

B – Education

C – Previous Work History

D – Experiences of Work

E – Current Employment Status

F – Trade Union Involvement

G – Attitudes to Women and Work

H – Home

J – Childcare

K – Other Dependant Relatives

WOMEN & EMPLOYMENT 1990

This questionnaire deals with your experience and attitudes towards work. The questionnaire is broken down into a number of sections and you will often be asked to reply to a series of questions in each section. Sometimes a whole section or large parts of a section will not apply to you. In which case, the interviewer will move straight on to the next section. Once more, thank you for your help.

CARD NUMBER   1

SERIAL NUMBER   *2-5

SECTION A

GENERAL INFORMATION

District Council Area: _____

Ward: _____   6-7

8-9

Location:		
Inner City	1	
Outer City	2	
Town	3	10
Village	4	
Country	5	

Interviewer code: 11-12

Date of interview: 13-16   day   mth

Time:		
Morning	1	
Afternoon (to 5.00pm)	2	
Early evening (to 7.00pm)	3	17
Late evening (after 7.00pm)	4	

A1 *Is your home?*

	Owner/occupier (with or without mortgage)	1
	Housing executive accommodation	2
CODE	Privately rented accommodation	3	18
ONE	Accommodation provided with job	4
	Other (please specify)	5

A2 Apart from children and / or husband / partner, who else lives permanently with you at this address?

CODE ALL

Grandparents [number]	19
Other relatives [number]	20
Other non-relatives [number]	21

A3 In which year were you born?   22-23 | 1 | 9 |

A4 What is your present marital status?

CODE ONE

Single	1
Married/Co-habiting	2
Divorced/Separated	3
Widowed	4

24

If SINGLE > GO TO A6
OTHERS > CONTINUE

A5 List below dates of all marriages.
CODING: If only one marriage and still continuing, enter first marriage start only.
For previous marriages, year start (cols 1&2); year finish (cols 3 & 4); if divorced / separated (1); widowed (2) (col 5)

	Start	End	Div/Sep	Widowed		Yr start	Yr end	D/W
1st marriage	19_	19_	1	2	25-29			
2nd marriage	19_	19_	1	2	30-34			
3rd marriage	19_	19_	1	2	35-39			

A6 Do you have any children?

DON'T   YES
CODE   NO

If NO > GO TO A8
If YES > CONTINUE

A7 Could I ask you for a few details about your children?
This includes children of whatever age and who may no longer be living with you or who may have died since birth.
CODING: Col 1 = Sex (M = 1; F = 2); Cols 2&3 = Age in years;
Col 4 = Present circumstances (At home = 1; living elsewhere = 2; deceased = 3).
Begin with eldest child and work through to youngest.

	Sex	Age (yrs)	At home?	Elsewhere?	Deceased?	
1.	M(1) F(2)	___	1	2	3	40-43
2.	M(1) F(2)	___	1	2	3	44-47
3.	M(1) F(2)	___	1	2	3	48-51
4.	M(1) F(2)	___	1	2	3	52-55
5.	M(1) F(2)	___	1	2	3	56-59
6.	M(1) F(2)	___	1	2	3	60-63
7.	M(1) F(2)	___	1	2	3	64-67
8.	M(1) F(2)	___	1	2	3	68-71
9.	M(1) F(2)	___	1	2	3	72-75
10.	M(1) F(2)	___	1	2	3	76-79

Sex   Age   At home

A8 What religion are you? (Only answer this question if you wish.)

Protestant	1
Catholic	2
Other	3
None	4

80

GO TO SECTION B

SECTION B

CARD NUMBER   [ ] 1

SERIAL NUMBER   [ ][ ][ ][ ] *2-5

EDUCATION

B1 *Did you leave school after primary school / elementary school?*

DON'T   YES   1
CODE   NO   2

> If YES > GO TO B4
> If NO > CONTINUE

Was/is the secondary / post-primary school which you attended for the longest period of time?

CODE   Outside Northern Ireland 1
ONE   In Northern Ireland 2   [ ] 6

Was/is this school?

CODE ONE
Mixed-sex grammar 1
Mixed-sex secondary 2
Single-sex grammar 3
Single-sex secondary 4
Mixed-sex comprehensive 5
Single-sex comprehensive 6
Other (specify) 7   [ ] 7

To check, Are you still at school full-time?

DON'T   YES   1
CODE   NO   2

> If YES > GO TO B24
> If NO > CONTINUE

B2 *In which year did you leave school?*   [ ][ ] 8-9

B3 *At what age did you leave school?*

CODE ONE
14 or under 1
15 2
16 3
17 4
18+ 5
Don't know 6   [ ] 10

B4 *What examination qualifications did you have when you left school?*
Code highest that applies.

CODE HIGHEST
THAT APPLIES
None 01
Secondary level certificates 02
Higher secondary level certificates 03
CSE(s) (no Grade 1 passes) 04
CSE(s) (with Grade 1 passes) 05
GCE 'O'/GCSE (1 - 4 subjects passed) 06
GCE 'O'/GCSE (5+ subjects passed) 07
GCE 'A' level (1 subject passed) 08
GCE 'A' level (2+ subjects passed) 09
Other (specify) 10   [ ][ ] 11-12

B5 *Apart from training (including YTP), did you continue full-time or part-time education (other than for recreation and courses less than 3 months) after school?*

CODE   YES, immediately 1
ONE   YES, not immediately but within 5 years 2
      YES, not immediately but after 5 years 3
      NO 4   [ ] 13

> If NO > GO TO B6
> If YES > CONTINUE

Was this education?

CODE ONE
Full-time study 1
Part-time study 2
Both full-time and part-time 3   [ ] 14

> For Full-time or Both > GO TO B11
> For Part-time > GO TO B16

B6 *Did you decide not to continue full-time or part-time education after leaving school because* (Choose one):

CODE ONE
You wanted to start work 1
Parents/relatives/friends advised you to leave 2
You did not like school 3
Don't know / can't remember 4
Other (specify) 5   [ ] 15

B7 *Do you now regret leaving full-time education at this age?*

CODE ONE

YES, mainly because I enjoyed school work — 1

YES, mainly because I did not achieve what I felt I could have achieved at school — 2

YES, mainly because my career prospects were/are now affected — 3

NO — 4

[box 16]

B8 *Are you thinking about continuing your education at some time in the future?*

CODE ONE

Definitely — 1

Probably — 2

Possibly — 3

No — 4

Don't know — 5

[box 17]

If NO or Don't know > GO TO B21
If YES > CONTINUE

B9 SHOW CARD B1

What sort of courses are you thinking of taking?

1 GCSE
2 GCE 'A' level
3 Teaching qualification
4 Social work qualification
5 Nursing qualification
6 Clerical & commercial/secretarial qualification
7 Training for skilled occupations
8 Course and training in childcare
9 City & Guilds
10 Degree or equivalent
11 Membership of professional institution
12 HND
13 HNC
14 B Tec
15 Community Education course
16 Women's Education course
17 Other (specify) ....

LIST ALL THAT APPLY
*18-19

B10 SHOW CARD B2

What are your main reasons for thinking of continuing your education?

1 Boredom
2 To improve my job prospects at work
3 A change of job
4 Personal development / to learn more
5 To help me return to work
6 Don't know

LIST ALL THAT APPLY

> GO TO B21

*20-21

For those continuing education, Full-time

B11 SHOW CARD B2

What were / are your main reasons for continuing your education?

1 Boredom
2 To improve my job prospects at work
3 A change of job
4 Personal development / to learn more
5 To help me return to work
6 Don't know

LIST ALL THAT APPLY
*22-23

B12 SHOW CARD B3

Was / is your further education at?

1 F.E. / Technical College
2 Teacher Training College
3 University / Polytechnic
4 Nursing School
5 Secretarial / Business School
6 Other (specify) ....

LIST ALL THAT APPLY
SHOW CARD B1
*24-25

What qualification did you gain / are you hoping to gain?

1 GCSE
2 GCE 'A' level
3 Teaching qualification
4 Social work qualification
5 Nursing qualification
6 Clerical & commercial/secretarial qualification
7 Training for skilled occupations
8 Course and training in childcare
9 City & Guilds
10 Degree or equivalent
11 Membership of professional institution
12 HND
13 HNC
14 B Tec
15 Community Education course
16 Women's Education course
17 Other (specify) ....

LIST ALL THAT APPLY

*26-27

B13 To check, *Are you still in full-time education?*

DON'T CODE   YES
                  NO

IF YES > GO TO B15
IF NO > CONTINUE

B14 *At what age did you leave full-time education?*

14 or under   1
15-16   2
17-18   3
19-20   4
21 - 30   5
31+   6

CODE ONE

28

> GO TO B21

B15 *Are you studying part-time as well as full-time at present?*

DON'T CODE   YES
                  NO

IF NO > GO TO B21
IF YES > CONTINUE

B16   SHOW CARD B2

What were / are your main reasons for continuing your part-time education?

1 Boredom
2 To improve my job prospects at work
3 A change of job
4 Personal development / to learn more
5 To help me return to work
6 Don't know

LIST ALL THAT APPLY

*29-30

SHOW CARD B3

Was / is your further education at?

1 F.E. / Technical College
2 Teacher Training College
3 University / Polytechnic
4 Nursing School
5 Secretarial / Business School
6 Other (specify) ....

LIST ALL THAT APPLY

*31-32

B17 *Was/is this mainly?*

CODE ONE   Evenings and/or Week-ends   1
           Day and/or Block release   2
           Both   3

33

B18   SHOW CARD B1

What qualification(s) did you gain / do you hope to gain?

1 GCSE
2 GCE 'A' level
3 Teaching qualification
4 Social work qualification
5 Nursing qualification
6 Clerical & commercial/secretarial qualification
7 Training for skilled occupations
8 Course and training in childcare
9 City & Guilds
10 Degree or equivalent
11 Membership of professional institution
12 HND
13 HNC
14 B Tech
15 Community Education course
16 Women's Education course
17 Other (specify) ....

LIST ALL THAT APPLY

*34-35

B19 *Are you still in part-time education?*

CODE ONE

YES	1	
NO	2	36

If YES > GO TO B20
If NO > CONTINUE

At what age did you leave part-time education?

16 or under	1	
17 - 18	2	
CODE ONE 19 - 20	3	37
21 - 30	4	
31+	5	

B20 *Were you / are you mainly working in paid employment whilst studying part-time?*

NO	1	
YES, under 8hrs per week	2	
YES, over 8hrs but less than 16hrs per week	3	
CODE ONE YES, over 16hrs but less than 30hrs per week	4	38
YES, over 30hrs but less than 40hrs per week	5	
YES, over 40hrs per week	6	
Don't know / can't remember	7	

B21 *Have you ever taken part in any government training courses?*

CODE ONE

YES	1	
NO	2	39

If NO > GO TO B24
If YES > CONTINUE

B22 *What is/are was/were the name(s) of the course(s)?*

LIST
ALL
THAT
APPLY

*40-41

B23 *In terms of work opportunities, overall did you find the course(s)?*

Very useful	1	
Quite useful	2	
CODE ONE Of little use	3	42
Of no use	4	

B24 *Did your own mother (or substitute) work outside the home after her marriage?*

CODE ONE

YES	1	
NO	2	43
Don't know	3	

If YES > CONTINUE
If NO > GO TO NEXT SECTION (C)

B25 *Did your mother work after the birth of her first child?*

CODE ONE

YES, full-time	1	
YES, part-time	2	44
NO	3	
Don't know	4	

B26 *Did your mother work after the birth of her last child?*

CODE ONE

YES, full-time	1	
YES, part-time	2	45
NO	3	
Don't know	4	

RECORDING SHEET

Serial Number *

PERIOD NUMBER:

DATES: FROM (YEAR)

      TO (YEAR)

ECONOMIC STATUS: (refer to CARD C1)

IF IN WORK.   Unsociable hours?   3 = Always; 2 = Often; 1 = Sometimes; 0 = Never

     Working at home?   1 = YES; 2 = NO

     Actively seeking other work?   1 = YES; 2 = NO

     Industry?   *

     Job title?   *

IF NOT IN WORK.   Registered as unemployed?   1 = YES; 2 = NO

     Actively seeking work?   1 = YES; 2 = NO

Reason for change of economic status to next period: *

_____

PERIOD NUMBER:

DATES: FROM (YEAR)

      TO (YEAR)

ECONOMIC STATUS: (refer to CARD C1)

IF IN WORK.   Unsociable hours?   3 = Always; 2 = Often; 1 = Sometimes; 0 = Never

     Working at home?   1 = YES; 2 = NO

     Actively seeking other work?   1 = YES; 2 = NO

     Industry?   *

     Job title?   *

IF NOT IN WORK.   Registered as unemployed?   1 = YES; 2 = NO

     Actively seeking work?   1 = YES; 2 = NO

Reason for change of economic status to next period: *

SECTION C

PREVIOUS WORK HISTORY

NOTES FOR INTERVIEWERS

In this section you should direct respondents to divide their career from the time of leaving school into periods of being in employment (full-time or part-time) or periods of not working. Employment refers chiefly to paid work. Therefore unpaid childcare, housework etc should not normally be coded as periods of employment.

Whether in or out of work, it is important that all details are included for each period. Change of employment status refers not only to movement in and out of work but also changes between full-time and part-time work or between jobs where there has been a significant change in pay, working conditions, hours worked etc.

For each period, ask the respondent to refer to CARD C1, and code the period as appropriate.

CARD C1
ECONOMIC STATUS

01   Self-employed (alone)
02   Self-employed (with staff)
03   Full-time employee
04   Part-time employee
05   YTP
06   Unemployed
07   Full-time education
08   Temporarily unavailable for work (sickness/illness)
09   Permanently unavailable for work (sickness/illness/disability)
10   Unavailable for work (looking after own children)
11   Unavailable for work (looking after other relative, including children)
12   Unavailable for work (looking after home)
13   Retired

When asking about reasons for change of economic status, the following prompts may be useful but are not to be followed rigidly. Remember, change can refer to - in work to out of work; part-time to full-time; full-time to part-time; or out of work to in work.

Contract ended
Laid off / made redundant
Dismissed
Illness / injury
Unhappy with type of work
Unhappy with hours
Sexual harassment
Better offer / opportunity elsewhere
To continue education
Marriage
Pregnancy
Moved house
Domestic responsibilities (children)
Domestic responsibilities (other dependents)
Needed the money / better money / needed the money / don't need money
Promotion, better prospects elsewhere
Health
To have more time at home
Enjoyed work
To further my career
For the company / to meet people
Boredom
Children were grown up / at school

SECTION D

CARD NUMBER [1]

SERIAL NUMBER *2-5 [ ][ ][ ][ ]

EXPERIENCES OF WORK

(i) *Applying for jobs*
D1 *How many jobs would you estimate that you have applied for since leaving school?*

None	0
1 - 2	1
3 - 5	2
6 - 10	3
11 - 20	4
21 - 30	5
31 - 50	6
50+	7

CODE ONE 6 [ ]

If None	>	GO TO D6
Others	>	CONTINUE

D2 *How many jobs would you estimate that you have applied for in the last five years?*

None	0
1 - 2	1
3 - 5	2
6 - 10	3
11 - 20	4
21 - 30	5
31 - 50	6
50+	7

CODE ONE 7 [ ]

If None	>	GO TO D6
Others	>	CONTINUE

D3 **SHOW CARD D1**

When looking for work, which of the following have you used?

1 Newspaper advertisement
2 From friends/relatives/word of mouth
3 Made approach to previous employer after break
4 Approached by previous employer after break
5 Approached new employer directly
6 Private employment agency
7 Jobcentre/employment exchange
8 Internal advertisement
9 Don't know / can't remember

LIST ALL THAT APPLY *8-9 [ ][ ][ ]

D4 **SHOW CARD D2**

When applying for jobs, which of the following are important to you?

1 Work you like doing
2 Job gives you status in the community
3 Good prospects
4 Convenient hours of work
5 Good rate of pay
6 Secure job
7 Friendly people to work with
8 Pleasant work environment
9 Convenient to home
10 Opportunity to use your ability
11 Familiar work
12 Good child care facilities
13 Support from husband / partner

LIST ALL THAT APPLY *10-11 [ ][ ]

D5 **SHOW CARD D3**

If you think you have ever failed to get a job because you were a woman, which of the following do you think were important in the eyes of prospective employers?

1 You may leave to start a family
2 You would take too much time off work
3 You were generally not committed / serious about the job
4 You could not cope with the job and looking after the home
5 You were not strong enough
6 Don't know
7 Other (specify) ....

LIST ALL THAT APPLY *12-13 [ ][ ]

D6 *To check. Have you ever worked since leaving school?*

CODE ONE	YES	1
	NO	2

14 [ ]

If NO	>	GO TO NEXT SECTION (E)
If YES	>	CONTINUE

(ii) *Promotion*

The following questions deal with promotion within your place of work. Promotion here does not mean moving 'sideways' from one position or set of responsibilities to another roughly similar post with similar salary or wage. It refers instead to changing jobs where either your status, pay or prospects have improved as a result of this move.

With this in mind, have you ever been promoted at work?

CODE ONE	YES, once	1
	YES, more than once	2
	NO	3
	Don't know	4

15 [ ]

D7 *Have you ever refused promotion or deliberately avoided promotion?*

CODE ONE
YES, more than once   1
YES, once   2
NO   3
Don't know   4   ☐ 16

> If NO or Don't know > GO TO NEXT SECTION (E)
> If YES > CONTINUE

D8   **SHOW CARD D4**

Which of the following reasons were important in making you decide not to try for promotion?

1 Did not want more responsibility / don't like giving orders
2 Interfered with family commitments (hours etc.)
3 Happy in post/like the job I'm doing
4 Expected to leave job soon
5 Would prefer transfer to promotion
6 Did not like new work
7 Was not sufficiently qualified
8 Did not want to be 'above' fellow workers
9 Did not want to supervise men
10 Too old
11 Other (specify) ....

LIST ALL THAT APPLY   ☐☐☐☐ *17-18

SECTION E

CURRENT EMPLOYMENT STATUS

E1   **SHOW CARD E1**

At the present time (and including those still in work but absent through temporary illness [less than 3 months], holidays or maternity leave), what sort of job do you currently have, if any?

01 Full-time work
02 Part-time work
03 Waiting to take up work
04 YTP
05 Unemployed (available for work)
06 Full-time education
07 Temporarily unavailable for work (sickness/illness)
08 Permanently unavailable for work (sickness/illness/disability)
09 Unavailable for work (looking after children)
10 Unavailable for work (looking after other relative)
11 Unavailable for work (looking after home)
12 Retired

CODE ONE   ☐☐ 19-20

> If in work (categories 1 or 2) > GO TO E4
> All others > CONTINUE

E2 *Are you currently registered as unemployed?*

CODE ONE
YES   1
NO   2
Don't know   3   ☐ 21

> IF YES > GO TO E3
> IF NO > CONTINUE

Is this because?

You don't think you are eligible for benefits   1
You know you are not eligible for benefits   2
CODE ONE   You cannot be bothered   3
You don't think it is worth it   4   ☐ 22
Other (specify) ....

E3 *Do you have any occasional paid work (e.g. childminding, outwork, seasonal jobs)?*

CODE
ONE
YES   1
NO   2   ☐ 23

> IF YES > CONTINUE
> IF NO > GO TO E3a

How long have you been with your present employer?

Less than thirteen weeks	1
Thirteen weeks but less than twenty-six weeks	2
Twenty-six weeks but less than one year	3
One year but less than two years	4
Two years but less than five years	5
Five years but less than ten years	6
Ten years or over	7

CODE ONE   45

E6 *Did you start work in this job?*

After finishing full-time education	1
After not-working for domestic reasons (e.g. child care)	2
After not working for non-domestic reasons	3
Immediately after leaving another job	4

CODE ONE   46

E7   **SHOW CARD E3**

How did you find out about this job?

1 Newspaper advertisement
2 From friends / relatives / word of mouth
3 Made approach to previous employer after break
4 Approached by previous employer after break
5 Approached new employer directly
6 Private employment agency
7 Jobcentre / employment exchange
8 Internal advertisement
9 Don't know / can't remember

LIST ALL THAT APPLY   *47-48

E8   **SHOW CARD E4**

Which of the following factors were important in making you decide to take this job?

1 Work you like doing
2 Job gives you status in the community
3 Good prospects
4 Convenient hours of work
5 Good rate of pay
6 Secure job
7 Friendly people to work with
8 Pleasant work environment
9 Convenient to home
10 Opportunity to use your ability
11 Familiar work
12 Good child care facilities
13 Support from husband / partner

LIST ALL THAT APPLY   *49-50

Please give details of this occasional paid work

Job Title: _____   *24-26

Industry: _____   *27-29

Hours per week (on average): _____ hrs   30-31

Does this involve you working at home?

YES	1
NO	2

CODE ONE   32

E3a To check, *are you presently waiting to take up work?*

YES	
NO	

DON'T CODE

If YES > GO TO E7
If NO > GO TO E60

33

E4 *Do you earn money from any other paid work, apart from your main job?*

YES	1
NO	2

CODE ONE

If YES > CONTINUE
If NO > GO TO E5

Please give details of this other work

Job Title: _____   *34-36

Industry: _____   *37-39

Hours per week (on average): _____ hrs   40-41

Does this involve you working at home?

YES	1
NO	2

CODE ONE   42

E5   **SHOW CARD E2**

Referring now to your main job, what are the main reasons why you are working at present?

1 I need the money
2 I like the stimulation of going out to work
3 Working makes me feel I'm doing something useful
4 I spend too much time with my family and friends
5 I often get bored and fed up without work
6 I have too much time on my hands without work
7 My husband / partner likes me to work

LIST ALL THAT APPLY   *43-44

E9 *What is your job title?* _____ *51-53

What type of industry? *54-56

What is your status at work?

Self-employed (alone)	0
Self-employed (with employees)	1
Permanent employee (professional / manager)	2
CODE ONE Permanent employee (supervisor)	3
Permanent employee (non-manual / manual worker)	4
Temporary employee (professional / manager)	5
Temporary employee (supervisor)	6
Temporary employee (non-manual / manual worker)	7

57

Those waiting to start work > GO TO E53
Others > CONTINUE

E10 *During your time in this job, have you worked?*

Always full-time	1
Always part-time	2
CODE ONE Full-time, now part-time	3
Part-time, now full-time	4

58

If always full-time OR always part-time > GO TO E11
If full-time to part-time > E10a
If part-time to full-time > E10b

E10a **If full-time to part-time   SHOW CARD E5**

Which of the following were important in making you change?

1 Greater domestic responsibilities (i.e. children)
2 Greater domestic responsibilities (i.e. other dependents)
3 Health
4 Money no longer so important
5 To have more time at home
6 To reduce hours worked
7 Other (specify) ....

LIST ALL THAT APPLY   *59-60

E10b **If part-time to full-time   SHOW CARD E6**

Which of the following were important in making you change?

1 Better money
2 Fewer domestic responsibilities (children)
3 Fewer domestic responsibilities (other dependents)
4 Promotion, better prospects
5 Better health
6 To work more hours
7 Other (specify) ....

LIST ALL THAT APPLY   *61-62

E11 *How far from your work do you live?*

Work at home	1
Less than 1 mile	2
1 - 3 miles	3
CODE ONE 4 - 10 miles	4
11 - 30 miles	5
More than 30 miles	6
Varies	7

63

If work at home > GO TO E13
Others > CONTINUE

E12 *What is your main means of getting to and from work?*

Walk	1
Bicycle	2
Bus	3
CODE ONE Train	4
Car (as driver)	5
Car (as passenger)	6
Varies	7
Other (specify)	

64

SERIAL NUMBER   *1-3

Working Conditions

(i) HOURS

E13 At present (or if off work temporarily, most recent work), which days of the week do you work and how many hours per day? Use the last full working week as a guide. Record start and finish times working to a 24 hour clock. Overtime to be recorded in minutes.

	START Hours	Mins	FINISH Hours	Mins	OVERTIME Mins	
MONDAY						4-14
TUESDAY						15-25
WEDNESDAY						26-36
THURSDAY						37-47
FRIDAY						48-58
SATURDAY						59-69
SUNDAY						70-80

CARD NUMBER   1   5

SERIAL NUMBER   *2-5

E14 Apart from overtime, most weeks do you normally work outside the hours 8am-6pm, Monday to Friday?   6

CODE ONE	YES, very frequently	1
	YES, quite often	2
	YES, occasionally	3
	NO, never	4

If YES, usually which of the following?   7

CODE ONE	1 - 4 evenings per week	1
	5+ evenings per week	2
	Weekends	3
	Night-shift	4
	Varies	5
	Other (specify)	

To check, *Are you self-employed?*

DON'T CODE   YES / NO

If YES > GO TO E35
If NO > CONTINUE

E15 *How many hours per week are you contracted to work?*   8-9 hrs

E16 *How many hours per week would you prefer to work (assuming that your pay would be based on the same hourly rate)?*   10-11 hrs

E17 *Do you ever do any paid overtime?*   12

CODE ONE   YES 1 / NO 2

If NO > GO TO E19
If YES > CONTINUE

Is paid overtime available?   13

CODE ONE	Every week	1
	Most weeks	2
	Occasionally	3
	Varies considerably	4

E18 *On average, how many hours paid overtime do you work?*   14

CODE ONE	1 - 5 hours per week	1
	6 - 10 hours per week	2
	11+ hours per week	3
	Varies considerably	4

E19 *On average, how many hours unpaid overtime do you feel you work?*   15

CODE ONE	None	1
	Varies considerably	2
	Occasional hours	3
	1 - 5 hours per week	4
	6 - 10 hours per week	5
	11+ hours per week	6

E20 *Would you welcome the opportunity for paid overtime / more paid overtime?*   16

CODE ONE	YES	1
	NO	2

If YES, *How many hours / more hours per week?*   17-18 hrs

E21 *At your work, would you say that paid overtime is available for?*

	Mainly men	1
	Mainly women	2
	Only men	3
CODE ONE	Only women	4
	Men and women	5
	Not applicable	6
	Don't know	7

☐ 19

E22 *Are you allowed to choose the time you begin and end work (flexitime), or do you have to work a set day?*

CODE ONE	Fixed set day	1
	Flexitime	2

☐ 20

If Fixed day > GO TO E23
If Flexitime > GO TO E24

E23 *Would you welcome the introduction of flexible start and finish times (with the same total working hours)?*

	YES	1
CODE ONE	NO	2
	Don't know	3

☐ 21

(ii) BENEFITS

E24 *Do you receive pay when you are off sick?*

	YES, full pay	1
CODE ONE	YES, less than full pay	2
	NO	3

☐ 22

If YES > GO TO E25
If NO > CONTINUE

Do you know why you don't receive sick pay?

SHOW CARD E7

	01	Don't know / not sure
	02	Not available to any employees
	03	Not available to my type of job
	04	Part-time workers not eligible
CODE MOST	05	Temporary workers not eligible
IMPORTANT	06	Not in work long enough
	07	Don't work enough hours
	08	Too young
	09	Too old
	10	Alternatives more attractive
	11	Other (specify) ....

CODE ONE

☐☐ 23-24

E25 *Does your employer run an occupational pensions scheme (not state scheme)?*

	YES	1
CODE ONE	NO	2
	Don't know	3

☐ 25

If YES > CONTINUE
If NO / Don't know > GO TO E26

Do you belong to the scheme?

	YES	1
CODE ONE	NO	2
	Don't know	3

☐ 26

If YES > GO TO E26
If NO > CONTINUE

Why do you not belong?

SHOW CARD E7

	01	Don't know / not sure
	02	Not available to any employees
	03	Not available to my type of job
	04	Part-time workers not eligible
CODE MOST	05	Temporary workers not eligible
IMPORTANT	06	Not in work long enough
	07	Don't work enough hours
	08	Too young
	09	Too old
	10	Alternatives more attractive
	11	Other (specify) ....

CODE ONE

☐☐ 27-28

E26 *How many days holiday (paid or unpaid) are you entitled to each year, including bank holidays?*

_____ days

☐☐ 29-30

E27 *How many days holiday do you normally take each year (if different from above)?*

_____ days

☐☐ 31-32

E28 *Are you entitled to any paid holidays (apart from bank holidays)?*

	YES, all are paid	1
	YES, some are paid	2
CODE ONE	NO	3
	Don't know	4

☐ 33

E29 *Does your employer provide maternity leave?*

YES (unpaid)	1
YES (part salary)	2
YES (full salary)	3
NO	4
Don't know	5

CODE ONE

34 ☐

If YES, *Would you be eligible for this scheme, if pregnant and having worked for two years?*

YES (presumed in work for two years)	1
NO	2
Don't know	3

CODE ONE

35 ☐

If NO, *Why do you think that you would not be eligible?*

SHOW CARD E7

01 Don't know / not sure
02 Not available to any employees
03 Not available to my type of job
04 Part-time workers not eligible
05 Temporary workers not eligible
06 Not in work long enough
07 Don't work enough hours
08 Too young
09 Too old
10 Alternatives more attractive
11 Other (specify) ....

CODE MOST IMPORTANT

36-37 ☐☐

E30 *Does your employer run a day nursery or creche?*

YES	1
NO	2
Don't know	3

CODE ONE

38 ☐

If NO or Don't know > GO TO E32
If YES > CONTINUE

Do you know how much this costs per child per day?

CODE TO NEAREST POUND

£ 39-40 ☐☐

E31 *If you have pre-school children, do you in fact use this service?*

CODE ONE

YES	1
NO	2

41 ☐

If NO, *Why not?*

SHOW CARD E7

01 Don't know / not sure
02 Not available to any employees
03 Not available to my type of job
04 Part-time workers not eligible
05 Temporary workers not eligible
06 Not in work long enough
07 Don't work enough hours
08 Too young
09 Too old
10 Alternatives more attractive
11 Other (specify) ....

CODE MOST IMPORTANT

CODE ONE

42-43 ☐☐

E32 *Has your employer provided you with a written contract of employment?*

CODE ONE

YES	1
NO	2
Don't know	3

44 ☐

If NO, *Why not?*

SHOW CARD E7

01 Don't know / not sure
02 Not available to any employees
03 Not available to my type of job
04 Part-time workers not eligible
05 Temporary workers not eligible
06 Not in work long enough
07 Don't work enough hours
08 Too young
09 Too old
10 Alternatives more attractive
11 Other (specify) ....

CODE MOST IMPORTANT

CODE ONE

45-46 ☐☐

E33 Which of the following do you have?

SHOW CARD E8

1	Specified salary or wage rate
2	Bonus / Merit scheme / Other Payments in kind
3	Paid holiday
4	Rest and refreshment break(s)
5	Payment for unsocial hours
6	Preferential mortgage scheme
7	Preferential loan scheme
8	Profit sharing scheme
9	Career break scheme
10	Company car
11	Travel allowance
12	Occupational pension scheme
13	Other (specify) ....

LIST ALL THAT APPLY

*47-48

(iii) EARNINGS

In order to build up a comprehensive picture of women's employment in Northern Ireland, it is important that we ask a few questions about pay. Please rest assured that this information will be treated in the strictest confidence by the research team.

E34 Are you paid?

The same amount per week or month (salary)	1
By the hours you work (hourly rate)	2
By how much you produce (piecework)	3
On fixed sum plus commission	4
On fixed sum plus productivity bonus	5
On commission alone	6
Other (specify)	7

CODE ONE

49

E35 At present, how much do you earn per week (or month/year) *before* any compulsory deductions (e.g. tax; National Insurance)?

SHOW CARD E9

Code	Per week £	(Per month) £	(Per annum) £
01	Up to £25	Up to £100	Up to £1,200
02	26 - 50	101 - 200	1,200 - 2,400
03	51 - 75	201 - 300	2,401 - 3,600
04	76 - 100	301 - 400	3,601 - 4,800
05	101 - 125	401 - 500	4,801 - 6,000
06	126 - 150	501 - 600	6,001 - 7,200
07	151 - 175	601 - 700	7,201 - 8,400
08	176 - 200	701 - 800	8,401 - 9,600
09	201 - 250	801 - 1000	9,601 - 12,000
10	251 - 300	1001 - 1200	12,001 - 14,400
11	301 - 350	1201 - 1400	14,401 - 16,800
12	351 - 400	1401 - 1600	16,801 - 19,200
13	401 - 500	1601 - 2000	19,201 - 24,000
14	501 - 700	2001 - 2800	24,001 - 33,600
15	701 - 900	2801 - 3600	33,601 - 43,200
16	over £900	over £3600	over £43,200

CODE ONE

50-51

E36 At present, how much do you earn per week (month/year) *after* any deductions (e.g. tax; National Insurance)?

SHOW CARD E9

Code	Per week £	(Per month) £	(Per annum) £
01	Up to £25	Up to £100	Up to £1,200
02	25 - 50	101 - 200	1,200 - 2,400
03	51 - 75	201 - 300	2,401 - 3,600
04	76 - 100	301 - 400	3,601 - 4,800
05	101 - 125	401 - 500	4,801 - 6,000
06	126 - 150	501 - 600	6,001 - 7,200
07	151 - 175	601 - 700	7,201 - 8,400
08	176 - 200	701 - 800	8,401 - 9,600
09	201 - 250	801 - 1000	9,601 - 12,000
10	251 - 300	1001 - 1200	12,001 - 14,400
11	301 - 350	1201 - 1400	14,401 - 16,800
12	351 - 400	1401 - 1600	16,801 - 19,200
13	401 - 500	1601 - 2000	19,201 - 24,000
14	501 - 700	2001 - 2800	24,001 - 33,600
15	701 - 900	2801 - 3600	33,601 - 43,200
16	over £900	over £3600	over £43,200

CODE ONE

52-53

E37 *Do you pay?*

Both Income Tax & National Insurance	1
National Insurance Only	2
CODE ONE Income Tax Only	3
Neither Income Tax nor National Insurance	4
Don't know	5
Refusal	6

54 ☐

E38 *To check, are you self employed?*

DON'T
CODE YES
NO

If YES > GO TO E48
If NO > CONTINUE

(iv) TRAINING

This section is concerned with the amount of vocational training you have received in connection with your present work. This does not include general further and higher education but training particularly related to your current employment. For those in professional employment (e.g. teachers; managers; nurses; doctors), include training for professional qualifications only where these are directly relevant to your present work, and where training was given whilst in post.

E39 *How much formal training (i.e. time set aside for learning the job, courses etc.) have you received from your employer in connection with your present job, that is the post which you are working in at present?*

None	1
Half a day or less	2
One day	3
CODE ONE Two days but under one week	4
One week but under one month	5
One month but under six months	6
Over six months	7

55 ☐

If None > GO TO E40
Others > CONTINUE

Was this training?

Mainly training courses at work	1
Mainly training courses (day / block release)	2
CODE ONE Mainly training courses (residential)	3
Mainly on-the-job training	4
Courses for professional qualifications	5
Both courses and on-the-job training	6

56 ☐

E40 *In comparison with men at your place of work, do you believe that you have received?*

Much more training	1
More training	2
About the same amount of training	3
CODE ONE Less training	4
Much less training	5
Don't know	6
Not applicable	7

57 ☐

E41 *Are there any opportunities for you to receive further training at work?*

YES, but only for new jobs / more complex jobs	1
CODE ONE YES, for my present job	2
NO	3

58 ☐

E42 *Would you welcome the opportunity to receive further training?*

YES, preferably day release / in-house training	1
YES, preferably residential courses (away from home)	2
CODE ONE NO	3

59 ☐

(v) PROMOTION

E43 *Is it possible for you to gain promotion from the job you are currently doing?*

YES	1
CODE ONE NO	2
Don't know	3

60 ☐

If NO > GO TO E46
If YES > CONTINUE

Have you ever been promoted in your present work?

CODE ONE YES	1
NO	2

61 ☐

E44 *Would you welcome the opportunity of being promoted?*

YES, definitely	1
YES, probably	2
CODE ONE YES, possible	3
NO	4
Don't know	5

62 ☐

If YES > GO TO E46
If NO > CONTINUE

E45   SHOW CARD E10

Which of the following are / were important to you in making this decision?

1 Do / did not want more responsibility
2 Interferes / interfered with family commitments
3 Happy in present post
4 Expect to leave job soon
5 Would prefer transfer to promotion
6 Would not like new work
7 Not sufficiently qualified
8 Do / did not want to be 'above' fellow workers
9 Do / did not want to supervise/manage men
10 Too old
11 Other (specify) ....

LIST ALL THAT APPLY   ☐ ☐ ☐ ☐ ☐   *63-64

(vi) EQUAL OPPORTUNITIES

E46 To check, are you working at home?

DONT   YES
CODE   NO

If YES > GO TO E48
If NO > CONTINUE

E47 At your place of work, do you work?

Alongside men	1	
CODE Alongside women	2	
ONE Alongside men and women	3	☐ 65
Alone	4	

If Alongside Men OR Men and Women > CONTINUE
Others > GO TO E48

If you work alongside men, are they mainly:

Doing similar work to you	1	
In better jobs than you	2	
CODE ONE In worse jobs than you	3	☐ 66
In different work	4	
Varies	5	
Don't know	6	

(vii) ATTITUDES TO WORKING AND JOB SATISFACTION

Below are a series of statements dealing with your attitudes to different aspects of work. For each statement, indicate how you feel in general about your work.
CODING: Circle each answer. At end of each section, add total for section and enter in boxes

E48 Your pay

	YES	UNSURE	NO
I am under paid for what I do	1	2	3
My pay is adequate for my needs	3	2	1
My pay is far too low	1	2	3
I am quite highly paid	3	2	1
My pay is fairly satisfactory	3	2	1
My pay is poor	1	2	3
I am well paid	3	2	1
I am paid less than I deserve	1	2	3

TOTAL = _____   ☐☐ 67-68

CODE TOTAL SCORE

E49 The job itself

	YES	UNSURE	NO
The work is the same day after day	1	2	3
It is the wrong sort of job for me	1	2	3
The work is worthwhile	3	2	1
The work is routine	1	2	3
Time passes quickly	3	2	1
The work is satisfying	3	2	1
The work seems endless	1	2	3

TOTAL = _____   ☐☐ 69-70

CODE TOTAL SCORE

If self-employed > GO TO E53

E50 Your immediate superior / boss

	YES	UNSURE	NO
He/she lets you know where you stand	3	2	1
He/she does a good job	3	2	1
He/she interferes too much	1	2	3
He/she is always too busy to see you	1	2	3
He/she stands up for you	3	2	1
He/she is quick tempered	1	2	3
You can discuss problems with him/her	3	2	1
He/she is hard to please	1	2	3

TOTAL = _____   ☐☐ 71-72

CODE TOTAL SCORE

E51 The organization you work for

Take the unit within which the person directly works as the organization (e.g. school; shop; factory; section; hospital)

	YES	UNSURE	NO
As a whole it looks after its employees	3	2	1
It is a poor organization to work for	1	2	3
It treats you like a number	1	2	3
It has a good reputation	3	2	1
It has too much class distinction	1	2	3
It is an organization where you feel you belong	3	2	1
It needs some fresh people at the top	1	2	3
It is the best organization I have worked for	3	2	1

CODE TOTAL SCORE   TOTAL = _____   73-74

E52 Opportunities

	YES	UNSURE	NO
The system of promotion is fair	3	2	1
Prospects are very limited	1	2	3
It is easy to get on	3	2	1
There is too much favouritism in promotion	1	2	3
There are good opportunities for promotion	3	2	1
My experience increases my prospects	3	2	1
This is a dead end job	1	2	3
The good jobs are usually taken before you hear of them	1	2	3

CODE TOTAL SCORE   TOTAL = _____   75-76

CARD NUMBER   1   6

SERIAL NUMBER   *2-5

(viii) CHILDCARE

E53 To check, *do you expect to have any children/any more children?*

	YES
DON'T CODE	NO
	Don't know

If NO or Don't know > GO TO E57
If YES > CONTINUE

E54 *Which of the following do you think is the likeliest to happen?*

CODE ONE

Continue working (apart from maternity leave)	1
Give up work, start again some time before youngest child starts primary school	2
Give up work, start again when youngest child starts primary school	3
Give up work, start again before youngest child leaves secondary school	4
Give up work, start again when youngest child leaves secondary school	5
Give up work completely	6
Don't know	7
Other (specify)	

[box] 6

E55 *If you expect to continue working, how soon after the baby's birth would you like to start work again?*

CODE ONE

Immediately after maternity leave	1
Within one month	2
Between one month and two months	3
Between two months and four months	4
After four months	5
Don't know	6

[box] 7

E56 *After pregnancy, do you think you would like to return to your old job?*

CODE ONE

YES, full-time	1
YES, part-time	2
Don't know	3
NO	4

[box] 8

(ix) FUTURE PLANS

E57 *For any reason, do you plan or expect to leave your present job within the next year?*

CODE ONE

YES	1
NO	2
Don't know	3

[box] 9

If NO or Don't know > GO TO E59
If YES > CONTINUE

SHOW CARD E11

Why do you expect to leave?

1 Retirement
2 Contract end/temporary job
3 Don't like the job
4 Moving away
5 To raise a family / spend more time with family
6 Start full-time education
7 Other (specify) ....

CODE ONE   ☐ 10

E58 *Do you expect to look for other work immediately after leaving this job?*

YES 1
NO 2
Don't know 3

CODE ONE   ☐ 11

| If NO or Don't know > GO TO E59 |
| If YES > CONTINUE |

How easy do you think it will be to find another job?

Very easy 1
Fairly easy 2
Fairly difficult 3
Very difficult 4
Don't know 5

CODE ONE   ☐ 12

E59 *Do you expect that you will continue working / looking for work, until retirement age?*

YES 1
NO 2
Don't know 3

CODE ONE   ☐ 13

If NO,   ## SHOW CARD E12

Will this be because?

1 Won't need the money
2 Want to spend more time with husband/family/at home
3 Health reasons/tiring job
4 Will lose job
5 Don't enjoy working
6 Don't know
7 Concentrate on other interests
8 Other (specify) ....

LIST ALL THAT APPLY   *14-15

To check, are you presently waiting to start work?

DON'T   YES
CODE   NO

| If YES > GO TO E65 |
| If NO (those working) > GO TO NEXT SECTION (F) |

Women Not in Paid Work

SHOW CARD E13

E60   *What are the main reasons why you are not working at present?*

1 Contract ended
2 Laid off/made redundant
3 Dismissed
4 Illness/injury
5 Unhappy with work (general)
6 Unhappy with hours
7 Sexual harassment
8 Better offer / opportunity will turn up
9 To continue education
10 Marriage
11 To start a family
12 Moved house
13 Domestic responsibilities (children)
14 Domestic responsibilities (other dependents)
15 Other (specify) ....

LIST ALL THAT APPLY   *16-17

E61 *How long is it since you last worked?*

Under 13 weeks 1
13 weeks but less than 26 weeks 2
26 weeks but less than one year 3
One year but under two years 4
Two years but under five years 5
Five years or more 6

CODE ONE   ☐ 18

E62 *Do you still pay into a private / company pension scheme?*

YES 1
NO 2
Don't know 3

CODE ONE   ☐ 19

E63 *How soon do you think you will start work again, if at all?*

Within six months 1
6 months but less than 1 year 2
1 year but less than 2 years 3
2 years but less than 5 years 4
5 years or more 5
Never 6

CODE ONE   ☐ 20

E64 *Are you looking for a paid job at the moment?*

| CODE | YES | 1 |
| ONE | NO | 2 |

[ ] 21

> If YES > GO TO E65
> If NO > CONTINUE

How soon do you think you might start applying for jobs again?

	Within six months	1
	6 mths but less than 1 yr	2
	1 yr but less than 2 yrs	3
CODE ONE	2 yrs but less than 5 yrs	4
	Over 5 yrs	5
	Never	6
	Don't know	7

[ ] 22

> If Never or Don't know > GO TO NEXT SECTION (F)
> Others > GO TO E69

E65 *How long have you been looking for a job?*

	Less than 2 weeks	1
	2 weeks but less than 4 weeks	2
CODE ONE	1 month but less than 3 months	3
	3 months but less than 6 months	4
	6 months or more	5

[ ] 23

E66 *How hard have you been trying to find work during this period?*

	Occasionally / Off and on	1
CODE ONE	Frequently	2
	Continually	3

[ ] 24

> For those waiting to start work > GO TO E69

E67 *How many jobs have you applied for in the last year (approximately)?*

	None	1
	1 - 2	2
CODE ONE	3 - 4	3
	5 - 9	4
	10 or more	5

[ ] 25

E68   **SHOW CARD E14**

Which of the following has made it difficult for you to find work?

1 No suitable jobs in this region for my skills
2 Too many people looking for work
3 No jobs with the right hours / working conditions
4 I don't have enough / the right qualifications
5 I have too many qualifications
6 I am too young/too old
7 I lack relevant experience
8 My husband / partner doesn't want me to work

LIST ALL THAT APPLY

[ ][ ] *26-27

E69   **SHOW CARD E4**

Which of the following factors are important in making you decide to apply for a particular job?

1 Work you like doing
2 Job gives you status in the community
3 Good prospects
4 Convenient hours of work
5 Good rate of pay
6 Secure job
7 Friendly people to work with
8 Pleasant work environment
9 Convenient to home
10 Opportunity to use your ability
11 Familiar work
12 Good child care facilities
13 Support from husband / partner

LIST ALL THAT APPLY

[ ][ ] *28-29

E70   **SHOW CARD E2**

Why are you seeking work at present?

1 I need the money
2 I like the stimulation of going out to work
3 Working makes me feel I'm doing something useful
4 I spend too much time with my family and friends
5 I often get bored and fed up without work
6 I have too much time on my hands without work
7 My husband / partner likes me to work

LIST ALL THAT APPLY

[ ][ ] *30-31

E71 *To check, do you expect to have any children / any more children?*

	YES	1
CODE ONE	NO	2
	Don't know	3

[ ] 32

> If NO or don't know > GO TO E73
> If YES > CONTINUE

Which of the following would you like to happen?

CODE ONE

Continue working (apart from maternity leave)	1
Give up work, start again some time before youngest child starts primary school	2
Give up work, start again when youngest child starts primary school	3
Give up work, start again before youngest child leaves secondary school	4 · 33
Give up work, start again when youngest child leaves secondary school	5
Give up work completely	6
Don't know/refusal	7
Other (specify)	

To check, *do you ever expect to work again?*

DON'T   YES
CODE   NO

If NO > GO TO NEXT SECTION (F)
If YES > CONTINUE

E72 *If you expect to continue working, how soon after the baby's birth would you like to start work again?*

Don't know	1
Immediately	2
CODE ONE Within one month	3 · 34
One month but less than two months	4
Two months but less than four months	5
Four months or later	6

E73 *If you return to work, would you prefer to work?*

Full-time, permanent	1
Part-time, permanent	2
Full-time, temporary	3
CODE ONE Part-time, temporary	4 · 35
Don't know	5

To check, *have you ever worked before?*

DON'T   YES
CODE   NO

If NO > GO TO E75
If YES > CONTINUE

E74 *Would you like to return to your old job?*

YES	1
CODE ONE NO	2 · 36
Don't know	3

E75 *If you could make suitable arrangements for looking after your child(ren) while at work, would you prefer to start a paid job sooner?*

YES	1
CODE ONE NO	2 · 37
Don't know	3

SECTION F

TRADE UNION INVOLVEMENT

Are you currently in paid work?

DON'T
CODE

YES   1
NO   2   *38

If NO > GO TO F2
If YES > CONTINUE

F1 *Is there a Trade Union or Staff Association which you can join if you wish?*

CODE ONE

YES   1
NO   2
Don't know   3

If YES or Don't know > GO TO F2
If NO > CONTINUE

If not available, do you wish there was a trade union that you could join?

DON'T
CODE

YES   1
NO   2   *39-40

If NO > GO TO F2
If YES > CONTINUE

SHOW CARD F1

Why would you like to join a trade union?

1   To improve general working conditions
2   To improve pay
3   To secure jobs
4   Because working people should belong to a union
5   As a matter of principle
6   Other (specify) ....

LIST ALL THAT APPLY   *41

F2 *Have you ever been a member of a Trade Union or Staff Association?*

CODE
ONE

YES   1
NO   2

If YES > GO TO F3
If NO > CONTINUE

SHOW CARD F2

If you have never been a member was this because?

1   Not in work
2   Never available at my work
3   I object to unions on principle
4   Union subscription are/were too high
5   I cannot see the point of joining
6   Part-time workers aren't eligible
7   Don't know
8   Other (specify) ....

LIST ALL THAT APPLY   *42-43

> GO TO NEXT SECTION (G)

F3 *Have you ever held any union office e.g. shop steward; committee member?*

CODE ONE

YES   1
NO   2   44

In total for how long were you / have you been a union member?

CODE ONE

Under five years   1
5 - 10 years   2
11 - 20 years   3
21 years +   4
Don't know   5   45

F4 *Are you still a trade union member?*

CODE
ONE

YES   1
NO   2   46

If YES > GO TO F5
If NO > CONTINUE

SHOW CARD F3

Are you no longer a member because?

1   Not in work
2   Never available at my work
3   I object to unions on principle
4   Union subscription are/were too high
5   I cannot see the point of joining
6   Part-time workers aren't eligible
7   Don't know
8   Other (specify) ....

LIST ALL THAT APPLY   *47-48

At the present time, would you like to be in a Trade Union?

CODE ONE   YES 1
         NO   2

| | 49 |

> GO TO NEXT SECTION (G)

F5 *Which union do you belong to?*

*50-51

F6 *How often do you attend union meetings?*

   Always   1
CODE ONE Often   2
      Occasionally 3
      Never   4

| | 52 |

If Always > GO TO NEXT SECTION (G)
Others   > CONTINUE

F7   **SHOW CARD F3**

If you do not always attend union meetings, which of the following is the most important reason for you not attending?

1 Not interested / find them boring
2 No meetings / don't know of meetings
3 Inconvenient times (e.g. lunchtime; evenings)
4 Do not believe in unions
5 Other (specify) ....

CODE ONE

| | 53 |

SECTION G

ATTITUDES TO WOMEN AND WORK

G1 *People's views about whether a woman ought to work or not often vary. For each of the situations described below, choose the one statement that best fits your views about what a woman should do.*

0 = Don't know / can't say / no response
1 = It is up to her to decide
2 = She should go if she really needs the money
3 = She ought to stay at home
4 = She should do what her husband/partner tells her

A married woman whose children have all left home.	0	1	2	3	4	54
A married woman whose children are all at school.	0	1	2	3	4	55
A married woman with children under school age.	0	1	2	3	4	56
A married woman with no children.	0	1	2	3	4	57
A single woman with no family responsibilities.	0	1	2	3	4	58

G2 *For each statement please circle the response which best describes how you feel. There are no right or wrong answers, we are just interested in your opinions.*

1 = strongly agree; 2 = agree; 3 = neutral; 4 = disagree; 5 = strongly disagree

1 There should be more women leaders in important jobs in public life, such as politics. (R)	1	2	3	4	5	59
2 If a woman goes out to work her husband should share the housework, such as washing dishes, cleaning and cooking. (R)	1	2	3	4	5	60
3 Women should have completely equal opportunities in getting jobs and promotion as men. (R)	1	2	3	4	5	61
4 Women should worry less about being equal with men and more about becoming good wives and mothers.	1	2	3	4	5	62
5 Women should not be bosses in important jobs in business and industry.	1	2	3	4	5	63
6 Daughters in a family should be encouraged to stay on at school and go to college as much as the sons in the family. (R)	1	2	3	4	5	64
7 It would be ridiculous for a woman to drive a train or for a man to sew on shirt buttons.	1	2	3	4	5	65
8 A women's place is in the home looking after her family, rather than following a career of her own.	1	2	3	4	5	66
9 Women have less to offer than men in the world of business and industry.	1	2	3	4	5	67
10 There are many jobs that men can do better than women.	1	2	3	4	5	68
11 Girls should have as much opportunity to do apprenticeships and learn a trade as the boys. (R)	1	2	3	4	5	69

SECTION H

CARD NUMBER 1

SERIAL NUMBER   *2-5

HOME

H1 To check, *are you married or living permanently with someone?*

DON'T   YES
CODE   NO

If NO > GO TO H25
If YES > CONTINUE

H2 *How old is your husband/partner?*

CODE IN YEARS   6-7   [ ] yrs

H3 *At what age did your husband/partner finish full-time education?*

Still in full-time education   1
Under 14 (or none)   2
14-15   3   8
CODE ONE   16-17   4
18-19   5
20+   6
Don't know   7

H4   SHOW CARD H1

Which of the following qualifications does he have?

1   GCSE
2   GCE 'A' level
3   Teaching qualification
4   Social work qualification
5   Nursing qualification
6   Clerical & commercial/secretarial qualification
7   Training for skilled occupations (not apprenticeship)
8   Course and training in childcare
9   City & Guilds
10   Degree or equivalent
11   Membership of professional institution
12   HND
13   HNC
14   B Tec
15   Community Education course
16   Apprenticeship
17   Other (specify) ....

LIST ALL THAT APPLY   *9-10

If still in full-time education > GO TO H15
Others > CONTINUE

G4 To check, *are you currently in paid work?*

DON'T   YES
CODE   NO

If NO > GO TO NEXT SECTION (H)
If YES > CONTINUE

G5 *Please indicate how true each question on the card is for you at present.*

0 = don't know / can't remember / refusal
1 = definitely true
2 = partly true
3 = not true

	0	1	2	3	
I/my family could not manage unless I was earning	0	1	2	3	70
I don't need to work for the money	0	1	2	3	71
If I lost my job I would look for another straight away	0	1	2	3	72
It wouldn't bother me if I lost my job and I couldn't find another one	0	1	2	3	73
I like the stimulation of going out to work	0	1	2	3	74
I wish I didn't go out to work	0	1	2	3	75
Working makes me feel I'm doing something useful	0	1	2	3	76
I have less time than I would like to spend with my family and friends	0	1	2	3	77
I often get very tired because of my work	0	1	2	3	78
I never have enough time for everything	0	1	2	3	79
I would not continue to work if my partner disapproved	0	1	2	3	80

H5 Is he in paid work at the moment (including holiday, temporary illness [less than 3 months] etc.)?

CODE YES 1
ONE   NO   2   11

If YES > GO TO H7
If NO   > CONTINUE

How long has he been out of work?

Less than 6 mths   1
6mths but less than 1 yr   2
1 yr but less than 3 yrs   3
3 years but less than 5 yrs   4
5 yrs or more   5

CODE ONE   12

H6 Is he currently?

Actively seeking work   1
Waiting to take up a job   2
Temporarily sick   3
Permanently unable to work   4
Retired   5

CODE ONE   13

Has your husband/partner ever worked?

YES   1
NO   2
Don't know   3

CODE ONE   14

If NO or Don't know > GO TO H15
If YES > CONTINUE

H7 What is / was his present / most recent job, or what job is he waiting to take up?

Job title: _____   *15-17

Industry: _____   *18-20

H8 Is / was he / will he be?

Self-employed (alone)   1
Self-employed (with employees)   2
Employee (professional/manager)   3
Employee (supervisor)   4
Employee (non-manual/manual worker)   5
Don't know/refusal   6

CODE ONE   21

To check, is he working at present?

DON'T
CODE   YES   NO

If NO > GO TO H15
If YES > CONTINUE

H9 On average, how many hours per week does your husband/partner work (excluding breaks)?

Under 8hrs per week   1
Over 8hrs but less than 16hrs per week   2
Over 16hrs but less than 30hrs per week 3
Over 30hrs but less than 40hrs per week 4
Over 40hrs per week   5
Don't know / can't remember   6

CODE ONE   22

H10 On average, how many hours paid overtime does this normally include?

Varies considerably   1
1 hr - 5hrs   2
6hrs - 10hrs   3
11hrs +   4
Don't know   5

CODE ONE   23

H11 Has your husband / partner's job affected your availability for work or the sort of job you do?

YES, entirely   1
YES, partially   2
NO   3

CODE ONE   24

If NO > GO TO H13
If YES > CONTINUE

H12 How has his work affected you?

....
....   *25-26

H13 In an average week, would your husband/partner be working (outside the home):

Varies   0
1 - 2 evenings per week   1
3 - 4 evenings per week   2
5+ evenings per week   3
Either Saturday or Sunday   4
Both Saturday and Sunday   5
Night-shift   6
Not applicable (fixed sociable hours)   7

CODE ONE   27

H14   SHOW CARD H2

At present, how much does he earn per week/month/year after any deductions (e.g. tax; National Insurance)?

Code	Per week £	(Per month) £	(Per annum) £
01	Up to £25	Up to £100	Up to £1,200
02	25 - 50	101 - 200	1,200 - 2,400
03	51 - 75	201 - 300	2,401 - 3,600
04	76 - 100	301 - 400	3,601 - 4,800
05	101 - 125	401 - 500	4,801 - 6,000
06	126 - 150	501 - 600	6,001 - 7,200
07	151 - 175	601 - 700	7,201 - 8,400
08	176 - 200	701 - 800	8,401 - 9,600
09	201 - 250	801 - 1000	9,601 - 12,000
10	251 - 300	1001 - 1200	12,001 - 14,400
11	301 - 350	1201 - 1400	14,401 - 16,800
12	351 - 400	1401 - 1600	16,801 - 19,200
13	401 - 500	1601 - 2000	19,201 - 24,000
14	501 - 700	2001 - 2800	24,001 - 33,600
15	701 - 900	2801 - 3600	33,601 - 43,200
16	over £900	over £3600	over £43,200

CODE ONE

28-29 ☐☐

H15   SHOW CARD H3

Are you or your husband/partner at present receiving any of these benefits or allowances?

1   Child benefit / family allowance
2   Unemployment benefit
3   State retirement or widow's pension
4   Sickness/industrial injury benefit
5   Disability/ invalidity allowance or pension
6   Maternity benefit
7   Income support
8   Attendance allowance
9   Housing benefit / rates relief

LIST ALL THAT APPLY   ☐☐ ☐☐   *30-31

H16   SHOW CARD H4

Apart from earnings and benefits, do you or your husband/partner receive any regular income from the following?

1   Pension from former employer
2   Private pension/income
3   Educational grant / training allowance
4   Allowance from parents
5   Money from lodgers
6   Money from family members in house
7   Rent from properties
8   Maintenance payments
9   Interest from building society/dividends/investments
10 Other   (specify) ....

LIST ALL THAT APPLY   ☐☐ ☐☐   *32-33

H17   SHOW CARD H2

Could you look at this card and tell me into which group you and your husband/partner's net income falls. That is, the total amount which comes into the home per week, including benefits etc., after deductions for tax, National Insurance and other statutory deductions?

Code	Per week £	(Per month) £	(Per annum) £
01	Up to £25	Up to £100	Up to £1,200
02	25 - 50	101 - 200	1,200 - 2,400
03	51 - 75	201 - 300	2,401 - 3,600
04	76 - 100	301 - 400	3,601 - 4,800
05	101 - 125	401 - 500	4,801 - 6,000
06	126 - 150	501 - 600	6,001 - 7,200
07	151 - 175	601 - 700	7,201 - 8,400
08	176 - 200	701 - 800	8,401 - 9,600
09	201 - 250	801 - 1000	9,601 - 12,000
10	251 - 300	1001 - 1200	12,001 - 14,400
11	301 - 350	1201 - 1400	14,401 - 16,800
12	351 - 400	1401 - 1600	16,801 - 19,200
13	401 - 500	1601 - 2000	19,201 - 24,000
14	501 - 700	2001 - 2800	24,001 - 33,600
15	701 - 900	2801 - 3600	33,601 - 43,200
16	over £900	over £3600	over £43,200

CODE ONE

34-35 ☐☐

H18   *How do you organize household finances?*

We share all money	1
He gives me an allowance	2
I give him an allowance	3
Other (specify)	4

CODE ONE   36 ☐

H19   *Thinking about your financial situation, do you?*

Manage reasonably well	1
Manage, but with little money to spare	2
Often find it difficult to manage	3
Do not manage on the money coming in	4

CODE ONE   37 ☐

H20   *Would you say you worry about money?*

Almost all the time	1
Quite often	2
Sometimes	3
Never/almost never	4

CODE ONE   38 ☐

H21 *Thinking about the jobs that need to be done around the home, such as shopping, cooking and cleaning. How is the work shared between you and your partner/husband?*

CODE ONE	I do it all	1
	I do most of it	2
	It is shared equally	3
	He does most of it	4
	He does it all	5

[box] 39

H22 *How often does your husband/partner do the following?*
3 = Often; 2 = Sometimes; 1 = Never

	Washing	3 2 1	40
	Ironing	3 2 1	41
CODE ALL	Cooking	3 2 1	42
	Cleaning/vacuuming	3 2 1	43
	Shopping	3 2 1	44

H23 *Given the choice, do you think that at present your husband/partner would prefer?*

	That you were working full-time	1
	That you were working part-time	2
CODE ONE	That you were not working	3
	He has no view	4
	Don't know	5

[box] 45

H24 *For each of the following statements, choose the one that you feel best fits your husband's/partner's views about whether a woman should work in the following circumstances.*

0 = Don't know / can't say / no response
1 = It is up to her to decide
2 = She should go if she really needs the money
3 = She ought to stay at home
4 = She should do what her husband/partner tells her

A married woman whose children have all left home.	0	1	2	3	4	46
A married woman whose children are all at school.	0	1	2	3	4	47
A married woman with children under school age.	0	1	2	3	4	48
A married woman with no children.	0	1	2	3	4	49
A single woman with no family responsibilities.	0	1	2	3	4	50

> GO TO NEXT SECTION (J)

For those without a husband / partner

H25 *At present, are you:*

	Living alone	1
CODE	Living with your children	2
ONE	Living with other relatives (e.g. parents)	3
	Sharing accommodation with non-relatives	4

[box] 51

H26   **SHOW CARD H3**

Are you at present receiving any of these benefits or allowances?

1 Child benefit / family allowance
2 Unemployment benefit
3 State retirement or widow's pension
4 Sickness/industrial injury benefit
5 Disability/invalidity allowance or pension
6 Maternity benefit
7 Income support
8 Attendance allowance
9 Housing benefit / rates relief

LIST ALL THAT APPLY   [boxes] *52-53

H27   **SHOW CARD H4**

Apart from earnings and benefits, do you personally receive any regular income from the following?

1 Pension from former employer
2 Private pension/income
3 Educational grant / training allowance
4 Allowance from parents
5 Money from lodgers 5
6 Money from family members in house
7 Rent from properties
8 Maintenance payments
9 Interest from building society/dividends/investments
10 Other (specify)............

LIST ALL THAT APPLY   [boxes] *54-55

SECTION J

CARD NUMBER 1 [8]

SERIAL NUMBER

*2-5

CHILDCARE

J1 To check, *do you currently have any child(ren) aged 16 or under 16 living at home?*

DON'T CODE
   YES
   NO

If YES > GO TO J2
If NO > CONTINUE

To check, *in the past have you had children aged 16 or under living at home?*

DON'T CODE
   YES
   NO

If YES > GO TO J2
If NO > CONTINUE

To check, *are you pregnant?*

DON'T CODE
   YES
   NO

If NO > GO TO NEXT SECTION (K)
If YES > CONTINUE

To check, *are you working at the moment (including being on maternity leave)?*

DON'T CODE
   YES
   NO

If YES > GO TO J8
If NO > GO TO J23

J2 *Has bringing up a family influenced your availability for work?*

YES, it has hindered a lot	1
YES, it has hindered a little	2
CODE ONE NO, no effect	3
YES, it has helped a little	4
YES, it has helped a lot	5

6

To check, *are / were you mainly a single parent whilst your children were / are under 16?*

DON'T CODE
   YES
   NO

If YES > GO TO J5
If NO > CONTINUE

H28   **SHOW CARD H2**

Could you look at this card and tell me into which group your net income falls. That is, the total amount which comes into the home per week, including benefits etc., after deductions for tax, National Insurance and other statutory deductions?

Code	Per week £	(Per month) £	(Per annum) £
01	Up to £25	Up to £100	Up to £1,200
02	25 - 50	101 - 200	1,200 - 2,400
03	51 - 75	201 - 300	2,401 - 3,600
04	76 - 100	301 - 400	3,601 - 4,800
05	101 - 125	401 - 500	4,801 - 6,000
06	126 - 150	501 - 600	6,001 - 7,200
07	151 - 175	601 - 700	7,201 - 8,400
08	176 - 200	701 - 800	8,401 - 9,600
09	201 - 250	801 - 1000	9,601 - 12,000
10	251 - 300	1001 - 1200	12,001 - 14,400
11	301 - 350	1201 - 1400	14,401 - 16,800
12	351 - 400	1401 - 1600	16,801 - 19,200
13	401 - 500	1601 - 2000	19,201 - 24,000
14	501 - 700	2001 - 2800	24,001 - 33,600
15	701 - 900	2801 - 3600	33,601 - 43,200
16	over £900	over £3600	over £43,200

CODE ONE   56-57

H29 *Thinking about your financial situation, at the moment do you?*

Manage and have money to save	1
CODE ONE Manage, but with little money to spare	2
Find it difficult to manage	3
Do not manage on the money coming in	4

58

H30 *Would you say you worry about money?*

Almost all the time	1
CODE ONE Quite often	2
Sometimes	3
Never/almost never	4

59

J8 *If your child(ren) is / are ill or need(s) to be taken anywhere by you, can you get time off work?*

	Yes, easily	1
CODE	Yes, with difficulty	2
ONE	No	3
	Don't know	4

□ 18

If NO or Don't know > GO TO NEXT SECTION (K)
If YES > CONTINUE

J9 *Is this time off work normally taken as?*

	Part of your holidays	1
CODE	Part of your sick leave	2
ONE	Compassionate leave/informally allowed by employer	3
	Hasn't happened	4
	Varies	5

□ 19

J10 *Do you get paid for any time you take off for the children?*

	YES	1
CODE	NO	2
ONE	Varies	3
	Don't know	4

□ 20

J11 *Do you have children aged under 5, and / or are you pregnant?*

DON'T
CODE   YES
                NO

If NO > GO TO J17
If YES > CONTINUE

J3 *Thinking about looking after the children, how much of this is / was shared between you and your husband / partner?*

	I do / did it all	1
	I do / did most of it	2
CODE ONE	It is / was shared 50/50	3
	He does / did most of it	4
	He does / did it all	5
	Don't know / refusal	6

□ 7

J4 *How often has your husband / partner done the following?*
3 = Often; 2 = Sometimes; 1 = Never

	Fed the child(ren) alone	3	2	1	8
	Taken the child(ren) to bed	3	2	1	9
CODE ALL	Washed/bathed the child(ren)	3	2	1	10
	Read to him/her/them	3	2	1	11
	Played with him/her/them	3	2	1	12
	Taken the child(ren) to the doctor	3	2	1	13
	Taken the child(ren) to or from school	3	2	1	14
	Changed a nappy	3	2	1	15
	Got up in the night to look after him/her	3	2	1	16

J5 *To check, are your children currently under 16 and / or are you pregnant?*

DON'T
CODE   YES
                NO

If NO > GO TO NEXT SECTION (K)
If YES > CONTINUE

J6 *Do you intend to resume work before your youngest child is 16?*

	YES	1
CODE ONE	NO	2
	Don't know	3

□ 17

If NO or Don't know > GO TO J26
If YES > CONTINUE

J7 *Are you working at the moment (including being on maternity leave)?*

DON'T
CODE   YES
                NO

If NO > GO TO J23
If YES > CONTINUE

J12   SHOW CARD J1

With regard to those of your children aged under 5, which of the following arrangements apply or will apply?

1 Work at home
2 Take child to work
3 Only work outside school hours and term time
4 Husband looks after
5 Older brother/sister looks after
6 Mother/mother in law looks after
7 Other relative looks after
8 Childminder (in childminder's own home)
9 Childminder (in respondent's home)
10 Friend/neighbour on exchange basis
11 Day nursery / creche run by employer
12 Day nursery / creche run by social services / community group
13 Private day nursery / creche
14 State nursery school / class
15 Private nursery school / class
16 Maintained/church nursery school / class
17 Playgroup / Mothers and Toddlers
18 Primary school
19 Other (specify) ....

CHILDREN AGED UNDER 3

LIST ALL THAT APPLY   *21-22

CHILDREN AGED 3 - 4

LIST ALL THAT APPLY   *23-24

How much does / will this cost you each week in total?

TO NEAREST POUND   £   25-27

J13 *How satisfied are you with these arrangements?*

For children aged under 3?

Very satisfied	1
Quite satisfied	2
Not satisfied	3
Not applicable	4

28

For children aged 3 or 4?

Very satisfied	1
Quite satisfied	2
Not satisfied	3
Not applicable	4

29

If Not satisfied > CONTINUE
Others > GO TO J15

J14   SHOW CARD J2

If for any reason you are not satisfied, which of the following are problems?

1 Cost
2 Quality of care
3 Taking and collecting child(ren)
4 Uncertainty of arrangements
5 Distance from home
6 Distance from work
7 Available hours
8 Other (specify) ....

CHILDREN AGED UNDER 3

LIST ALL THAT APPLY   *30-31

CHILDREN AGED 3 - 4

LIST ALL THAT APPLY   *32-33

J15   SHOW CARD J1

If you could choose, which of these arrangements or combination of arrangements would you prefer for the child(ren)?

1 Work at home
2 Take child to work
3 Only work outside school hours and term time
4 Husband looks after
5 Older brother/sister looks after
6 Mother/mother in law looks after
7 Other relative looks after
8 Childminder (in childminder's own home)
9 Childminder (in respondent's home)
10 Friend/neighbour on exchange basis
11 Day nursery / creche run by employer
12 Day nursery / creche run by social services / community group
13 Private day nursery / creche
14 State nursery school / class
15 Private nursery school / class
16 Maintained/church nursery school / class
17 Playgroup / Mothers and Toddlers
18 Primary school
19 Other (specify) ....

CHILDREN AGED UNDER 3

LIST ALL THAT APPLY   *34-35

CHILDREN AGED 3 - 4

LIST ALL THAT APPLY   *36-37

J16 *If you could change the hours you are at work, without working fewer hours in total, to help you to manage your responsibilities for the child(ren) aged under five, which of the following would you change?*

		YES	NO	
CODE	Time of day	1	2	38
EACH	Days of week	1	2	39
	Work more hours during term-time / fewer in holidays	1	2	40

To check, do you currently have any children aged five or over?

DON'T   YES
CODE   NO

If NO > GO TO NEXT SECTION (K)
If YES > CONTINUE

J17   **SHOW CARD J3**

For your children aged five and over, which of the following arrangements apply to you at the moment?

1   Only work outside school hours and term time
2   Husband looks after
3   Older brother / sister looks after
4   Mother / mother in law looks after
5   Other relative looks after
6   Childminder (in childminder's home)
7   Childminder (in own home)
8   Friend / neighbour on exchange basis
9   Work at home
10 Other (specify) ....

LIST ALL THAT APPLY   *41-42

J18 *How satisfied are you with these arrangements?*

Very satisfied   1
Quite satisfied   2   43
Not satisfied   3

If Not satisfied > CONTINUE
Others > GO TO J20

J19   **SHOW CARD J2**

If you are not satisfied, which of the following are problems?

1   Cost
2   Quality of care
3   Taking and collecting child(ren)
4   Uncertainty of arrangements
5   Distance from home
6   Distance from work
7   Available hours
8   Other (specify) ....

LIST ALL THAT APPLY   *44-45

J20 *How much does this cost you each week, altogether?*

TO NEAREST POUND   £   46-48

J21   **SHOW CARD J3**

If you could choose, which of these arrangements or combination of arrangements would you prefer for the child(ren) aged five and over?

1   Only work outside school hours and term time
2   Husband looks after
3   Older brother / sister looks after
4   Mother / mother in law looks after
5   Other relative looks after
6   Childminder (in childminder's home)
7   Childminder (in own home)
8   Friend / neighbour on exchange basis
9   Work at home
10 Other (specify) ....

LIST ALL THAT APPLY   *49-50

J22 *If you could change the hours you are at work, without working fewer hours in total, to help you to manage your responsibilities for the child(ren) aged five and over, which of the following would you change?*

		YES	NO	
		1	2	
CODE	Time of day	1	2	51
	Days of week	1	2	52
EACH	Work more hours during term-time / fewer in holidays	1	2	53

> GO TO NEXT SECTION (K)

For Those Not Currently in Work

J23 *Do you intend to start work*

DON'T   1 Before your youngest child is aged 5
CODE   2 When your youngest child is aged 5 or older

If 1 > CONTINUE
If 2 > GO TO J25

J24   **SHOW CARD J1**

When you start work / find a job, which of the following arrangements will probably apply when your children are under five years old?

1 Work at home
2 Take child to work
3 Only work outside school hours and term time
4 Husband looks after
5 Older brother/sister looks after
6 Mother/mother in law looks after
7 Other relative looks after
8 Childminder (in childminder's own home)
9 Childminder (in respondent's home)
10 Friend/neighbour on exchange basis
11 Day nursery / creche run by employer
12 Day nursery / creche run by social services
    / community group
13 Private day nursery / creche
14 State nursery school / class
15 Private nursery school / class
16 Maintained/church nursery school / class
17 Playgroup / Mothers and Toddlers
18 Primary school
19 Other (specify) ....

LIST ALL THAT APPLY   CHILDREN AGED UNDER 3   *54-55

LIST ALL THAT APPLY   CHILDREN AGED 3 - 4   *56-57

| **Card J1 - Childcare Arrangements for Under 5's** |

J25   **SHOW CARD J3**

When you start work / find a job, which of the following arrangements will probably apply when your children are aged 5 and over?

1 Only work outside school hours and term time
2 Husband looks after
3 Older brother / sister looks after
4 Mother / mother in law looks after
5 Other relative looks after
6 Childminder (in childminder's home)
7 Childminder (in own home)
8 Friend / neighbour on exchange basis
9 Work at home
10 Other (specify) ....

LIST ALL THAT APPLY   CHILDREN AGED 5 AND OVER   *58-59

J26 *How important has the lack of suitable child care facilities been in influencing your decision not to work at the moment?*

	Very important	1
CODE ONE	Fairly important	2
	Not important	3

60

| **If Not important > GO TO NEXT SECTION (K)** |
| **Others > CONTINUE** |

J27   **SHOW CARD J2**

Which of the following problems with childcare arrangements have been / are important?

1 Cost
2 Quality of care
3 Taking and collecting child(ren)
4 Uncertainty of arrangements
5 Distance from home
6 Distance from work
7 Available hours
8 Other (specify) ....

LIST ALL THAT APPLY   *61-62

J28 *What kind of arrangements would you consider necessary in order for you to consider returning to work?*

For children under five years old   SHOW CARD J1

1 Work at home
2 Take child to work
3 Only work outside school hours and term time
4 Husband looks after
5 Older brother/sister looks after
6 Mother/mother in law looks after
7 Other relative looks after
8 Childminder (in childminder's own home)
9 Childminder (in respondent's home)
10 Friend/neighbour on exchange basis
11 Day nursery / creche run by employer
12 Day nursery / creche run by social services
   / community group
13 Private day nursery / creche
14 State nursery school / class
15 Private nursery school / class
16 Maintained/church nursery school / class
17 Playgroup / Mothers and Toddlers
18 Primary school
19 Other (specify) ....

CHILDREN AGED UNDER 3

LIST ALL THAT APPLY   *63-64

CHILDREN AGED 3 - 4

LIST ALL THAT APPLY   *65-66

For children aged five years and over   SHOW CARD J3

1 Only work outside school hours and term time
2 Husband looks after
3 Older brother / sister looks after
4 Mother / mother in law looks after
5 Other relative looks after
6 Childminder (in childminder's home)
7 Childminder (in own home)
8 Friend / neighbour on exchange basis
9 Work at home
10 Other (specify) ....

CHILDREN AGED 5 AND OVER

LIST ALL THAT APPLY   *67-68

SECTION K

OTHER DEPENDANT RELATIVES

K1 *Apart from normal family commitments, is there anyone who depends on you to provide some regular help or care for them?*

CODE ONE   YES   1
                  NO   2   69

┌─────────────────────────┐
│ IF NO > GO TO END   │
│ IF YES > CONTINUE   │
└─────────────────────────┘

Who is this person / are these people?

                  Husband   1
                  Child   2
                  Mother   3
CIRCLE   Father   4
UP TO   Mother-in-law   5
TWO   Father-in-law   6   *70-71
                  Grandparent   7
                  Other relative   8
                  Friend / neighbour   9
                  Other (specify, including more than one)   11

K2 *Does he/she live with you?*

CODE ONE   YES   1
                  NO   2   72

K3 *What is the nature of their complaint?*

                  Sickness/poor physical health   1
CODE   Mental health   2
ONE   Physical handicap   3   73
                  Old age   4
                  Other (specify)................. 5

K4 *How often do you see him/her/them?*

                  Daily   1
                  Several times a week   2
CODE   Once/twice a week   3   74
ONE   Less than once a week   4
                  Varies   5

K5 *What do you do for thim / her / them? Choose the category which best fits your help.*

Generally keep an eye on him / her / them   1
Look after him / her / them completely   2
CODE   Household chores (cooking, cleaning, odd jobs)   3
ONE   Shopping, transport   4
Provide company, visit   5

75 ☐

K6 *On the days you are with this person, about how long do you spend doing this each day?*

Varies considerably   0
Up to one hour   1
CODE   One hour but less than two   2
ONE   Two hours but less than four   3
Over four hours   4

76 ☐

K7 *About how long do you spend doing this altogether each week?*

Varies considerably   0
Up to one hour   1
One hour but less than two hours   2
CODE   Two hours but less than four hours   3
ONE   Four hours but less than eight hours   4
Eight hours but less than sixteen hours   5
Sixteen hours but less than thirty hours   6
Over thirty hours   7

77 ☐

K8 *Has the care which you provide affected whether you have been able to go out to work?*

YES   1
CODE ONE   NO   2
Don't know   3

78 ☐

If YES,   <u>**SHOW CARD K1**</u>

Has this?

1   Prevented you from going out to work
2   Restricted the number of hours you can work
3   Regularly involved taking days off work to care for dependant(s)
4   Using all holidays to care for dependant(s)
5   Meant working only part-time
6   Seriously affected your career

LIST ALL THAT APPLY   ☐☐☐☐☐   *79-80 ☐

Author Index

Subject index

Printed in the United Kingdom for HMSO
Dd. 303627, C10, 12/92.